Political Ideologies
and the Democratic Ideal

Political Ideologies and the Democratic Ideal

TERENCE BALL
University of Minnesota

RICHARD DAGGER
Arizona State University

HarperCollins*Publishers*

ACKNOWLEDGMENTS

Unless otherwise acknowledged, all photographs are the property of Scott, Foresman.

27, Alinari/Art Resource, N.Y.; 32, Alinari/Art Resource, N.Y.; 38, The Bettmann Archive; 58, National Portrait Gallery, London; 60, The Bettmann Archive; 73, The Bettmann Archive; 95, The Bettmann Archive; 153, Historical Pictures Service; 157, AP/Wide World Photos; 161, UPI/Bettmann Newsphotos; 186, AP/Wide World Photos; 190, The Bettmann Archive; 203, John Tweedle; 208, The Bettmann Archive.

Sponsoring Editor: Lauren Silverman
Project Editors: B. Pelner, Diane Rowell
Design Supervisor: Heather A. Ziegler
Cover Design: Circa 86, Inc.
Cover Photo: Stephen Ferry/Gamma-Liaison
Photo Research: Nina Page
Production: Willie Lane/Sunaina Sehwani
Compositor: David E. Seham Inc.
Printer and Binder: R. R. Donnelley & Sons Company
Cover Printer: New England Book Components, Inc.

Political Ideologies and the Democratic Ideal
Copyright © 1991 by HarperCollins Publishers Inc.

Library of Congress Cataloging-in-Publication Data
Ball, Terence.
    Political Ideologies and the Democratic Ideal / Terence Ball, Richard Dagger.
      p. cm.
    Includes index.
    ISBN 0-06-040473-6
    1. Political science—History. 2. Democracy—History. 3. Right and left (Political science)—History. 4. Ideology—History.
I. Dagger, Richard. II. Title.
JA81.B25 1991
320.5'09—dc20   90-46507
                                    CIP

90 91 92 93 9 8 7 6 5 4 3 2 1

To
Jonathan and Stephen Ball
and
Emily and Elizabeth Dagger

Contents

PART TWO   THE DEVELOPMENT OF POLITICAL IDEOLOGIES

Chapter 3   Liberalism   49

Chapter 4   Conservatism   91

Preface

Although there are already a number of "modern ideologies" texts in print, we believe that there is not only room, but a definite need for yet another. This belief grows out of long experience—more than a quarter-century between us—of regularly teaching courses in political ideologies. Throughout that time we have looked for a textbook that combines a concise characterization and analysis of contemporary political ideologies with an account of their origins and development. This second feature became increasingly important as we discovered more and more students whose ignorance of history is overwhelming—students who seem never to have heard of the French Revolution, for instance, or who believe that Thomas Jefferson wrote the Constitution of the United States. So, failing to find a textbook that suited our students' needs, we finally decided to write our own.

The aims of *Political Ideologies and the Democratic Ideal* are twofold. We want, first, to supply an informed and accessible overview of the major ideologies that have shaped, and continue to reshape, the political landscape of this century. Beyond that, the second aim is to show how these ideologies began and how and why they have changed over time. Like people and concepts, ideologies have histories, and students need to know something about these histories if they are to comprehend the ideological divisions and contests of their own time. In addition, then, to examining the major modern "isms"—liberalism, conservatism, socialism, and fascism—we provide the reader with a sense of the history, structure, supporting arguments, and internal complexities of these and other, recently emerging, ideologies.

We begin by constructing a fourfold framework—a definition of "ideology" in terms of the four functions that all ideologies perform—within which to compare, contrast, and analyze the various ideologies. We also show how each ideology interprets "democracy" and "freedom" in its own way. Democracy is not, in our view, simply one ideology among others, but an *ideal* that different ideologies interpret in different ways. Each ideology also has its own particular conception of, and its own program for promoting, freedom. We use a simple three-part model to illustrate this, comparing and contrasting each ideology's view of freedom in terms of agent, obstacle, and goal. In every chapter devoted to a particular ideology, then, we explain its basic conception of freedom in terms of the triadic model, discuss the origin and development of the ideology, examine its interpretation of the democratic ideal, and conclude by showing how it performs the four functions of political ideologies.

We do this, moreover, not only with liberalism, conservatism, socialism, and fascism, but also with the more recent ideologies. These include "liberation ideologies"—black liberation, women's liberation, gay liberation, liberation theology, and animal liberation—and a newly emerging environmental or "green" ideology.

This text forms the first leg of a tripod. The second leg is an accompanying anthology, *Ideals and Ideologies: A Reader*, also published by HarperCollins. The third leg is Terence Ball's "Contemporary Political Ideologies," a public television series comprising ten half-hour episodes. (To obtain videotape copies of this series, write to: The Director, Media-Assisted Instruction, Independent Studies, 45 Westbrook Hall, University of Minnesota, Minneapolis, Minnesota, 55455.) Each section of the anthology and each half-hour video program corresponds to, and complements, successive chapters in this text. Although each of these "legs" is able to stand alone, we like to think that, taken together, they form a coherent, stable, and sturdy structure one fit for the end of this century and the beginning of the next.

We undertook this collaborative effort in the belief that two heads are better than one. What we have found is that a project of this sort requires many more, or better, heads than the authors could muster between themselves. To those who shared their time, energy, and wisdom with us, we extend our deepest thanks.

HarperCollins secured helpful reviews at three different stages in the development of the manuscript. For contributing their critical judgment and expertise to this project, we are most grateful to William T. Bluhm, University of Rochester; Robert E. Calvert, DePauw University; Phillip C. Chapman, University of Arizona; Peter Diamond, University of Utah; Larry Elowitz, Georgia College; Alan Gilbert, University of Denver; Timothy W. Luke, Virginia Polytechnic Institute and State University; William McGuire, Normandale Community College; Andrew Raposa, Westfield State College; and Joel D. Schwartz, College of William and Mary. We did not always follow the advice these reviewers offered—indeed, we could not when one reviewer's suggestions directly contradicted another's—but their comments forced us to do a fair bit of rethinking and rewriting. Whatever its faults, this book is much the better for their contributions.

We also enjoyed the benefit of comments from and conversations with a number of friends and colleagues. Professor Lawrence Biskowski of the University of Georgia in particular deserves our gratitude for commenting on early outlines and an early draft of the entire manuscript. We are also grateful to Jeffrey M. Nelson for contributing the title; to Professor Jack Crittenden of Arizona State University for his comments on Chapters 1 and 2; to Professor John Pottenger of the University of Alabama-Huntsville for sharing his knowledge of liberation theology with us; to Professor Terrell Carver of the University of Bristol (England) for commenting on an earlier version of Chapter 5; to Regents Professor Emeritus John Turner of the University of Minnesota for helpful suggestions regarding Chapter 6; to Professor Qi Xiyu of the People's University of Beijing for his very helpful comments on portions of Chapter 6; to Professor Gary Thomas of the University of Minnesota for his knowledge of "gay" politics and for commenting helpfully on Chapter 8; to Professor James Farr of the University of Minnesota for many stimulating conversations about Marx, Marxism, and ideology in general; to Professors Mary Dietz, Sara Evans, and Naomi Scheman of the University of Minnesota for making us more aware of the history, variety, and complexity of feminist theory and practice; to Charles Betz, Andrew Davison, and William Lynn of the University of Minnesota for conversations about and comments on Chapter 9. Special thanks are due the students in the Spring 1989 sections of our political ideologies courses who offered comments, criticisms, and suggestions for improving an earlier version of this book.

We also want to thank Andrew Davison for preparing the index.

We received assistance of a different sort from the staff at HarperCollins, especially our sponsoring editor, Lauren Silverman, who skillfully guided us through the labyrinth of textbook publishing.

Finally, for their assistance in preparing the manuscript, we are grateful to William Otting and Barbara Dagger.

Terence Ball
Richard Dagger

To the Reader

We want to call three features of this book to your attention. The first is that a number of key words and phrases in the text are set in **boldface** type. Definitions of these words and phrases appear in the Glossary at the back of the book, just before the Index.

Second, many of the primary works quoted or cited in the text are also reprinted, in whole or in part, in a companion volume edited by the authors, *Ideals and Ideologies: A Reader*. When we cite one of these primary works in this text, we include in the footnote a reference to the corresponding selection in *Ideals and Ideologies*.

Finally, the study of political ideologies is in many ways the study of words. For this reason we frequently call attention to the use political thinkers and leaders make of such terms as "democracy" and "freedom." In doing so we have found it convenient to adopt the philosophers' convention of using quotation marks to refer to words—as in "democracy" and "freedom."

T.B.
R.D.

IDEOLOGY AND DEMOCRACY

Chapter
1

Ideology and Ideologies

[T]he ideas of economists and political philosophers, both when they are right and when they are wrong, are more powerful than is commonly understood. Indeed the world is ruled by little else. Practical men, who believe themselves to be quite exempt from any intellectual influences, are usually the slaves of some defunct economist. Madmen in authority, who hear voices in the air, are distilling their frenzy from some academic scribbler of a few years back.

John Maynard Keynes

*L*ate in 1989 the communist government of the German Democratic Republic (East Germany) opened the Berlin Wall. For some thirty years the Wall had stood as an ugly symbol not only of the division of Germany, but of a deep ideological division that threatened the peace of the whole world. Then, suddenly, in one of the most remarkable events of a remarkable year, the Wall was open and everything seemed to change. The Cold War finally appears to be over, and yesterday's threats—the "communist menace" and the "evil empire"—seem almost as distant as the earlier threat of fascism.

But if these threats are gone, they should not be forgotten. As the philosopher George Santayana remarked, those who forget the past may be doomed to repeat its mistakes. Those who forget the past, moreover, can hardly hope to understand themselves or the world in which they live. Our minds, our thoughts, our beliefs and attitudes—all have been forged in the fires and shaped on the anvil of earlier ideological conflicts. If we wish to act effectively and live peacefully, then, we need to know something about the political ideologies that have influenced so profoundly our own and other people's political attitudes and actions.

It is also important to note that the apparent demise of communism in Eastern Europe and even the Soviet Union does not signal the end of all ideologies and ideological conflict. In the same year that the Berlin Wall opened, the communist government of China ordered—in the name of ideological purity—the massacre of peaceful protesters in Beijing's Tiananmen Square. Ideological conflicts also contributed to bloodshed in the deserts of the Middle East and the jungles of Latin America. Conflicts of a less intense and more peaceful sort occurred throughout the world in parliaments and congresses—and sometimes in the streets—and these, too, often grew out of ideological differences. Ideologies have not only shaped our world, but they continue to reshape it. To understand our world, then, we must understand the many forms political ideologies have taken.

Our aim in this book is to provide the basis for this understanding. In this introductory chapter we clarify the concept of ideology itself. In subsequent chapters we go on to examine the various ideologies that have played an important part in shaping, and sometimes radically reshaping, the political landscape on which we live. We discuss liberalism, conservatism, socialism, fascism, and other ideologies in turn, in each case relating the birth and growth of the ideology to its historical context. We proceed in this way because political ideologies do not appear out of nowhere. They arise in particular historical circumstances, and then take shape and change in response to changes in those circumstances. These changes sometimes lead to perplexing results—for instance, today's conservatives sometimes seem to have more in common with earlier liberals than today's liberals do. But this is because political ideologies, far from being fixed or frozen in place, respond to the changes in the world around them.

This is not to say that ideologies react passively, like weathervanes, to every shift in the political winds. On the contrary, ideologies try to shape and direct social change. The men and women who follow and promote political ideologies—and almost all of us do this in one way or another—are attempting to make sense of the world, to understand society and politics and economics, in order either to change it for the better or to resist changes that they think will make it worse. But to act upon the world in this way, they must react to the changes that are always taking place, including the changes brought about by rival ideologies.

Political ideologies, then, are dynamic. They do not stand still. This can be frustrating for anyone who wishes to understand *exactly* what a liberal or a conservative is, say, for it makes it impossible to define liberalism or conservatism or any other ideology with mathematical precision. But once we recognize that political ideologies are rooted in, change with, and themselves help to shape historical circumstances, we are on the way to grasping what any particular ideology is about.

THE HISTORY OF "IDEOLOGY"

Let us begin with the word itself. There is at first sight something strange about the word *ideology*. Other terms ending in *-ology* name fields of scientific study. For example, biology—the prefix coming from the Greek *bios*, or life—is the scientific study of life. Psychology is the study of psyche, or mind. And sociology is the study of society. It seems only logical, then, that ideology would be the scientific study of ideas. And that is just what ideology originally meant when the term was coined in the eighteenth century.

The word *ideology* is the invention of a French scholar, Antoine Destutt de Tracy (1754–1836), who tried in the 1790s and early 1800s to found a systematic study of the sources or origins of ideas.[1] De Tracy believed that this study, *ideologie,* could be every bit as scientific as biology, geology, or zoology. Like many other French *philosophes,* or philosophers, of the eighteenth century, he drew heavily on the ideas of an English philosopher, John Locke (1632–1704). In his *Essay Concerning Human Understanding* (1690), Locke had argued that the human mind at birth is like a *tabula rasa,* or blank tablet, in that people are born with no knowledge and no ideas. Everything we know and every idea we have is something we acquire as a result of the experience of our senses. Through sight, touch, and the other senses, the blank tablet of our minds is gradually filled with ideas. Thus babies are born with no idea of what a butterfly is, for example; through sensory experience, however—by seeing, touching, or even tasting butterflies—the idea of "butterfly" is impressed on their minds. It also follows, of course, that someone who never sees, reads about, or hears of a butterfly cannot possibly have the idea of "butterfly."

De Tracy used Locke's argument as the starting point of his own science of ideas. If ideas are the result of experience, he reasoned, it must be possible to discover their sources and thus to explain why different people have different ideas. Since people of different nationalities, cultures, social classes, and ethnic origins have formative experiences in their early years that are in some respects significantly different, so too must their ideas differ. A person's knowledge of the world can therefore be expected to vary with his or her social position or perspective. Princes and peasants, Persians and Frenchmen—all have different experiences and, therefore, different ideas and outlooks.

But for de Tracy, *ideologie* did not stop with explanations. He wanted to use this knowledge of the sources of ideas to reform and improve society. Many ideas are false and misleading, he argued, including religious ideas, which he regarded as mere superstitions that prevent people from seeing the world as it really is. But, according to de Tracy, the new science of ideology will enable us to remove these and other misleading ideas, thus making it possible to teach people the right kind of ideas—the kind that will lead to a rational and happy society.

Not surprisingly, the Catholic church, the nobility, and some powerful political figures of the time viewed *ideologie* and the *ideologues,* as de Tracy's associates were called, with some alarm. With its emphasis on rationality and science, *ideologie* posed a threat to traditional authority in politics and society as well as in religion. In conservative or traditional circles, in fact, the word *ideologie* quickly began to acquire negative connotations as something false, seductive, and downright dangerous. But it was Napoleon Bonaparte who decisively attacked de Tracy's attempt to found a reforming science of ideas. Once a supporter of the *ideologues,* Napoleon changed positions in the early 1800s when, as self-proclaimed Emperor of France, he needed the support of the church and nobility. Denouncing ideology as "sinister metaphysics," he declared the new science to be nothing but a mask to cover the subversive political plans of his opponents and critics.

It is in this sense of "hiding" or "masking" that Karl Marx (1818–1883) used the notion of ideology some forty years later. In Marx's hands the concept came to refer to a set or system of ideas whose function is to justify and legitimize the rule of a dominant class in society. The dominant class will differ from one form of society to another, but it will always be the class that controls the material forces—the resources needed to produce food and other goods. Ideology masks the rule of this class by portraying existing social relations as normal, natural, necessary, and eternal. As Marx and his coauthor, Friedrich Engels, observed,

> The ideas of the ruling class are in every epoch the ruling ideas, i.e., the class which is the ruling *material* force of society, is at the same time its ruling *intellectual* force. The class which has the means of material production at its disposal, has control at the same time over the means of mental production, so that thereby, generally speaking, the ideas of those who lack the means of mental production are subject to it.[2]

The task of Marx's theory, as he saw it, was to unmask and expose "the illusion of the epoch"—an illusion shared by ruler and ruled alike, but working to the advantage of the former at the expense of the latter. Once the illusion of permanence is exposed, its legitimating function is lost. Once the class or classes at the bottom of society begin to realize that the ruling class need not be the ruling class—that is, once they *see through* the ideology that supports the ruling class—then revolution becomes a real political possibility.

A further feature of Marx's conception of ideology is worth noting. Although his critical theory is meant to expose "ideology" in its negative sense, the *intent* of Marx's theory is "ideological" in de Tracy's original sense of the word. That is, Marxian theory attempts to trace moral, political, and economic ideas to their class-based social sources. But, unlike the French *ideologues*, Marx's purpose was not to trace any and all ideas to their sources, but only the "ruling ideas" of the dominant class to their privileged social and economic position.

Marx's theory, and his conception of ideology in particular, was not politically neutral. It was, as he readily acknowledged, intended to be a "weapon" in the "class struggle." But Marx thought it was a particularly powerful weapon because it revealed the truth. In other words, Marx believed that the prevailing ways of thinking about social relations throughout history were *nothing but* ideologies—complex and subtle defenses of the power and privileges of the dominant classes. Yet his own ideas were not, in his view, biased or ideological in this way. On the contrary, Marx thought of his ideas as "scientific." He thought they promoted the interests of the oppressed and exploited class, certainly, but Marx maintained—for reasons we explore in Chapter 5—that the interests of the exploited class in his day were the interests of all humanity. To expose "the illusion of the epoch" as mere ideology, then, was to speak the truth and open the way to a classless society in which ideology and illusion disappear.

For Marx, then, as for Napoleon, "ideology" was a pejorative term. But this began to change when Karl Mannheim and others pointed out that Marx's use of "ideology" as a weapon against the dominant class could be turned against Marx's theory itself. For if Marx is right when he says that the ruling ideas of society serve to justify the dominance of the ruling class, is it not also likely that the ideas of other social classes arise out of *their* interests and aspirations? If so, then all ideas and beliefs about society can be traced not to some objective truth, but to their origins in social or historical relations. What people think—not just the ruling class, but *everyone*—may depend upon their social position. Mannheim took up this theme in his *Ideology and Utopia*, calling for a *sociology of knowledge* to trace the social origins of ideas and beliefs.[3]

According to Mannheim, the sociology of knowledge requires us to draw a distinction between the "particular" and the "total" conceptions of ideology. We employ the *particular conception*, he said, when we say that the ideas and positions of a specific group of people we oppose, such as a political party or an interest group, are ideological. This is what happens, for example, when critics of the National Rifle Association claim that the NRA's efforts to stop gun control are biased, self-interested, or ideological. In this sense, "ideology" remains a weapon to use against one's opponents. The "total conception of ideology," by contrast, refers to the characteristic ways of thinking of an entire class or society or historical period, such as medieval society or the modern age. Because these ways of thought are so broad and encompassing, Mannheim doubted that anyone could ever stand outside them, entirely removed from the web of social and economic interests, and thus be in a position to unmask the ideological sources of *all* ideas and beliefs. In this way he raised the disturbing possibility that all our thinking about society and social relations is ideological. Mannheim did believe that intellectuals may be able to achieve a synthesis, or combination, of opposing perspectives that comes closer to the whole truth; but even then, he said, it would be the truth of a particular historical time and place, not the truth for all time and all places.

For our purposes, Mannheim's conception of ideology is important for two reasons. First, he raised the possibility that all social thought is ideological, which implies that there is no purely scientific or objective understanding of social arrangements. In doing this, however, he stretched the notion of ideology to mean something like a system of beliefs about the social world, or a *Weltanschauung* (world view). This is the second reason for Mannheim's importance here, for he made it possible to think of an ideology as something more than a defense of the interests of the dominant class.

By stretching the notion in this way, of course, Mannheim may have made it harder to determine just what an ideology is. The term may simply be too vague to be useful. At least this is the view of some twentieth century social scientists. Because "ideology" has meant different things to different people at different times, these social scientists have suggested that it be replaced by a less loaded term, such as *belief system*.[4]

Their suggestion has not been widely accepted. "Ideology" is too important and too powerful a word to be abandoned, it seems. But it also seems to resist definition. To many people, "ideology" remains a pejorative term. In their view, ideologies always simplify and distort matters. Worse yet, ideologues encourage their followers to believe that their particular ideology has a monopoly on the truth. Anyone who disagrees, then, must be an enemy who stands in the way of truth, justice, and progress—an enemy who must either be converted or defeated. "The trouble is," one critic says,

> . . . that ideologists are "terrible simplifiers." Ideology makes it unnecessary for people to confront individual issues on their individual merits. One simply turns to the ideological vending machine, and out comes the prepared formulae. And when these beliefs are suffused by apocalyptic fervor, ideas become weapons, and with dreadful results.[5]

If "ideology" continues to carry negative connotations for many, however, there is growing evidence that many others use the word in a neutral fashion to mean something akin to "belief system." In the 1988 U.S. presidential campaign, for example, George Bush sought to emphasize an ideological difference between himself and his opponent, Michael Dukakis, whom Bush portrayed as a "big-spending liberal." Judge the candidates not only in terms of their competence, Bush urged the voters, but also in terms of their ideology. "Competence is important," he said, "but so is ideology." In saying this, of course, Bush was saying that he had an ideology. He would not have said this if he thought of ideology as something sinister, distorted, or dangerous. In his eyes, and in the eyes of many others, an ideology is simply a more or less consistent set of ideas, beliefs, and convictions about how the world is and how it ought to be.

Which of these two conceptions of ideology is correct? This is a question we cannot settle here. As our history of the concept shows, both views of ideology are defensible. For our purposes in this book, however, we prefer the second conception. By following this view we can give ideology in general, as well as the specific ideologies we discuss, as fair a hearing as possible. What we need, then, is a useful definition of a term that is notoriously difficult to define. Such a definition must be broad enough to encompass what most people have in mind when they talk about ideologies, but not so broad as to include anything and everything related to social and political thought. With these conditions in mind, we offer the following definition.

A WORKING DEFINITION OF "IDEOLOGY"

An ideology is a fairly coherent and comprehensive set of ideas that explains and evaluates social conditions, helps people understand their place in society, and provides a program for social and political action. An ideology, in other words, performs four functions for people who hold it: the (1) explanatory, (2) evaluative, (3) orientative, and (4) programmatic functions. Just how it performs them can best be seen by looking directly at the functions themselves.

Explanation   An ideology offers an explanation of why social, political, and economic conditions are as they are. If everything seems to be going well in society, most people are not likely to worry about these conditions. When there is a crisis, however, or a sense that things are somehow out of order, people will search, sometimes frantically, for some explanation of what is happening. Why are there wars? Why do depressions occur? What causes unemployment? Why are some people rich and others poor? Why are relations between different races so often strained and difficult? To these and many other questions different ideologies supply different answers. But in one way or another, every ideology tries to answer these questions and to make sense of the complicated world in which we live. A Marxist might explain wars as an outgrowth of **capitalists'** competition for foreign markets, for instance, while a fascist is apt to explain them as tests of one nation's *will* against another's. Sometimes the explanation may be highly abstract and technical—as in Marx's *Capital*, for example. Ideologies typically want to reach as many people as possible, however, and this leads many ideologists to offer simpler, sometimes simplistic, explanations of puzzling events and circumstances.

Evaluation   Besides explaining why things are the way they are, ideologies tell us what we should think about them. They go beyond explanation, that is, to supply standards for evaluating social conditions and propose solutions for improving them. Are all wars evils to be avoided, or are some wars morally justifiable? Are depressions a normal part of the business cycle or a symptom of a sick economic system? Is full employment a reasonable ideal or a naive pipe dream? Are vast disparities of wealth between rich and poor a good or a bad thing? Are racial tensions inevitable or are they avoidable? Again, an ideology supplies its followers with the criteria required for answering these and other questions. If you are a libertarian, for example, you are likely to evaluate a proposed policy by asking if it increases or decreases the role of government in the lives of individuals. If it increases government's role, the policy is undesirable. If you are a feminist you will probably ask whether this proposed policy will work for or against the interests of women, then either approve or disapprove of it on that basis. Or if you are a communist, you are apt to ask how this proposal affects the working class and whether it raises or lowers the prospects of their victory in the class struggle. This means that those who follow one ideology may evaluate favorably something that the followers of a different ideology greatly dislike—communists look upon class struggle as a good thing, for instance, while fascists regard it as an evil. Whatever the position may be, however, it is clear that all ideologies provide standards or cues that help people decide whether some social policy or condition is good, bad, or indifferent.

Orientation   An ideology supplies its holder with an orientation and a sense of identity—of who he or she is, where he or she belongs, and how he or she is related to the rest of the world. If you are a communist, for example, you most likely think of yourself as a member of the working class who belongs to a party devoted to freeing workers from capitalist exploitation and oppression, and are therefore implacably opposed to the ruling capitalist class. Or if you are a Nazi you probably think of yourself as a white person and member of a party dedicated to preserving racial purity and enslaving or even eliminating "inferior" races. Or suppose that you are a feminist. If so, you are apt to think of yourself as first and foremost a woman (or a man sympathetic to women's problems) who belongs to a movement aiming to end sexual oppression and exploitation. Other ideologies enable their adherents to see their situation or position in society in still other ways, but all perform the function of orientation.

Political Program   An ideology, finally, tells its followers what to do and how to proceed. It performs a programmatic function by setting out a general program of social and political action. If you are a communist, for example, you believe it important to raise working-class consciousness or awareness in order to prepare for the overthrow of capitalism, the seizure of state power, and the eventual creation of a cooperative, communist society. If you are a nazi, however, you think it important for the "superior" white race to isolate, separate, subordinate, and perhaps even exterminate Jews, blacks, and other "inferior" peoples. If you are a libertarian your political program will include proposals for reducing or eliminating government interference in people's lives. But if you are a traditional conservative, you may want the state or government to intervene in order to promote morality or traditional values. Again, different ideologies will recommend very different programs of action, but all will recommend a program of some sort.

Political ideologies perform these four functions because they try to link thought, or ideas and beliefs, to action. Every ideology provides a vision of the social and political world as it is, and as it should be, in hopes of inspiring people to act either to change or preserve their way of life. If it does not do this—if it does not perform all four functions—it is not a political ideology. In this way our functional definition helps to sharpen our picture of what an ideology is by showing us what it is—and is not.

One thing an ideology is *not* is a scientific theory. To be sure, the distinction between an ideology and a scientific theory is sometimes difficult to draw, partly because the proponents of political ideologies often claim that their views are truly scientific. Another reason is that scientists, particularly social scientists, sometimes fail to see that their ideological biases are shaping their theories. And political ideologies frequently borrow from scientific theories to help explain why the world is as it is. Some anarchists and some liberals have used Darwin's theory of evolution for their own purposes, for instance, as have nazis.

Difficult as it may sometimes be to separate the two, there is still a difference between a theory, such as Darwin's, and an ideology that draws on and often distorts the theory. Scientific theories are **empirical** in nature, which means that they are concerned with describing and explaining some feature or features of the world, not with prescribing what people ought to do. To the extent that these theories carry implications for how people *can* live, of course, they also carry implications for the **normative** problem of how people *should* live. This is especially true of theories of society, where empirical and normative concerns are remarkably difficult, some say impossible, to separate. But to agree that scientific theories have implications for action is not to admit that they are ideologies. The scientist is not directly concerned *as a scientist* with these implications, but the ideologue certainly is.

We can also use our functional definition to distinguish political ideologies from some of the other "isms," such as terrorism, that are occasionally mistaken for ideologies. Because the names of the most prominent ideologies end with the suffix *ism*, some people conclude that all "isms" must be political ideologies. This is clearly a mistake. Whatever else they are, alcoholism, magnetism, and hypnotism are not political ideologies. Nor is terrorism. Terrorism may offer a program for social and political action, thus performing the programmatic function, but it does not itself explain and evaluate conditions or provide people with an orientation. Terrorism is a strategy that some ideologues use to try to advance their causes, but it is not an ideology itself.

This functional definition, finally, helps to distinguish democracy from political ideologies. Unlike socialism, conservatism, and the other ideologies, democracy offers no explanation of why things are the way they are, and it is only in a loose sense that we can say that democracy serves the evaluative, orientative, or programmatic functions. Furthermore, almost all political ideologies claim to be democratic, a claim they could hardly make if democracy were an ideology itself. One can claim to be a conservative democrat, a liberal democrat, or a social(ist) democrat, for instance, much more easily than one can claim to be a socialist conservative, say, or a liberal fascist. This suggests that democracy, or rule by the people, is an *ideal* rather than an ideology—a topic we pursue further in the next chapter.

In these three cases, the functional definition helps to clarify what an ideology is by eliminating possibilities that do not perform all four functions. There are other cases, however, where our functional definition is not so helpful. The task of distinguishing a political theory or philosophy from an ideology is one of them. In this case the functional definition offers no help, for political theories typically perform the same four functions. The chief difference is that they do so at a higher, more abstract, and perhaps more dispassionate level. The great works of political philosophy, such as Plato's *Republic* and Rousseau's *Social Contract*, certainly attempt to explain and evaluate social conditions, just as they try to provide the reader with a sense of his or her place in the world. They even prescribe programs for action of a very general sort. But masterpieces of political philosophy tend to be highly abstract and complex—and not, therefore, the kind of writing that stirs great numbers of people into action. Political ideologies draw on the works of the great political philosophers, much as they draw on scientific theories to promote their causes. But because their concern to link thought to action is so immediate, political ideologies tend to simplify the ideas of political philosophers to make them accessible, and inspiring, to masses of people. The difference between a political philosophy and a political ideology, then, is largely a difference of degree. They accomplish the same things, but political ideologies do so in simpler, less abstract ways, because their focus is more tightly fixed on the importance of action.

Similar problems arise with regard to religion. Most religions, perhaps all, perform the explanatory, evaluative, orientative, and programmatic functions for their followers. Does this mean they are ideologies? It does if we define an ideology simply as a *belief system*. Many scholars and quite a few ideologues have noted, moreover, the ways in which political ideologies take on the characteristics of a religion for their followers. One account of **communism** by former communists, for instance, is called *The God that Failed*.[6] And there is no denying that religious concerns have played, and continue to play, a major role in ideological conflicts—as is noted in subsequent chapters. Still, there is an important difference between religions and political ideologies. Religions are often concerned with the supernatural and divine—with God (or gods) and the after-life (or after-lives)—whereas ideologies are much more interested in the here and now, with this life on this earth. Rather than prepare people for a better life in the next world, in other words, political ideologies stress the importance of helping them to live as well as possible in this world.

This difference, again, is a matter of degree. Most religions take an active interest in how people live on earth, but this is neither always nor necessarily their abiding concern. For a political ideology, it is. Even so, drawing sharp and clear distinctions between political ideologies, on the one hand, and scientific theories, political philosophies, and religions, on the other, is not the most important point for someone who wants to understand ideologies. The most important point is to see how the different ideologies perform the four functions—and how they make use of various theories, philosophies, and religious beliefs in order to do so.

HUMAN NATURE AND FREEDOM

For a political ideology to perform these four functions—the explanatory, evaluative, orientative, and programmatic—it must draw on some deeper conception of human potential, of what human beings are capable of achieving. This means that implicit in every ideology are two further features: (1) a set of basic beliefs about *human nature* and (2) a conception of *freedom*.

Human Nature

Some conception of human nature—an account of basic human drives, motivations, limitations, and possibilities—is present, at least implicitly, in every ideology. Some ideologies assume that it is the nature of human beings to compete with one another in hopes of acquiring the greatest possible share of scarce resources; others hold that people are *naturally* inclined to cooperate with each other and to share what they have with others. For example, a classical liberal, or a contemporary libertarian, is likely to believe that human beings are "naturally" competitive and acquisitive. A communist, by contrast, will hold that competitiveness and acquisitiveness are "unnatural" and nasty vices nurtured by a deformed and deforming capitalist system, a system that warps people whose true nature is to be cooperative and generous. Still, other ideologies take it for granted that human beings have a natural or innate racial consciousness that compels them to associate with their own kind and to avoid associating or even sympathizing with members of other races. Thus nazis maintain that it is natural for races to struggle for dominance and unnatural to seek interracial peace and harmony.

These conceptions of human nature are important to the understanding of political ideologies because they play a large part in determining how each ideology performs the four functions. They are especially important because each ideology's notion of human nature sets the limits of what it considers to be politically possible. When a communist says that you ought to work to bring about a classless society, for instance, this implies that he or she believes that a classless society is something human beings are capable of achieving—and something, therefore, that human nature does not rule out. When a conservative urges you to cherish and defend traditional social arrangements, on the other hand, this implies that he or she believes that human beings are weak and fallible creatures who are more likely to damage society than to improve it. Other ideologies take other views of human nature, but in every case the program a political ideology prescribes is directly related to its core conception of human nature, or to its notion of what human beings are truly like and what they are capable of doing.

Freedom

Strange as it may seem, every ideology claims to defend and extend *freedom* (or its synonym *liberty*). Freedom figures in the performance of both the evaluative and programmatic functions, with all ideologies condemning societies that do not promote freedom and promising to take steps to promote it themselves. But different ideologies define "freedom" in different, and sometimes radically divergent, ways. A classical conservative's understanding of freedom differs from a classical liberal's or contemporary libertarian's understanding, for instance; both, in turn, disagree with a communist's view of freedom; and all three diverge radically from a nazi's notion of freedom. This is because freedom is an **essentially contested concept**. What counts as being free is a matter of controversy, in other words, because there is no one, indisputably correct, definition of *freedom*.

Because every ideology claims to promote freedom, that concept provides a convenient basis for comparing and contrasting different ideologies. In later chapters, therefore, we explicate every ideology's conception of freedom by fitting it within the triadic, or three-cornered, model proposed by Gerald Mac-Callum.[7] According to MacCallum, every conception of freedom necessarily refers to three features: (A) an agent, (B) a barrier or obstacle blocking the agent, and (C) a goal at which the agent aims. And every statement about freedom can take the following form: "(A) is (or is not) free from (B) to achieve, be or become (C)."

To say that someone is free, in other words, is to say that he or she is *free from* something and therefore *free to do* something. The *agent* is the person, thing, or group who is free. But a person is not simply free; to be free, a person must be *free to* pursue a *goal*, whether it is speaking one's mind, practicing one's religion, or merely going for a stroll in the park. No one can be free to pursue a goal, however, unless he or she is also free from particular *obstacles* (or barriers, or restraints). These may take a wide variety of forms—walls, chains, prejudices, and poverty, to name a few—but the point is that no one can be free when there are obstacles that prevent one from doing what one wants to do. So "freedom" refers to a relationship involving an agent who is both free from some obstacle and free to achieve some goal.

We can visualize this relationship in a diagram (See Figure 1.1). Consider how these three aspects of freedom are present even in so ordinary a question as "Are you free tonight?" The agent in this case is *you*, the person to whom the question is addressed. There are no obvious obstacles or goals specified in the question, but that is because the point of the question is to learn whether some obstacle keeps the agent from pursuing a particular goal. When we ask someone whether he or she is free tonight, in other words, we are trying to determine whether anything—such as the need to study for a test, to go to work, or to keep a promise to someone else—prevents that person from doing something. If not, then the agent in this instance is free.

But what of *political* freedom? According to MacCallum, people have different views of what counts as freedom in politics because they identify A, B, and C in different ways. Let us examine each of these, beginning with the

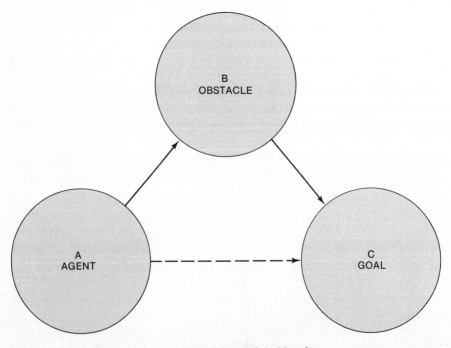

Figure 1.1 The triadic model of freedom.

agent, proceeding to a consideration of the agent's goals, and returning to examine the barriers or obstacles facing the agent in pursuing those goals.

The Agent   The agent can be an individual, a class, a group, a nation, a sex, a race, or even a species. As noted in Chapter 3, liberals typically talk of freedom as the freedom of the individual. Marx and the Marxists, by contrast, focus their attention on the freedom of a particular class, the working class. Mussolini and the Italian Fascists identified the agent as a nation-state; German fascists (Nazis) as a race. For feminists the gender identity of the agent is all-important.

The Goal   Agents have goals. Different kinds of agents have different kinds of goals. A nazi's goal is the "purity" and supremacy of the white race. A communist's goal is the achievement of a classless communist society. A liberal's goal is to live in his or her own way, without undue interference from others. A feminist's goal is to live in a society that recognizes and rewards the capacities and worth of women.

Obstacles   In pursuing their goals, agents often encounter obstacles in their path. These obstacles can take various forms: material or physical conditions (poverty or physical disabilities, for instance); crime; social, political, and economic ideas, ideologies, institutions, practices, traditions, and beliefs. Women confront sexism and sexual discrimination. Communists confront the apathy and "false consciousness" of the workers and the wealth and power of the capitalist class. Nazis confront Jews, blacks, and other "inferior" races and the non-racially based ideologies of communism and liberalism. To the extent that these agents can overcome or remove these obstacles, they are said to be "free." To the degree that they are unable to do so, they are not free, but "unfree." And when the individuals—or class, or race, or gender a political ideology takes as its agent—are not free to realize their goals, then the ideology will call for action to remove the obstacles to their freedom. Throughout the history of political ideologies, that action has often taken the form of revolution.

IDEOLOGY AND REVOLUTION

Like "ideology," the word **revolution** is a relatively recent addition to the vocabulary of politics. Until 1688, the primary use of the term was in astronomy, as in the earth's revolution around the sun. To undergo a revolution, in this sense, is simply to revolve, and thus to return to some starting point. It was this sense of revolution that led to its first use to describe a set of political events, the Glorious Revolution of 1688. Believing that their king was attempting to deprive them of their liberties, the English forcibly drove King James II from the country and "restored" the liberties of Englishmen. Because they saw this as a return to the condition they had enjoyed before James II tried to take all power into his own hands, the English regarded their uprising as a revolution.

In its first political use, then, "revolution" did not refer to the attempt to do anything new or radical. But after the American and French revolutions, this is exactly what it came to mean. The American Revolution may have begun as an attempt to restore the colonists' rights as Englishmen, but it ended with the creation of a new country with a new system of government. Then, while that new system was still taking shape, the French Revolution began with the intention not of returning to the old ways, but of introducing a radically new social and political order. As we shall see in Chapter 3, this revolution went further than the men who launched it intended and ended in a way none of them wanted. But it did bring about sweeping changes in the social, economic, and political life of France. Indeed, the French Revolution sent shock waves through all of Europe and much of the rest of the world, waves so strong that their effects are still very much with us. One sign of this is the way political positions are now commonly described as **left**, **right**, or **center**. These terms come from the seating arrangements in the National Assembly of the revolutionary period. Moderates sat in the center, those who favored radical change congregated on the left of the chamber, and those who argued against change gathered on the right. Thus people all over the world now think of politics in categories—leftists, centrists, right-wingers—bequeathed to them by the French Revolution. The idea of a revolution as an attempt to overthrow the old order of society in order to replace it with something new and fundamentally different is part of this heritage.

Revolutions are radical. Their aim is not simply to replace one set of rulers or leaders with another, nor to make minor changes or reforms in the political structure. Revolutionaries want to overthrow the old order because they believe it is fundamentally rotten or corrupt. Changes or reforms are not enough, in their view, if the government and society are diseased at the roots. When this is the case, they say, the only solution is to uproot the whole social order and replace it with something better. This is literally a radical approach, for "radical" comes from the Latin *radix*, meaning root.

Of course, no one will undertake anything so radical as a revolution unless he or she believes that it is indeed possible to bring about a fundamental change for the better in society. This is why conservatives are so suspicious of revolutions—except, perhaps, when they seek to revolve back to their vision of the way things used to be, as in President Reagan's and Prime Minister Thatcher's "revolutions" of the 1980s. But conservatives' low estimate of human nature generally leads them to believe that sweeping improvements in society are practically impossible. Conservatism is very different from the other ideologies in this respect, however. All the others hold to the view that human reason and action can bring about great advances in society, politics, and the quality of life. Each ideology has its own idea of what counts as an advance or improvement, to be sure, but all except conservatism have been generally optimistic about the possibility of dramatic progress and significant improvement in the quality of human life.

In this respect political ideologies are products of the modern world. In the ancient and medieval periods of history, most people had every reason to believe that their lives would be much the same as their parents' and grandparents' lives. Most of them made their living from the soil or the sea, and changes in their ways of life were so slow in coming that they usually had little reason to believe that their children's or grandchildren's lives would be significantly different from their own. In the modern world, however, the pace of change has become so rapid that we now have people, futurists or futurologists, who make careers of anticipating the changes to come; others, meanwhile, fear that they will not be able to adjust or keep up with change as their jobs and perhaps even their attitudes become obsolete. For better or worse, we live in an age of innovation. And this, for better or worse, is also an age of ideology.

Ideologies and innovation are connected in an important way. The scientific, technical, and even artistic advances that mark the beginnings of the modern world in Europe instilled in many people a faith in progress, a belief that life on earth could become far more rewarding for many more people than it had ever been before. Before people could enjoy the fruits of progress, however, society itself would have to be reordered. The old ways of life retarded progress, especially when they prevented creative and vigorous individuals from using their energies and initiative to improve life for themselves and others. So the institutions that upheld the old ways of life, notably the Roman Catholic church and the economic order of feudalism, came under attack from those who sought to free individuals to make the most of themselves in a new world of opportunity, progress, and reason. This attack took a number of forms, including the philosophical movement known as the Enlightenment. Inspired by the scientific discoveries of Sir Isaac Newton (1642–1727) and Locke's *Essay Concerning Human Understanding* (1690), the Enlightenment philosophers saw the world as something to be comprehended by human reason and perfected by human action. Their writings served, in turn, to inspire Destutt de Tracy, at the end of the eighteenth century, to devise the new science of *ideölogie*.

The attack on the old way of life also took the form, even before the Enlightenment, of liberalism, the first of the political ideologies. How liberalism arose as a reaction against religious conformity and feudalism in the name of tolerance and opportunity is a story that is told in Chapter 3. For now, the important point is that first liberalism, then all the other political ideologies except conservatism, grew out of a conviction that human life and society can and should be dramatically changed. It is this conviction that leads some people to try to inspire others to join in movements of one kind or another to reshape and even revolutionize their social and political systems. It is this conviction, in short, that gives rise to political ideologies.

NATIONALISM AND ANARCHISM

Two more important features of the age of ideology remain to be discussed. These features, **nationalism** and **anarchism**, are often considered ideologies in their own right. We have no quarrel with this, especially since one can plausibly argue that both nationalism and anarchism perform the four functions that define a political ideology. But nationalism and anarchism take so many forms and are so entwined with so many different ideologies that we think it better not to treat them as distinct ideologies. Few nationalists are simply nationalists, for instance. They are, instead, liberal or conservative or communist or fascist nationalists. Anarchists also are divided in this way, with most of them following either liberalism or socialism to the radical conclusions that mark them as anarchists. For these reasons, it seems better to weave the discussions of nationalism and anarchism into the discussions of those ideologies most closely connected with them. But first we need to have some idea of what nationalism and anarchism are.

Nationalism

One of the most powerful forces in modern politics, nationalism grows out of the sense that the people of the world fall more or less naturally into distinct groups, or nations. A person's nationality, in this view, is not something he or she chooses, but something acquired at birth. Indeed, *nation* and *nationality* come from the Latin word for birth, *natus*. A nation, then, is a group of people who in some sense share a common birth. In this way a person's nationality may be separate from his or her citizenship. A member of the Cherokee nation, for example, may also be a citizen of the United States. From the perspective of the ardent nationalist, however, nationality and citizenship *should not* be separate. The people who share a common birth, who belong to the same nation, should also share citizenship in the same political unit, or state. This is the source of the idea of the **nation-state**, a sovereign, self-governing political unit that binds together and expresses the feelings and needs of a single nation.

Although nationalistic sentiments have been present through much of history, they became especially powerful following the Napoleonic Wars of the early 1800s. As Napoleon's French armies conquered most of Europe, they stirred the resentment, and sometimes the envy, of many of the conquered peoples. This was particularly true in Germany and Italy, neither of which was a unified country at the time. Germany was a scattered collection of separate political units, ranging in size and strength from the Kingdom of Prussia and the Austrian Empire to tiny duchies or baronies ruled by the local nobility. Even so, the people of these scattered communities spoke a common language and shared a common literature, as well as many customs and traditions. Italy's condition was similar. The victories of Napoleon's armies—the victories of the French *nation*—created a backlash that inspired many people in Germany, Italy, and elsewhere to recognize their respective nationalities and to struggle for unified nation-states of their own.

In the nineteenth and twentieth centuries this nationalistic struggle spread to virtually every part of the globe. Nationalistic sentiments and antagonisms helped to provoke World Wars I and II, for example, as well as the anticolonial "wars of national liberation" in Asia and Africa. For all their emotional power and political force, however, the ideas of nation and nationalism are plagued by difficulties. One is the difficulty of determining just what a nation is. What marks a group of people as members of the same nationality, in other words? There is no clear answer to this question, although nationalists often appeal to such characteristics as shared race, ethnicity, culture, language, religion, customs, or history. These traits, however, are themselves notoriously difficult to define.

Even if we can determine what nationality is, another difficulty remains for nationalism. Many states—Canada, Switzerland, the Soviet Union, and the United States among them—include people of apparently different nationalities. Should each group have its own state? Should Switzerland be taken apart, for instance, with France, Germany, and Italy absorbing the French-speaking, German-speaking, and Italian-speaking parts, respectively? Should this happen even though the Swiss seem to be prospering under their present arrangement? Or should we say that together they form a new nation, the Swiss? If so, when and how did these people, with their different languages and cultures, become a single nation?

Despite these difficulties, there is no doubt that many people not only feel the pull of national sentiment, but think of themselves primarily in terms of nationality. As long as this is true, nationalism is likely to remain a powerful force in politics, as will become clear in later chapters.

Anarchism

Considerable confusion surrounds the words *anarchy* and *anarchism*. Contrary to popular misconception, anarchy does not mean chaos or confusion, nor do anarchists favor chaos and confusion. The word comes from the Greek *an archos*, meaning "no rule" or "no government." An anarchist is, then, someone who advocates abolishing the state, replacing its coercive force with voluntary cooperation among freely consenting and cooperating individuals. As the anarchist sees it, government by its very nature is immoral and evil. All governments force people to do things they do not want to do, such as pay taxes, fight in wars, follow orders, and so on, so all governments engage in immoral, coercive actions. One could agree with this assessment, of course, yet maintain that government or the state is simply a necessary evil that people should continue to obey. The anarchist, however, believes that the state is not necessary, but simply evil. Given the chance, anarchists insist, people can live together peacefully and prosperously with no coercive authority over them.

All anarchists agree, then, that the state is an evil to be abolished in favor of a system of voluntary cooperation. But there the agreement ends. Some anarchists are radical individualists who advocate a competitive and capitalist, but stateless, society. Others are communalists who detest capitalism and believe that anarchism requires the common control of property. Some anarchists advocate the violent overthrow of the state; others are pacifists who believe that only a peaceful path can lead to a cooperative society. The disagreements and differences between anarchists, in short, overwhelm the single point on which they agree.

Like nationalism, anarchism has played a major part in the development of modern political ideologies. In the late nineteenth and early twentieth centuries, in particular, it was a significant political force in many parts of the world. Since then, however, its influence has waned. A number of theorists continue to argue that the state is immoral and that anarchy is possible, but few appear to be taking direct action against the state.

CONCLUSION

We began by noting how important ideologies are in the conflicts that characterize modern political life. We then looked at the term *ideology*, showing how its original meaning differs from current usage. An ideology, as we define the term, is a more or less coherent and comprehensive set of ideas that performs four functions for those who accept it: (1) it explains why social conditions are the way they are; (2) it evaluates those conditions; (3) it helps to orient people so they can see how they fit into society; and (4) it provides a program for social and political action. In every ideology, moreover, there are core assumptions about human nature and freedom—assumptions that have led most of them, at one time or another, to call for a revolution.

In later chapters we examine the history and structure of different ideologies. Before doing that, however, we must look more closely at democracy. As we argue in the following chapter, democracy is not itself an ideology, but an ideal that different ideologies either reject outright or, more often, pursue in different ways.

NOTES

1. For accounts of the origin and history of *ideology*, see Terrell Carver, "Ideology," in Terence Ball and Richard Dagger, eds., *Ideals and Ideologies: A Reader* (New York: HarperCollins, 1991), selection 1; Mark Goldie, "Ideology," in Terence Ball, James Farr, and Russell L. Hanson, eds., *Political Innovation and Conceptual Change* (Cambridge: Cambridge University Press, 1989), pp. 266–291; and George Lichtheim, *The Concept of Ideology, and Other Essays* (New York: Random House, 1967).
2. Karl Marx and Friedrich Engels, *The German Ideology*, ed. C. J. Arthur (New York: International Publishers, 1970), p. 64.
3. Karl Mannheim, *Ideology and Utopia*, trans. Louis Wirth and Edward Shils (New York: Harcourt, Brace & World, 1936); first German edition, 1929.
4. Philip Converse, "The Nature of Belief Systems in Mass Publics," in David Apter, ed., *Ideology and Discontent* (New York: Free Press, 1964).
5. Daniel Bell, *The End of Ideology; On the Exhaustion of Political Ideas in the Fifties* (New York: Collier Books, 1961), pp. 399–400.
6. Arthur Koestler et al., *The God that Failed*, ed. R. H. S. Crossman (Freeport, N.Y.: Books for Libraries Press, 1972; originally published 1949).
7. Gerald MacCallum, Jr., "Negative and Positive Freedom," *Philosophical Review*, 76 (1967): 312–334.

FOR FURTHER READING

Arendt, Hannah. *On Revolution* (New York: Viking, 1963).

Berlin, Isaiah. *Four Essays on Liberty* (Oxford: Oxford University Press, 1969).

————. "Nationalism: Past Neglect and Present Power," in I. Berlin, ed., *Against the Current: Essays in the History of Ideas* (Harmondsworth: Penguin, 1982).

Bookchin, Murray. *Post-Scarcity Anarchism* (London: Wildwood House, 1974).

Carter, April. *The Political Theory of Anarchism* (London: Routledge & Kegan Paul, 1971).

Dunn, John. "Revolution," in Terence Ball, James Farr, and Russell L. Hanson, eds., *Political Innovation and Conceptual Change* (Cambridge: Cambridge University Press, 1989).

Kohn, Hans. *Nationalism: Its Meaning and History* (Princeton, N.J.: D. Van Nostrand, 1955).

Lichtheim, George. *The Concept of Ideology, and Other Essays* (New York: Random House, 1967).

McLellan, David. *Ideology* (Minneapolis: University of Minnesota Press, 1986).

Miller, David. *Anarchism* (London: Dent, 1984).

Wolff, Robert Paul. *In Defense of Anarchism* (New York: Harper & Row, 1970).

Woodcock, George. *Anarchism* (Harmondsworth: Penguin, 1963).

Chapter
2

The Democratic Ideal

No one pretends that democracy is perfect or all-wise. Indeed, it has been said that democracy is the worst form of Government except all those other forms that have been tried from time to time.

Winston Churchill

O ne of the most striking features of contemporary politics is the astonishing popularity of democracy. There are few people nowadays, whether major political leaders or ordinary citizens and subjects, who do not praise democracy and claim to be democrats. Except for fascists, nazis, and a few others, in fact, everyone seems to agree that democracy is desirable. But this agreement comes in the midst of vigorous, sometimes violent, ideological conflict. How can this be? How can men and women of almost all ideological persuasions— liberal and socialist, communist and conservative—share this belief in the value of democracy?

One answer is to say that many people use the word *democracy* in a hypocritical or deceptive way. Democracy is so popular it seems that everyone will try to link his or her ideology, whatever it may be, to democracy. The formal title of East Germany before the collapse of its communist regime in 1989– 1990 was the German *Democratic* Republic, for instance. Yet the government of this "democracy" strictly limited freedom of speech and effectively outlawed competition for political office. With this and other examples in mind, some critics have complained that the word *democracy* has been misused so often as to rob it of any meaning.

A second answer is to say that followers of different ideologies simply have different ideas about how to achieve democracy. Almost all agree that democracy is a good thing, but they disagree about how best to bring it about. Most people in the United States regard a dictatorship as an obviously undemocratic regime, but Mao Ze-dong, the leader of the Chinese Communist party for more than forty years, maintained that his government was a "people's democratic dictatorship." Mao apparently saw no contradiction in this because he believed that China needed a period of dictatorship to prepare the way for democracy.

Perhaps, then, there is a genuine and widespread agreement that democracy is the true *end* or *goal* of ideological activity, with disagreement arising only over the proper *means* for achieving that end.

Although there may be merit in both these positions, we think a third answer provides a deeper insight into the problem: different people quite simply mean different things by "democracy." They may all want to achieve or promote democracy, but they disagree about *how* to do this because they disagree about *what* democracy truly is. With respect to political ideologies, we may say that democracy is an *ideal* that most ideologies espouse; but because they have very different understandings of what democracy is, they pursue it in very different ways. They may even come in conflict with one another in their attempts to achieve or promote what they take democracy to be.

Democracy, then, like freedom, is an **essentially contested concept.** The democratic ideal is itself deeply involved in the ideological conflict of the modern world. To understand this conflict, we need to know more about democracy and the democratic ideal. In particular, we need to know what the term originally meant and why it is only in the last 150 years or so that democracy has been widely regarded as a desirable form of government.

THE ORIGINS OF DEMOCRACY

Democracy, the word, and democracy, the form of political life, both began in ancient Greece. The word comes from a combination of the Greek noun *demos,* meaning common people, and the verb *kratein,* to rule. For the Greeks, *demokratia* meant specifically rule or government by the common people—that is, those who were uneducated, unsophisticated, and poor. Because these people made up the majority of the citizenry, democracy was identified, as it still is today, with majority rule. But it is important to note that this majority consisted mainly of a single class, the *demos.* Many Greeks thus understood democracy to be a form of class rule, government by and for the benefit of the lower or working class. As such, it stood in contrast to aristocracy, rule by the *aristoi,* or the "best," those supposedly most qualified to govern.

The center of activity in ancient Greece, which was not united under a single government, was the self-governing *polis,* or city-state. Athens, the largest *polis,* provides the best example of a democratic city-state. Throughout most of the second half of the fifth century B.C., sometimes called the Golden Age of Athens, Athenians regarded their *polis* as a democracy. Not everyone willingly accepted this state of affairs, but those who did seem to have embraced democracy enthusiastically. This is evident in the words attributed to Pericles, the most famous leader of the Athenian democracy, in his Funeral Oration.

> Our form of government does not enter into rivalry with the institutions of others. We do not copy our neighbours, but are an example to them. It is true that we are called a democracy, for the administration is in the hands of the many and not of the few. But while the law secures equal justice to all alike in their private disputes,

the claim of excellence is also recognized; and when a citizen is in any way distin-
guished, he is preferred [for] the public service, not as a matter of privilege, but
as the reward of merit. Neither is poverty a bar, but a man may benefit his country
[*polis*] whatever be the obscurity of his condition.[1]

Pericles' words hint at the tension between aristocrats and democrats in
ancient Athens. The aristocrats generally believed that only the well-estab-
lished citizens, those with substantial property and ties to the noble families,
were truly capable of governing. Pericles and the democrats, however, believed that most citizens were capable of governing if only they could afford to
take the time away from their farms and work. To this end, the Athenian democracy paid citizens an average day's wages to enable the poor as well as the
rich to go to the assembly, debate, and decide policy by their votes. Citizens
also were paid to serve on a jury, sometimes for as much as a year at a time.
As further testimony to their faith in the *demos,* the Athenians filled a number
of their political offices not by election, but by lottery.

Pericles' Funeral Oration also suggests another distinction of great significance to the Athenians, that between the citizen (*politēs*) and the private person (*idiotēs*). In Athens, Pericles said,

An Athenian citizen does not neglect the state [*polis*] because he takes care of his
own household; and even those of us who are engaged in business have a very fair
idea of politics. We alone regard a man who takes no interest in public affairs, not
as harmless, but as a useless character; and if few of us are originators, we are all
sound judges of a policy.[2]

Even more significant to Athenian democracy was another aspect of their
notion of citizenship. To be a citizen, one had to be an adult, free, male Athenian. Women, resident foreigners, and slaves (who may have made up a majority
of the population) were all excluded. In fact, only about one out of ten inhabitants of Athens was a citizen. From the vantage point of the late twentieth century, then, it appears that Athenian democracy was hardly democratic at all.

This judgment becomes even more striking when we consider that Athenian democracy provided little if any protection for minority rights. All *citizens*
were equal in the eyes of the law, to be sure, but this did not mean that any
citizen was free to express his opinions regardless of how unpopular those opinions might be. The Athenian assembly sometimes banished citizens temporar-
ily from Athens, without trial and even without legal charges being brought
against them, simply because the majority of the assembly thought these citizens posed a danger to the *polis.* This was the practice of *ostracism,* so called
because of the shell or piece of pottery (*ostrakon*) on which Athenian citizens
wrote the names of those they wished to banish.

Sometimes the punishment for voicing unpopular views was even harsher.
We know this especially from the case of Socrates (469–399 B.C.), the philosopher who saw himself as a gadfly whose mission was to sting the sluggish citizens of Athens out of complacency by raising questions about their beliefs. "I
never cease to rouse each and every one of you," he said, "to persuade and

reproach you all day long and everywhere I find myself in your company."[3] In 399 B.C., when the democratic faction was in control, some citizens stung back, accusing Socrates of religious impiety and corrupting the morals of the youth of Athens. Socrates was tried, convicted, and condemned to death by poison. Thus Athens, the first democracy, created the first martyr to the cause of free thought and free speech.

In the fifth and fourth centuries B.C., however, those who favored democracy found themselves facing a different criticism. This was the complaint that democracy is a dangerously unstable form of government. Foremost among those who made this complaint was Socrates' student and friend, Plato (427–347 B.C.).

Plato believed that democracy is dangerous because it puts political power into the hands of ignorant and envious people. Because they are ignorant, he argued, the people will not know how to use political power for the common good. Because they are envious, they will be concerned only with their own good, which they will seek to advance by plundering those who are better off. Because they are both ignorant and envious, they will be easily swayed by demagogues—literally, leaders of the *demos*—who will flatter them, appeal to their envy, and turn citizen against citizen. From democracy, in short, comes civil war and anarchy, the destruction of the city-state. When democracy has left the *polis* in this wretched condition, according to Plato's analysis, the people will cry out for law and order, rallying around anyone strong enough to bring an end to anarchy. But such a person will be a despot, Plato said, a tyrant who cares nothing about the *polis* or the people because he cares only for power. So from democracy, the rule of the people, it is but a series of short steps to despotism.[4]

This argument against democracy found favor with a number of political thinkers, including Plato's student Aristotle (384–322 B.C.). Aristotle maintained that democracy is one of six basic kinds of political regimes or constitutions. Governing power, he said in his *Politics*, must be in the hands of one person, a few people, or many; and this power may be exercised either for the good of the whole community, in which case it is good or true, or solely for the good of the rulers, in which case it is bad or corrupt. By combining these features, Aristotle arrived at the following scheme.

	True forms	Perverted forms
Rule by one	monarchy	tyranny
Rule by the few	aristocracy	oligarchy
Rule by the many	polity	democracy

Two features of Aristotle's classification of regimes are especially noteworthy. The first, of course, is that he followed Plato in considering democracy to be bad or undesirable. For Aristotle, democracy is a corrupt form of rule because the *demos* tends to be short-sighted and selfish. The common people will recklessly pursue their own interests by taking property, wealth, and power from the few with no regard for the peace and stability of the *polis* as a whole. But this serves their interests only in the short run, and in the end they will bring chaos, and ultimately despotism, on the whole *polis*.

The second noteworthy feature of Aristotle's classification is the inclusion of **polity,** a good form of rule by the many. For Aristotle, polity differs from democracy because it mixes elements of rule by the few with elements of rule by the many. The virtue of this **mixed constitution** (or **government**) is that each group can keep an eye on the other—the well-to-do few on the many, the many on the few—so that neither class can pursue its interest at the expense of the common good. Aristotle also suggested that polity may differ from democracy in its distribution of wealth and property. In a democracy, that is, the many will be poor. This is simply the way things usually are, according to Aristotle, and there is little one can do about it. However, in those rare but fortunate circumstances where most of the people are neither rich nor poor, but "have a moderate and sufficient property,"[5] one can expect the many to rule in a prudent manner. This is because the many, when they are "middle class," will avoid the excesses of the envious poor and the arrogant rich. Seeing the good of the *polis* as their own good, the middling many will work to maintain peace and stability in the city-state.

In the final analysis, Aristotle believed polity to be good—he even suggested that it is the best of the six regimes—and democracy bad. But he also argued that democracy is better than tyranny and oligarchy (rule by the few). This is largely because the many are better judges than the few. Even if none of the common people is an especially good judge of what is right or wrong, good or bad, beautiful or ugly, their collective judgment is still better than that of any individual or small group, including a group of experts. This is true, Aristotle said, in the same way that "a feast to which many contribute is better than a dinner provided out of a single purse."[6] Besides, democracy gives more men the chance to participate in the active life of the citizen—to rule and be ruled in turn, as he put it.

Yet even as Aristotle was celebrating the citizen and the *polis*, this way of life was falling victim to a much larger political unit, namely, the empire. First under the leadership of Philip of Macedonia (382—336 B.C.), then under his son (and Aristotle's student), Alexander the Great (356–323 B.C.), the Hellenic Empire spread across Greece, throughout the Middle East, and all the way to India and Egypt. As the empire concentrated power in the hands of the emperor, the self-governing city-state died, and rule by the many, whether in the form of democracy or polity, perished with it. Monarchy at best, tyranny at worst—that was the order of the day.

DEMOCRACY AND REPUBLIC

Popular government survived in the ancient world, but in the form of the *republic* rather than democracy. The word **republic** derives from the Latin *res publica*, which literally means the public thing, or public business. It took on

Aristotle (384–322 B.C.).

a more specific meaning, however, in the hands of the Greek historian Polybius (ca. 200–ca. 118 B.C.).

The Republic and Mixed Government

Polybius spent some 17 years in Rome as a hostage. This experience fed his interest in the growth of Roman power, which Polybius saw as part of a cycle of the rise and fall of great powers. Every powerful empire or country is doomed to decline, Polybius said, for both history and nature tell us that nothing lasts forever. Still, some hold their power far longer than others, and Polybius thought the example of Rome helped to explain why this is so.

The key to Rome's success, Polybius declared in his *Histories* (Book VI), was its *mixed government*. This was not an entirely new idea—Plato had hinted at it, as had Aristotle in his discussion of the polity—but Polybius developed it more clearly than his predecessors. The Roman Republic was a mixed government, he said, because neither one person, nor the few, nor the many held exclusive power. Instead, the Republic mixed or balanced these three regimes in a way that provided the benefits of each form while avoiding its defects. Rather than give all power to one person, or a few people, or the common people, in other words, the Roman Republic divided power among the three. The people as a whole exercised some control over policymaking through their assemblies, in which the free, adult males could participate. The aristocrats controlled the Senate. Then, in place of a monarch, the Republic relied on consuls to put the policies into effect. In this way, Polybius said, no group was able to pursue its own interest at the expense of the common good. Each kept watch over the others, and the result was a form of government that was free, stable, and long-lasting. Like an alloy that is stronger than any one of the metals that make it up, so Polybius believed that a mixed government will prove more durable than any unmixed or "pure" form of rule.

A republic, then, was a form of popular government, but it was not meant to be a democracy. Democracy promoted vice—the self-interested rule of the common people—whereas a republic promoted virtue. Republican virtue was the ability to rise above personal or class interest, to place the good of the whole community above one's own. Only active citizens could achieve this virtue, the republicans argued, citizens eager to exercise their liberty and ever vigilant to protect it against any person or group who might try to seize power. Mixed government served both these purposes by encouraging some degree of popular participation in government while making it difficult for anyone to acquire enough power to threaten liberty and the common good.

Within 100 years of Polybius's death, however, the Roman Republic had given way to the Roman Empire. Beginning with Julius Caesar (100–44 B.C.), a series of emperors drained the power from Rome's republican institutions and concentrated it in their own hands. Almost 1500 years would pass before the republican ideal was fully revived in the city-states of the Italian Renaissance. Another 400 years would pass before the democratic ideal experienced a revival of its own.

Christianity and Democracy

There were, of course, many significant developments in the intervening years, perhaps the most significant being the rise of Christianity. In some respects Christianity seems a natural ally of democracy, for it proclaims that every person, regardless of gender, nationality, or status, is a child of God. By the standards of the ancient world, certainly, Christianity stood for radical equality.

Rich or poor, slave or free, citizen or alien, Greek, Jew, or Roman, woman or man—none of these differences really mattered, the Christians preached, because all are equal in the eyes of God.

We might expect, then, that the early Christians would argue that everyone should have an equal voice in government. But they did not. This was not because the early Christians were antidemocratic, but because they were antipolitical. Christianity taught that life on earth is a preparation for the coming kingdom of God, a pilgrimage to the Christian's true home in heaven; so by themselves the affairs of this world have no true or lasting value or significance. Especially in the early years of Christianity, when Christians typically thought that the end of the world was near, this belief led some to take a lawless attitude. The common or orthodox position, however, was the one St. Paul stated: "Let every person be subject to the governing authorities. For there is no authority except from God, and those that exist have been instituted by God. Therefore he who resists the authorities resists what God has appointed, and those who resist will incur judgment."[7] Where politics was concerned, in other words, the Christian message was simply to obey those in power and seek no power yourself.

Matters could not remain so simple, however, particularly when various Roman emperors sought to destroy this new and (to their eyes) dangerous religion. And matters became quite complicated indeed when, in the fourth century A.D., Christianity survived the persecutions to become the official religion of the Roman Empire. Then, following the collapse of the Empire around 500 A.D., the Christian church became the dominant institution in Europe. It remained so throughout the period we know as the Middle Ages, that is, roughly 500 to 1400 A.D. With the disintegration of the Empire, the Church itself gradually divided into two wings: the Eastern Orthodox church, led by the Byzantine Emperor, who ruled from Constantinople (now known as Istanbul); and the Roman Catholic church, whose Bishop of Rome came to be known as the Pope. The rise and rapid spread of the Islamic faith throughout the Middle East, across Northern Africa, and into Spain in the seventh and eighth centuries also meant that much of the Mediterranean world was lost to Christianity. Yet the Roman church saw itself as the one true church—"catholic" means universal—and it preached its message and enforced its doctrines wherever possible.

The Roman church provided the spiritual bond that united most of western and central Europe throughout the Middle Ages, but there was no comparable political bond. The collapse of the Roman Empire had brought a return to localism, although not of the Greek city-state variety. There were some independent city-states in the Middle Ages—for instance, Rome, where the Pope ruled—but more common varieties of local rule developed around tribal loyalties or the old military regions of the fallen Empire. This happened, in the latter case, as some regional commanders of the Roman army managed to keep their forces together and their regions secure even as the Empire crumbled. From these *duces* and *comites*, who found themselves governing their territories as best they could, came the dukes and counts of the Middle Ages.

There were occasional attempts to revive a more nearly universal political bond in the form of a new empire, the most notable beginning on Christmas day in the year 800 when Pope Leo III placed a crown on Charlemagne, King of the Franks, and proclaimed him Emperor. Despite repeated efforts over the centuries, however, the new Holy Roman Empire never achieved the power and stature of the old; as the historian Edward Gibbon later quipped, it was neither holy, nor Roman, nor an empire. Local ties and loyalties simply proved stronger than the desire for a politically united Christendom.

These local ties and loyalties also encouraged **feudalism.** This form of social organization, rooted in the need for protection from marauding Vikings and Magyars, led to a great emphasis on status, one's station or position in society. A few people were aristocrats or nobles, some were free, and a great many were serfs—peasants who lived and worked in bondage to an aristocrat in exchange for protection. According to the medieval ideal, every person occupied a rank or station in society and was expected to perform the duties and enjoy the privileges of that rank or station. In this way everyone supposedly contributed to the common good, just as every bee in a hive does what is best for all by performing its own duties.

In such a society, there was little room for the democratic ideal. The outlook began to shift with the Renaissance, however, as a renewed concern for human achievement led to a revival of republicanism.

Renaissance and Republicanism

In the late Middle Ages, particularly in the thirteenth century, several developments prepared the way for the Renaissance. For our purposes, two of these are especially important. The first was Western civilization's renewed contact with the East. This came about partly through the Crusades, that is, the attempts to recapture the Christian holy land of the Middle East from the "infidel" Muslims, and partly through dealings with Islamic Spain, which Muslims had conquered in the early 700s. As often happens, contact with strange lands and people stimulated many in the West to examine their own customs and beliefs. The discovery that other people live in ways very different from what one has always assumed to be the natural, the only reasonable way to live, is often unsettling and disturbing. But it can also encourage creativity as people begin to see that it is possible to live in different, and perhaps better, ways. This happened most directly as Christian scholars rediscovered, through Spain, many works of ancient scholarship that had been lost to the West since the collapse of the Roman Empire. The most significant of these in political terms was Aristotle's *Politics*, which was translated into Latin in 1260—but only after the church convened a committee of scholars to determine whether the "pagan" philosopher's ideas were compatible with Christianity.

The second development preparing the way for the Renaissance was the revival of the city-state in Italy. Many Italian cities enjoyed a measure of independence before the thirteenth century, but they remained subject to the Germanic head of the Holy Roman Empire. After years of struggle, they became self-governing city-states upon the death of Emperor Frederick II in 1250.

This is significant, first, because the Renaissance began in the Italian city-states. It is also significant because the citizens of these city-states looked for a way to justify self-government at a time when empire and monarchy were the predominant forms of rule. They found this justification in the ancient theorists of republicanism.

These developments, among others, led to the flowering of Western culture in the fourteenth through sixteenth centuries that scholars of that time took to be a renaissance, a rebirth or revival. Under the inspiration of the ancient philosophers, they concluded that life on earth is not simply a vale of tears, a wearisome journey that the Christian must take on his or her way to the kingdom of God in heaven. On the contrary, life on earth, so rich and diverse, is not only worth living, but worth living fully. For human beings are capable of wondrous things—not the least of which is self-government.

Drawing on the writings of Aristotle and Polybius and the examples of the ancient republics of Rome and Sparta, the Renaissance republicans argued for a revival of civic life in which public-spirited citizens could take an active part in the governance of their independent city or country. The key concepts in this argument were *liberty, virtue,* and *corruption,* and nowhere were these concepts deployed more effectively than in the writings of Niccolò Machiavelli.

Machiavelli (1469–1527) was a prominent official in the republic of Florence in 1512, when the Medici family overthrew the republican government and installed themselves as rulers of the city-state. Implicated in a plot to overthrow the Medici and restore the republic, Machiavelli was arrested, tortured, and banished to his family estate in the countryside. While in exile, he wrote two books. The better known of the two is *The Prince,* the small book in which Machiavelli apparently instructs princes and petty tyrants to put conscience aside and do whatever it takes—lie, steal, even murder—to stay in power. Indeed, Machiavelli became so notorious that Shakespeare referred to him as "the murderous Machiavel"[8]; even today we sometimes call a cunning and unscrupulous person "machiavellian."

Whether this is a fair reading of Machiavelli's purposes in *The Prince* is something scholars continue to debate. But it definitely does *not* capture Machiavelli's purposes in the second, longer book, the *Discourses.* In this book Machiavelli makes clear his distrust of princes as he analyzes the factors that promote the longevity of a vital, virtuous, and free form of government—the republic.

For Machiavelli, as for Polybius, a republic is a mixed government in which no single class rules. Instead, all classes share power as each checks the potential excesses of the others. It is a system of government in which vigilant citizens jealously guard their liberties against encroachment by would-be tyrants in their midst. For liberty, as Machiavelli understands it, *is* self-government; it is something found not in private life, but in public action. But why must citizens be vigilant? Because as soon as they become complacent and indifferent to public affairs, they will find a tyrant waiting to relieve them of the burden of self-government and deprive them of their liberty. Thus Machiavelli insists that the greatest enemies of free government are complacent citizens.

These are citizens who care more for money and luxury than they care for the commonwealth. The love of wealth, luxury, and ease, together with a corresponding indifference to public affairs, is what Machiavelli calls "corruption." To keep corruption at bay, citizens must become and remain "virtuous." They must be attentive and alert to public affairs, in other words, and when they take part in these affairs they must strive to do what is best not for themselves as private persons, but what is best for the commonwealth. To be virtuous, then, the citizens must be free—free to assemble, to argue among themselves, to expose corruption and criticize their leaders and one another. If citizens neither enjoy nor exercise these essential liberties, no republic can long survive.

According to Machiavelli, the greatest danger a republic faces is that it will be destroyed from within by corruption. But because foreign enemies are also likely to threaten republics, a genuinely free republic must also require all able-bodied males—and only males could be citizens—to be members of a citizen militia, prepared to take up arms against any external threat to their liberty.

Niccolò Machiavelli (1469–1527).

Above all else, Machiavelli maintained that a free government must be ruled by law, not by the whim or caprice of any person or persons, not even of the majority of citizens. For a free government is a government of laws, not of men. A government of laws is more consistent, more concerned with fairness than a government of men. More importantly, laws are impersonal. We can depend upon the laws without losing our independence. When we depend upon people, however, even a majority of men, we are subject to their will— and this could hardly be called liberty. This is why Machiavelli, like Aristotle, considered democracy a bad form of government while regarding a republic as the best.

A mixed government, a virtuous citizenry, the rule of law—this was the ideal of the "republican" Machiavelli of the *Discourses*. If much of it sounds familiar, it is because this vision inspired what scholars now call the Atlantic Republican tradition—a way of thinking about politics that spread from Italy into Great Britain in the seventeenth century, and from there into Britain's American colonies in the eighteenth.

The Atlantic Republican Tradition

In Britain, the turmoil of the 1600s sparked interest in both republicanism and democracy. Civil war broke out in 1642 as King Charles I and the English Parliament, or legislative body, each sought to preserve and if possible extend its own power. The war ended with the Parliamentary forces victorious under the leadership of Oliver Cromwell, and in January, 1649, Charles I was beheaded. An attempt to establish a republic followed, but it failed as Cromwell assumed the powers, if not quite the title, of monarch. When Cromwell died in 1658, another attempt to establish a republic failed. Finally, the English Parliament called upon the son of the beheaded king to assume the throne, and this Charles II did in the Restoration of 1660.

In times as turbulent as these, it is hardly surprising that many turned their thoughts to public matters. One of these was James Harrington (1611–1677), who wrote *Oceana* apparently in hopes of persuading Cromwell to create a republic with a mixed or "balanced" system of government. More than a mixture of rule by one, by the few, and by the many, Harrington's "balance" included an effort to distribute land in a more nearly equal fashion so that no citizen would be dependent upon another for his livelihood. This would help to insure liberty under a government of laws, not of men. Harrington also called for regular and frequent elections and a system of representation in which representatives would be rotated in and out of office. This "rota" would protect liberty by preventing anyone from serving term after term in office, thereby acquiring too much personal power for the public good. It would also promote virtue by enabling more citizens to take an active and responsible part in the government of the commonwealth.

Harrington's ideas seem to have exercised great influence across the Atlantic in the colonies of British North America, as did those of other republican thinkers. Other influences were also at work, however, including the influence of men who had begun to speak favorably, for virtually the first time in 2000 years, of democracy. We shall see shortly how these influences intertwined to produce a "democratic republic" in the United States. But first we need to trace the reclamation of democracy.

THE RETURN OF DEMOCRACY

At the time of the English Civil War of the 1640s, some writers who supported the Parliamentary cause took the radical position of advocating democracy. They reached this position in part because of their religious convictions. Like most of northern Europe, Great Britain had legally forsaken Catholicism in the sixteenth century as the Protestant Reformation shattered the religious unity of Christendom. The new Protestant forms of Christianity emphasized a direct, immediate relationship between the individual person and God. According to Martin Luther, the priest who touched off the Reformation in 1517, what truly mattered was not strict conformity to Church doctrine, but faith and faith alone. Salvation did not come through priests, bishops, popes, and an elaborate church organization. All one needed was belief. Thus the true Christian church was simply the congregation of the faithful or, as Luther put it, "the priesthood of all believers."

Seventeenth Century Democrats

Although Luther did not conclude that this emphasis on individual conscience and faith made democracy desirable, some did. One was Roger Williams (1604–1683), a Protestant minister who left England for Massachusetts in 1631. In Massachusetts, Williams repeatedly ran afoul of the colony's Puritan authorities. He insisted that the colonists should pay the American Indians for the land taken from them, and he called for a separation of religious and civil leadership—a radical step in a colony where church and government were nearly one and the same. The authorities banished Williams from the colony in 1636, whereupon he and his followers moved to the south, bought land from the Indians, and established the colony of Rhode Island. Rhode Island became known for its defense of religious liberty, but it is also noteworthy that the government of the colony, according to its constitution of 1641, was a

> Democratical or Popular Government; that is to say, It is in the Power of the Body of Freemen, orderly assembled, or the major part of them, to make or constitute just Lawes, by which they will be regulated, and to depute from among themselves such Ministers [i.e., police officers, judges] as shall see them fairly executed between Man and Man.

The constitution of 1647 reaffirmed this commitment, proclaiming Rhode Island's form of government to be "Democraticall; that is to say, a Government held by ye free and voluntary consent of all, or the greater parte of the free inhabitants."[9]

Across the Atlantic in England, a group that came to be called the Levellers advanced similar ideas during the Civil War of the 1640s. The Levellers' position rested on the claim that political authority could be founded only on the consent of the people. For the Levellers, this meant that the franchise, the right to vote, had to be extended to all adult males, except for those who had surrendered this right either by committing crimes or by putting themselves, like servants and recipients of public charity, into dependence upon others. Such was the birthright of all men, the Levellers claimed, regardless of how much or how little property they owned. The most famous statement of this position came from Colonel Thomas Rainsborough of Oliver Cromwell's New Model Army.

> For really I think that the poorest he that is in England hath a life to live as the greatest he; and therefore truly, sir, I think it's clear, that every man that is to live under a government ought first by his own consent to put himself under that government; and I do think that the poorest man in England is not at all bound in a strict sense to that government that he hath not had a voice to put himself under. . . .[10]

But the Levellers failed to convince Cromwell and the others who came to power of the wisdom of their arguments. For the most part, those engaged in political activity and debates continued to regard democracy as a dangerously unstable form of government. Still, the efforts of the Levellers and the example of Rhode Island mark the beginning of a remarkable, although gradual, shift in attitude toward democracy.

The United States as Democratic Republic

Democratic ideas and arguments played a part in the American War of Independence against Great Britain, but there were relatively few favorable references to democracy either then or at the time the Constitution of the United States was drafted in 1787. In general, *democracy* continued to stand for a form of class or even mob rule. It was widely regarded as the bad form of popular government; the good form was the republic.

Throughout the quarrel with Great Britain that led to the Declaration of Independence in 1776, the American colonists typically couched their arguments in republican terms. They had no complaint against the form of British government, for the most part, because they believed it to be a model of republicanism. With the Crown, the House of Lords, and the House of Commons sharing the powers of government, the British constitution was a mixture or balance of rule by one, the few, and the many, just as republican theory prescribed. The problem, as the colonists saw it, was corruption. Corrupt British officials were working to upset the balanced constitution so that they could concentrate power in their own hands. Spurred by ambition and avarice, they aimed to replace a government of laws with a government of men, and their first target in this corrupt enterprise was the liberty of Britain's American colonists.[11]

The war that the colonists fought to defend their liberty as Englishmen soon became a war to secure their independence from England. Once they began to think about independence, however, the colonists also had to think about how best to organize the governments of the thirteen states. Faced with this problem, they drew again on the resources of republicanism. This is especially clear in John Adams's (1735–1826) *Thoughts on Government*, written early in 1776. Reading the works of republican writers, Adams said,

> . . . will convince any candid mind that there is no good government but what is republican. That the only valuable part of the British constitution is so because the very definition of a republic is "an empire of laws, and not of men." That, as a republic is the best of governments, so that particular arrangement of the powers of society . . . which is best contrived to secure an impartial and exact execution of the laws is the best of republics.[12]

In the beginning, then, the favored form of government in the United States was not democracy, but the republic. The U.S. Constitution itself testifies to this, for it makes no mention of democracy. But it does guarantee each state of the union "a Republican Form of Government . . ." (Article Four, section four). Nor do we have to look far for signs that the men who drafted the Constitution intended the government of the United States as a whole to be a republic.

The first sign is the separation of the government's powers into three branches, the legislative, executive, and judicial, with each branch put into position to check and balance the other two. This is a modification of the old idea of mixed or balanced government, where the executive branch is the monarchical element—rule by one; the judicial is the aristocratic—rule by the few; and the legislative is the popular—rule by the many. The correspondence is not quite this neat, however, as the legislative branch is itself a mixture of "aristocratic" and "democratic" elements. According to the original plan, the House of Representatives was to be a democratic body, closely responsive to the wishes of the people. Members of the House serve a two-year term of office, therefore, in the belief that the need to stand for reelection frequently will require them to stay in close contact with the voters. Members of the Senate, on the other hand, serve a six-year term precisely so that they may follow their own judgment rather than the voters' wishes. The "aristocratic" nature of the Senate was even clearer under the original Constitution, which placed election to the U.S. Senate in the hands of the state legislatures, not of the ordinary voters—a mode of election that did not change until the Seventeenth Amendment (1913) established the direct election of Senators.

This system of checks and balances also reflects the republican fear of corruption. Checks and balances are necessary, James Madison (1751–1836) observed in his defense of the new Constitution, because men are not angels. They are, on the contrary, ambitious and competitive, and the key to good government is to keep ambitious people from destroying the liberty of the rest. In Madison's words,

> Ambition must be made to counteract ambition. . . . It may be a reflection on human nature, that such devices should be necessary to control the abuses of gov-

ernment. But what is government itself, but the greatest of all reflections upon human nature? If men were angels, no government would be necessary. If angels were to govern men, neither external nor internal controls on government would be necessary. In framing a government which is to be administered by men over men, the great difficulty lies in this: you must first enable the government to control the governed; and in the next place oblige it to control itself.[13]

Other republican features of the Constitution appear in the Bill of Rights—the first ten amendments to the Constitution. The First Amendment, for instance, guarantees that Congress shall make no law depriving people of freedom of speech and assembly, two freedoms that republican writers saw as essential to the preservation of free government. The republican emphasis on a civil militia appears, too, in the Second Amendment: "A well-regulated militia being necessary to the security of a free state, the right of the people to keep and bear arms shall not be infringed."

So the Constitution created a popular government in which the popular element was checked and controlled by the Senate, the courts, and the president. Not everyone was entirely pleased with this arrangement. Alexander Hamilton (1755–1804) supported the proposed constitution, but thought it too democratic. Others, like Patrick Henry (1736–1799), opposed it because it was not democratic enough. He and other "Antifederalist" opponents of the Constitution objected that it took power from the state governments, which were closely connected to the wishes of the people, and concentrated it in the remote and dangerous federal government. It was largely in response to the Antifederalists' objections that the first Congress added the Bill of Rights to the original Constitution.

In the course of the debate over the ratification of the Constitution, the term *democracy* began to play a prominent part in political disputes. The Federalists, as those who favored the new Constitution were called, attacked their opponents as reckless democrats. The Antifederalists responded by blasting the "aristocratic" bias and pretensions of the Federalists. Once the Constitution was ratified, this dispute persisted in a new form as two political parties gradually emerged to challenge one another for political power. One party, the Federalists, followed Hamilton's lead in trying to strengthen the national government. In response, a second party joined former Antifederalists with some prominent supporters of the Constitution, notably Thomas Jefferson (1743–1826) and James Madison. This party, which won a great victory in 1800 with Jefferson's election to the presidency, was known first as the Republican party, then as the Democratic-Republican party, and finally, under the leadership of Andrew Jackson, president from 1829 to 1837, simply as the Democratic party.

Upon Jackson's election the United States entered a period known as Jacksonian Democracy and heralded as the age of the common man. The various state governments had abolished most property qualifications for voting, thus extending voting rights to almost all adult, white males—but not to women, slaves, and American Indians. In this era of Jacksonian Democracy, Americans celebrated not only the glories of liberty, but of equality as well. Many found this new emphasis on democracy and equality exhilarating, but some found it alarming. One observer, Alexis de Tocqueville, thought it a bit of both.

De Tocqueville on Democracy

De Tocqueville (1805–1859) was a French aristocrat who traveled throughout the United States in the early 1830s. Upon his return to France, he wrote *Democracy in America*, a two-volume work in which he analyzed democracy in the United States largely in order to foresee what the coming of democracy implied for Europe. De Tocqueville saw democracy as an irresistible force that was overwhelming the ranks, orders, and aristocratic privileges of the old way of life. In many ways de Tocqueville took this to be a change for the better. Democracy frees the common people and gives them an equal chance to make their way in the world, he said. But de Tocqueville also warned that democracy, with its overbearing emphasis on equality, threatens to produce mediocrity or despotism, or both.

Alexis de Tocqueville (1805–1859).

Democracy promotes mediocrity, de Tocqueville claimed, precisely because it celebrates equality. When everyone is supposed to be equal, there will be tremendous pressure to conform—to act and think as everyone else acts and thinks. No one will want to stand out, to rise above the crowd, for fear of being accused of putting on airs and trying to be better than everyone else. Rather than risk this, de Tocqueville warned, people will conform. The result will be a society where those who have something original or outstanding or out of the ordinary to contribute will remain silent because of the social pressure toward equality. De Tocqueville thought this pressure could be strong enough to call it "the tyranny of the majority."

Democracy also presents the threat of despotism, a more old-fashioned kind of tyranny, according to de Tocqueville. In an argument similar to the one Plato and Aristotle advanced more than 2000 years earlier, he warned that the common people are easily swayed by demagogues who flatter and mislead them in order to win power. An aristocracy helps to prevent this, he argued, because a class of people with inherited property and privileges will be on guard to protect its position against demagogues and despots. Once democracy and equality overwhelm this aristocratic barrier, however, there is little to prevent despotism from destroying liberty.

But de Tocqueville did see a positive possibility in democracy, one that joined republicanism to the democratic ideal. He believed that civic virtue could be promoted through participation in public affairs. The people who join with their neighbors to settle common problems and disputes, he reasoned, will learn the importance of cooperation, feel a strong attachment to their community, and develop those "habits of the heart" that lead them to identify their own welfare with the welfare of the community as a whole.[14] By offering the opportunity to participate to all citizens, democracy promises to cultivate a widespread and deeply rooted devotion to the common good. For this reason de Tocqueville was particularly impressed by two institutions of American democracy: the New England townships, where all citizens could participate directly in local government, and the shared responsibility of jury duty.

THE GROWTH OF DEMOCRACY

Despite de Tocqueville's concerns about the tendencies of democracies to degenerate into mediocrity and despotism, democracy became ever more popular throughout the nineteenth century and into the twentieth. Why it did so is not entirely clear, but the explanation probably has something to do with the growing faith in the abilities of the common man and woman. This faith, in turn, was related to a number of social and economic developments in the Industrial Revolution of the late eighteenth and nineteenth centuries. The most important of these developments include the growth of cities, the spread of public education, and improvements in communication technology, such as the telegraph. Each of these helped to spread literacy, information, and interest in political matters among the populations of Europe and America, thereby contributing to the growing faith in the common people's ability to participate knowledgeably in public affairs.

In England, the arguments for democracy tended to center on two concerns: self-protection and self-development. According to a group of philosophers known as the *Utilitarians*, the duty of government is to promote the greatest happiness of the greatest number of people. The best way to do this, they concluded, is through representative democracy, which will enable every man to vote for representatives who will protect his interests. One Utilitarian, John Stuart Mill, went on to argue in *The Subjection of Women* (1869) that this chance at self-protection through voting ought to extend to women as well.

Mill also maintained that political participation is valuable because of the opportunity it provides for self-development. Like de Tocqueville, Mill believed that democracy made it possible to strengthen civic virtue among the common people, thanks to what he called "the invigorating effect of freedom upon the character." Political participation—not merely voting for representatives, but direct participation at the local level—will educate and improve people by teaching them discipline, sharpening their intelligence, and even shaping their morality. Thus Mill drew attention to

> the moral part of the instruction afforded by the participation of the private citizen, if even rarely, in public functions. He is called upon, while so engaged, to weigh interests not his own; to be guided, in case of conflicting claims, by another rule than his private partialities; to apply, at every turn, principles and maxims which have for their reason of existence the common good: and he usually finds associated with him in the same work minds more familiarised than his own with these ideas and operations. . . . He is made to feel himself one of the public, and whatever is for their benefit will be for his benefit.[15]

Arguments like these helped to bring about a gradual extension of the franchise in the last 150 years. The right to vote came first to adult males—although this was not fully accomplished in Great Britain until 1885—then to male ex-slaves after the Civil War in the United States, and finally to women in the early 1900s in both countries. These extensions did not come swiftly—Switzerland, sometimes called the world's oldest continuous democracy, did not grant full voting rights to women until 1971[16]—nor did they always come calmly and peacefully. Often these changes came only after heated debate, protests, and violence. As late as the 1960s blacks in the American south were denied the right to vote and the right to run for public office. And some critics contend even now that women, blacks, and other minority groups are not fully included in the so-called democracies of the United States, Canada, Britain, and other Western countries.

This is a matter of some dispute, of course. What is beyond dispute, however, is that almost everyone in the so-called Western democracies accepts democracy as the best form of government. But so, too, do the leaders and peoples of many countries that are far from democratic by Western standards. How can we account for this?

DEMOCRACY AS AN IDEAL

As we noted at the beginning of this chapter, democracy is now so popular that most political ideologies claim to be democratic. Yet these supposedly democratic ideologies are in constant competition and occasional conflict with one another. The best explanation for this odd situation is to say that different ideologies do indeed pursue and promote democracy, but they do so in different ways because they disagree about what democracy is. They can do this because democracy is not a single thing, as our brief history of democracy makes clear. Rather than a specific kind of government that must take a definite form, democracy is, instead, an ideal.

To say that democracy is an ideal means it is something toward which people aim or aspire. In this respect it is like true love, inner peace, a perfect performance, or the surfer's perfect wave. Each is an ideal that inspires people to search or strive for it, but none is easy to find, or even to define. What one person takes to be true love, for instance, is likely to be quite different from another person's idea of it. So it is with democracy. There is general agreement, of course, that democracy is government or rule by the people, but exactly what that means is bound to be subject to sharp disagreement. Who are "the people" who are supposed to rule? Only the "common" people? Only those who own substantial property? Only adult males? Or should everyone who lives in a country—including resident foreigners, children, and convicted felons—have a formal voice in its government?

How, moreover, are the people to *rule*? Should every citizen vote directly on proposed policies, as the Athenians did, or should citizens vote for representatives, who will then make policy? If they elect representatives, do the people then cease to govern themselves? With or without representatives, should we follow majority rule? If we do, how can we protect the rights and interests of individuals or minorities, especially those who say and do things that anger or disturb the majority? But if we take steps to limit the power of the majority— if we create a mixed government, for instance, or a system of checks and balances—aren't we restricting or even retreating from democracy?

These are troublesome questions for anyone who claims to be a democrat. As our brief history of democracy suggests, they have been answered in very different ways over the centuries. Such questions have also led a number of political thinkers to worry about the instability of democracy, with a particular concern for its supposed tendency to degenerate into anarchy and despotism. This concern has been largely responsible for the creation of an alternative form of popular government, the republic. But the popularity of republicanism has waned as democracy has gained acceptance, and where it survives it is mostly in the hybrid form of *democratic* republicanism.[17]

Despite the difficulties of defining it, however, the ideal of rule by the people remains popular. This is due in part to its connection with freedom and equality, since democracy implies that in some sense every citizen will be both free and equal to every other. But exactly what freedom and equality are, or what form they should take, and how the two relate to one another, is open to interpretation. This is where political ideologies enter the picture. In some way all ideologies must come to terms with the democratic ideal, whether they accept or reject it. Coming to terms in this case means that political ideologies have to provide more definite notions of what democracy involves. They do this by drawing on their underlying conceptions of human nature and freedom to determine whether democracy is possible and desirable and, if so, what form it is to take.

To put the point in terms of our functional definition of ideology, we can say that an ideology's *explanation* of why things are the way they are largely shapes its attitude toward democracy. If an ideology holds, as fascism does, that society is often in turmoil because most people are incapable of governing themselves, it is hardly likely to advocate democracy. But if an ideology holds that most people have the capacity for freedom and self-government, as liberalism and socialism do, then the ideology will embrace the democratic ideal—as most of them have done. The ideology that does so will then *evaluate* existing social arrangements and provide a sense of *orientation* for individuals based largely on how democratic it takes these arrangements to be. If the individual seems to be an equal partner in a society where the people rule in some suitable sense, then all is well; but if he or she seems to be merely the pawn of those who hold the real power, then the ideology will encourage people to take action to reform or perhaps to overthrow the social and political order. This, finally, will require a *program* for change in what the ideology takes to be a democratic direction.

Every political ideology, then, has its own interpretation of the democratic ideal, which it defines, and may defend or pursue, according to its particular vision. In turn, the men and women who promote political ideologies will also use the democratic ideal, and their vision of it, to try to inspire others to join their cause or, at least, to see things as they see them.

Three Conceptions of Democracy

To clarify this connection between political ideologies and the democratic ideal, let us examine briefly the three principal versions of democracy in the twentieth century. Although these three share several features, their differences are sharp enough to make them distinctive and competing conceptions of democracy.

Liberal democracy   As the name suggests, **liberal democracy** emerged from liberalism, the ideology examined in our next chapter. As with liberalism in general, liberal democracy stresses the rights and liberty of the individual, and it is this form of democracy that is usually associated with the Western democracies. For liberals, democracy is certainly rule by the people, but an essential part of this rule includes the protection of individual rights and liberties. This means that limits must be set to majority rule. Democracy is rule by the majority of the people, in this view, but only as long as those in the majority do not try to deprive individuals of their basic civil rights. Freedom to speak and worship, the right to run for public office, the right to own property—these are among the civil rights and liberties that liberals have generally taken to be necessary to realize the democratic ideal as they understand it.

Social Democracy   Within the Western democracies, especially in Europe, the chief challenger to the liberal conception is **social democracy.** This view is linked to the ideology of socialism. From a "social democratic" or "democratic socialist" perspective, the key to democracy is *equality,* especially equal power in society and government. Social democrats argue that liberal democracy puts poor and working class people at the mercy of the rich. In the modern world, they say, money is a major source of power, and those who have wealth have power over those who do not. Wealth makes it possible to run for office and to influence government policies, for instance, so those who are well-to-do enjoy much greater influence when public policies are made. Yet this advantage, they insist, can hardly be democratic. Democracy is rule by the people, and the social democrats say that such rule requires that every person have a roughly equal influence over the government. This is what lies behind the slogan, "one person, one vote." But we will not really have this equal influence, they charge, unless we take steps to distribute power in a more nearly equal fashion. Nor can equality of political power exist unless there is a more nearly equal distribution of wealth or *economic* power. This is why the program of social democrats typically calls for the redistribution of wealth to promote equality, social rather than private control of natural resources and major industries, and workers' control of the workplace. Like liberals, then, social democrats want to preserve civil liberties and competition for political office. They simply do not believe that most people can be truly free or competition truly open when great inequalities of wealth and power prevail.

People's Democracy   In those countries that have called themselves communist, the prevailing version of the democratic ideal has been, until recently, **people's democracy.** In some ways people's democracy is closer to the original Greek idea of democracy—rule by and in the interests of the *demos*, the common people—than liberal or social democracy. From a communist perspective, the common people are the proletariat, or the working class, and democracy will not be achieved until government rules in their interest. This does not necessarily mean that the proletariat must itself directly control the government. As we explain in Chapter 6, communists used to call for **the revolutionary dictatorship of the proletariat,** a form of dictatorship that Marx described as ruling in the interests of the working class. The immediate purpose of this dictatorship would be to suppress the capitalists or bourgeoisie who have previously used their power and wealth to exploit the working class. By suppressing them, the dictatorship of the proletariat supposedly enables the common people to prepare themselves for the classless society of the communist future, when the state itself will "wither away." In the meantime, people's democracy

is to consist of rule by the Communist party for the good of the working majority. This is the sense in which Mao Zedong spoke of a "people's democratic
dictatorship" in the People's Republic of China.

By the end of the 1980s, as the Soviet Union relaxed its grip on Eastern
Europe and began to allow competition for public office at home, the idea of a
people's democracy seemed all but dead. Yet in the summer of 1989, after
ordering an attack on protesting students in Beijing's Tiananmen Square, the
leaders of the Chinese Communist party continued to insist on the need for a
people's democratic dictatorship. The alternative, they said, was "bourgeois
liberalization"—otherwise known as liberal democracy—and this they found
completely unacceptable.

CONCLUSION

Liberal democracy, social democracy, and people's democracy are not the only
visions of the democratic ideal in the world today. They have been, however,
the most influential. In this democratic age, then, it is important to understand
these visions and how they relate to various political ideologies. With this in
mind we explore in the next seven chapters the major ideologies of the modern
world—liberalism, conservatism, socialism, and fascism—and some of their recently emerging rivals. Each discussion will then conclude with an assessment
of the connection between the particular ideology and the democratic ideal.

NOTES

1. Pericles' Funeral Oration, from Thucydides, *History of the Peloponnesian War,* in
   Thucydides, vol. I, 2nd. ed., trans. Benjamin Jowett (Oxford: Clarendon Press,
   1900), pp. 127–128. Also in Terence Ball and Richard Dagger, eds., *Ideals and
   Ideologies: A Reader* (New York: HarperCollins, 1991), selection 3.
2. Ibid., p. 129.
3. Plato, *Apology,* 31; in *The Trial and Death of Socrates,* trans. G. M. A. Grube
   (Indianapolis: Hackett Publishing Co., 1983), p. 33.
4. For Plato's account of democracy, see Book 8 of his *Republic.*
5. Benjamin Jowett, ed. and trans., *The Politics of Aristotle* (New York: Modern Library, 1943), p. 192; also in Ball and Dagger, eds., *Ideals and Ideologies,* selection
   4.
6. Ibid., p. 146; *Ideals and Ideologies,* selection 4.
7. The New Testament, Romans 13: verses 1 and 2.
8. William Shakespeare, *King Henry the Sixth,* part 3, act 3, sc. 2.
9. Quotations from the Rhode Island constitutions are from Russell L. Hanson, "Democracy," in Terence Ball, James Farr, and Russell L. Hanson, eds., *Political Innovation and Conceptual Change* (Cambridge: Cambridge University Press, 1989), p.
   72f.
10. Rainsborough's remarks are from David Wooton, ed., *Divine Right and Democracy*
    (Harmondsworth: Penguin, 1986), p. 286.

11. For an elaboration of this analysis, see Bernard Bailyn, *The Ideological Origins of the American Revolution* (Cambridge, Mass.: Harvard University Press, 1967).

12. Charles Francis Adams, ed., *The Works of John Adams*, vol. 4 (Boston: Little and Brown, 1851), p. 194; also in Ball and Dagger, eds., *Ideals and Ideologies*, selection 6.

13. The Federalist Papers, #51.

14. For an analysis of American life in the late twentieth century that owes much to Tocqueville, see Robert Bellah, Richard Madsen, William Sullivan, Ann Swidley, and Steven Tipton, *Habits of the Heart: Individualism and Commitment in American Life* (New York: Harper & Row, 1986).

15. Both quotations are from Mill's *Considerations on Representative Government*, in John Stuart Mill, *Utilitarianism, Liberty, and Representative Government* (New York: E. P. Dutton, 1951), pp. 289 and 291; also in Ball and Dagger, eds., *Ideals and Ideologies*, selection 9.

16. For a discussion of democracy and liberty in Switzerland, see Benjamin R. Barber, *The Death of Communal Liberty* (Princeton: Princeton University Press, 1974).

17. See Russell L. Hanson, " 'Commons' and 'Commonwealth' at the American Founding: Democratic Republicanism as the New American Hybrid," in Terence Ball and J. G. A. Pocock, eds., *Conceptual Change and the Constitution* (Lawrence, Kans.: University Press of Kansas, 1988), pp. 165–193, for a discussion of the development of "democratic republicanism" in the United States.

FOR FURTHER READING

Gooch, G. P. *English Democratic Ideas in the Seventeenth Century*, 2nd ed. (New York: Harper & Brothers, 1959).

Gould, Carol C. *Rethinking Democracy* (Cambridge: Cambridge University Press, 1988).

Hanson, Russell L. *The Democratic Imagination in America: Conversations with Our Past* (Princeton: Princeton University Press, 1985).

Held, David. *Models of Democracy* (Stanford, Calif.: Stanford University Press, 1986).

Macpherson, C. B. *The Life and Times of Liberal Democracy* (Oxford: Oxford University Press, 1977).

——. *The Real World of Democracy* (Oxford: Oxford University Press, 1966).

Mansbridge, Jane. *Beyond Adversary Democracy* (Chicago: University of Chicago Press, 1983).

Pateman, Carole. *Participation and Democratic Theory* (Cambridge: Cambridge University Press, 1970).

Pocock, J. G. A. *The Machiavellian Moment: Florentine Political Thought and the Atlantic Republican Tradition* (Princeton: Princeton University Press, 1975).

Polybius, *Histories*, trans. Evelyn Schuckburgh (New York: Macmillan, 1889).

Skinner, Quentin. *The Foundations of Modern Political Thought*, 2 vols. (Cambridge: Cambridge University Press, 1978).

Walzer, Michael. *Radical Principles* (New York: Basic Books, 1980).

Wood, Gordon. *The Creation of the American Republic, 1776–1787* (Chapel Hill, N.C.: University of North Carolina Press, 1969).

PART
Two

THE DEVELOPMENT OF POLITICAL IDEOLOGIES

Chapter
3

Liberalism

Over himself, over his own body and mind, the individual is sovereign.

John Stuart Mill

*F*rom its beginning more than 300 years ago, the hallmark of liberalism has been the attempt to promote individual liberty. But this is a very broad goal, leaving room for liberals to disagree among themselves as to what exactly liberty is and how best to promote it. Indeed, this disagreement is now so sharp that liberalism is split into two rival camps of *neoclassical* and *welfare* liberals. Later in this chapter we shall see how this split occurred. But first we need to look at that broad area of common ground on which all liberals meet, the desire to promote individual liberty.

The words *liberal* and *liberty* both derive from the Latin *liber*, meaning free. "Liberal" did not enter the vocabulary of politics until early in the nineteenth century, however, long after "liberty" was widely used as a political term—and at least a century after ideas now regarded as liberal were in the air. Before the nineteenth century "liberal" was commonly used to mean generous or tolerant; this was an attitude that supposedly befit a "gentleman," just as the purpose of a "liberal education" was to prepare a young gentleman for life. "Liberal" still means generous or tolerant, of course, as when someone says that a teacher follows a liberal grading policy or a child has liberal parents. But nowadays, through an extension of this common use, the term more often refers to a political position or point of view.

The first clear sign of this extension occurred in the early 1800s when a faction of the Spanish legislature adopted the name *Liberales*. From there the term traveled to France and Great Britain, where the party known as the Whigs evolved by the 1840s into the Liberal party. These early liberals shared a desire for a more open and tolerant society in which people would be free to pursue their own ideas and interests with as little interference as possible. A liberal society was to be, in short, a *free* society. But what makes a society *free?* What *is* freedom and how can we best promote it? These questions have occupied liberals for more than three centuries now, providing the grounds not only for arguments among liberals, but also for disputes between liberalism and other ideologies.

LIBERALISM, HUMAN NATURE, AND FREEDOM

In Chapter 1 we noted that some conception of human nature provides the underpinnings for every political ideology. In the case of liberalism, the emphasis on individual liberty rests on the liberal conception of human beings as fundamentally rational individuals. There are significant differences among liberals on this point, but in general they stress individual liberty largely because they believe that most people are capable of living freely. This sets them apart from those who believe that human beings are at the mercy of uncontrollable passions and desires that push people in one direction, then pull them in another. Liberals acknowledge that people do have passions and desires, but they maintain that we also have the ability, through reason, to control and direct our desires. Most women and men, they insist, are rational beings who know what is in their own interests and are capable, given the opportunity, of acting to promote them.

Liberals generally agree that self-interest is the primary motive for most people. Some argue that self-interest should be given free rein, while others respond that it should be carefully directed to promote the good of all; but most hold that it is wisest to think of people as beings who are more interested in their own good than in the well-being of others. This implies, in turn, that all these rational, self-interested men and women will find themselves competing with one another in their attempts to promote their personal interests. This is healthy, liberals say, as long as the competition stays within proper bounds. Exactly where these proper bounds lie is a subject of sharp disagreement among liberals, as is the question of how best to encourage or enable people to compete. For the most part, though, liberals are inclined to regard competition as a natural feature of the human condition.

On the liberal view, then, human beings are typically rational, self-interested, and competitive. This implies that they are capable of living freely. But what does it mean to live in this way? How do liberals conceive of freedom? To answer this, let us employ the explanation from Chapter 1 of freedom as a triadic relationship involving an *agent* who is free from some *obstacle* to pursue some *goal*. In the case of liberalism, the agent is the individual. Liberals wish to promote the freedom of no particular group or class of people, but of each and every person as an individual. To do this, they have sought to free people from a variety of restrictions or obstacles. In the beginning liberals were most concerned with removing social and legal barriers to individual liberty, especially social customs, ties of feudal dependence, and religious conformity. Since then, other liberals have claimed that poverty, racial and sexual prejudice, ignorance, and illness are also obstacles to individual liberty. But whatever the differences in their views of the obstacles to freedom, liberals contend that the individual must be free to decide for himself—and, more recently, herself— what goals to pursue in life. The individual is the best judge of what is in his or her interest, according to most liberals, so each person ought to be free to live as he or she sees fit—as long as the person does not choose to interfere with the freedom of others to live as they see fit. (See Figure 3.1.)

This suggests that equality is also an important element in the liberal conception of freedom. In the liberal view, each person is to have an equal opportunity to enjoy liberty. No person's liberty is more important or valuable than any other's. This does not mean that everyone is to be equally successful in life or to have an equal share of the good things of life, whatever they may be. Liberalism seeks not equal success in life, but *an equal chance to succeed.* Liberalism thus stresses competition, for it wants individuals to be free to compete, on an equal footing, for whatever they count as success. Anything that prevents a person from having an equal opportunity—whether it be privileges for the aristocracy, monopolies that block economic competition, or discrimination based on race, religion, or gender—can be an obstacle to a person's freedom. And obstacles to equal opportunity ought to be removed.

Liberalism, in short, promotes individual liberty by trying to guarantee equality of opportunity within a tolerant society. In the English-speaking world, these are ideas that we usually take for granted. They are so much a part of our lives and our way of thinking that they seem natural. But this is

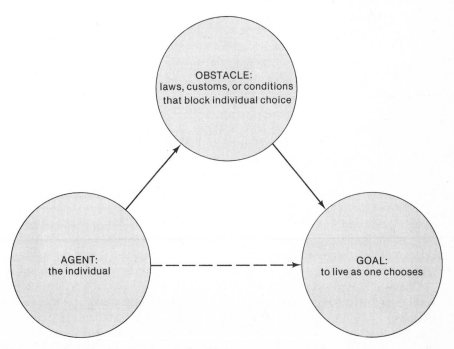

Figure 3.1 The liberal view of freedom.

because these liberal ideas are so much a part of our heritage in the English-speaking world and throughout Western civilization in general. These ideas were not always taken for granted, however, not even in England and Europe. To appreciate their full significance we need to see how liberalism began as a reaction against European society of the Middle Ages.

HISTORICAL BACKGROUND

The Medieval Background

The origins of liberalism can be traced to a reaction against two characteristic features of medieval society in Europe: **religious conformity** and **ascribed status.** This reaction did not come all at once. It developed over the course of centuries, and it took different forms at different times and places. By the time the word *liberal* entered the political vocabulary in the early nineteenth century, however, it was clear that a distinctive political viewpoint had emerged.

Religious Conformity   The new viewpoint called for freedom of religion and a separation of church and state. These ideas were foreign to the dominant ways of thinking in the Middle Ages, when church and state were supposed to be partners in the defense of Christendom. Indeed, there was no clear distinction between church and state in medieval Europe. For its part, the Christian Church saw its mission as saving souls for the kingdom of God—something that could best be done by teaching and upholding orthodoxy, or "correct belief." Those who took an unorthodox view of Christianity or rejected it altogether thus threatened the Church's attempts to do what it saw as the work and will of God. In response to these threats, the Church used its powers, and called on the kings and other secular authorities to use theirs, to enforce conformity to Church doctrine. For their part, the secular rulers were usually willing—either out of religious conviction or a desire to maintain order in their domains—to suppress those the Church considered heretics or infidels. Throughout medieval Europe, then, religious and political authorities joined to enforce conformity to the doctrines of the Roman church, which they believed to be the true and universal path to the kingdom of God.

Ascribed Status   The other feature of medieval society the early liberals reacted against was **ascribed status**. In a society based on ascribed status, a person's social standing is fixed, or ascribed, at birth, and there is little that he or she can do to change it. This stands in contrast to a society based on **achieved status,** where everyone is supposed to have an equal chance of working his or her way to the top—or, for that matter, to the bottom—of society. This is the kind of society liberals have historically fought for, but it was by no means the ideal of medieval society. To be sure, Christians in the Middle Ages professed that all people are born equal in the eyes of God, but this was compatible in their eyes with great inequalities in life here on earth. What counted was the state of one's soul, not one's status in society.

Yet status mattered very much in earthly life, for one's position and prospects were fixed by one's social "rank," "order," or "estate." This was especially true under **feudalism,** which became the main form of social and economic organization in Europe after the disintegration of Charlemagne's empire in the ninth century. Under feudalism, an intricate web of relationships developed in which a knight, the lord, would give the use of land to a lesser knight, the vassal, in return for military service. The vassal might then divide the land into parcels to be offered to others who then, in exchange for various services, became *his* vassals. In the beginning the original lord retained ownership of the land, with the vassal receiving only the right to use it and enjoy its fruits. These relationships gradually became hereditary, however, leading to a complicated network of ranks, status, and loyalties.

In one respect, though, feudalism simplified matters by reinforcing the existing tendency to divide society into two broad classes of people: nobles and commoners. As feudal relationships were passed down the generations, a distinct class of land-owning nobles or aristocrats took shape. These nobles thought themselves naturally superior to the commoners, who were the great majority of the people. They also believed that their nobility entitled them to exercise authority over the commoners and to enjoy privileges and liberties unavailable to common men and women.

This emphasis on social rank or estate was reflected in the parliaments or estates-general that began to appear in the late Middle Ages. These political bodies, usually summoned by kings, were called together to speak for the different orders of society. The Estates-General of France, for instance, which first convened in 1302, comprised representatives of the clergy (the first estate), the nobility (the second estate), and the commoners (the third estate). Because the members of this last group lived mostly in the cities and towns— *bourgs* in French—they were called the **bourgeoisie.** There were no representatives for those who were not free, such as the serfs.

Serfs (from the Latin *servus,* slave) were commoners, but they were not free. They were peasants, or agricultural laborers, but unlike free peasants they did not own land. Instead, they farmed plots of land owned by the lord of the manor, and from their plots they had to provide for their families and pay rent to the lord, typically in the form of crops.

What was most distinctive about serfdom, however, was the serfs' lack of freedom to choose where to live and what work to do. Serfs were often legally *attached* to the land or the person of the lord. By custom and law they were bound—hence the term, *bondsman*—either to remain on and work the land where they were born or, if attached to a person, to serve the lord wherever required. In exchange, serfs received protection from the lord. If they thought this a poor bargain, there was nothing they could do, as a rule, to earn release from serfdom. Some tried to win their freedom by force of arms; others ran away to the towns and cities; and still others accepted their condition as part of the natural course of life, although perhaps cherishing a hope that their lord would free them.

Whether a serf, a noble, or a free commoner, then, a person was born into a certain rank or estate in medieval Europe and could do little to change it.

The Church provided an exception to this rule, for people from all ranks of society could hope to find a place among the clergy. In other respects, though, medieval society was firmly rooted in ascribed status. Nobles were those born into the nobility, for the most part, while the children of free commoners and serfs were virtually locked into the social position of their parents, and no amount of effort or ability could significantly improve their stations in life. Even freedom was a matter of social position, with different liberties attached to different levels of status in society. For example, in the Magna Carta, the Great Charter of rights that the feudal barons of England forced King John to accept in 1215, the king agreed that "No free man shall be taken, or imprisoned, . . . or outlawed, or exiled, or in any way destroyed . . . except by lawful judgment of his peers or by the laws of the land." But in this case "free man" (*liber homo*) referred only to the barons and other nobles. Those of lesser rank could still be taken, imprisoned, or killed without the lawful judgment of their peers— without, that is, a trial by a jury.

Against this society rooted in ascribed status and religious conformity, liberalism emerged as the first distinctive political ideology. But this reaction did not take definite shape until a number of social, economic, and cultural changes disturbed the medieval order. Many of these were directly related to the outburst of creativity in the fourteenth and fifteenth centuries known as the Renaissance. But there was also the Black Death, an epidemic that devastated Europe from 1347 to 1351, killing about one of every three people. This epidemic opened new opportunities for survivors from the lower ranks of society and loosened the rigid medieval social structure. The expansion of trade and commerce in the late Middle Ages played a part in the breakdown of the medieval order, too, as did the wave of exploration set in motion by this expansion. Columbus's attempt to find a new trade route to Asia is noteworthy in this regard, for he discovered what was, for Europeans, an entirely new world—a new world that became a symbol of great new possibilities. But of all the historical developments that contributed to the decline of the medieval order and the rise of liberalism, the most important was the Protestant Reformation.

The Protestant Reformation

The Protestant Reformation can be dated from 1521, the year in which the Roman Church excommunicated Martin Luther. Luther (1483–1546) was a priest and professor of theology at the University of Wittenberg when he posted his famous 95 theses on the door of the church at Wittenberg in 1517. By themselves, the 95 theses were not a direct threat to the authority of the Church. Their immediate purpose was to call for a debate on the sale of "indulgences," which were issued on the authority of the Pope to raise money for Church projects—in 1517, the rebuilding of St. Peter's Basilica in Rome. Although the purchase of an indulgence was only supposed to release a sinner from some acts of penance, eager salesmen sometimes led people to believe that an indulgence could secure a place in heaven. This provoked Luther to issue his challenge to a debate.

With the aid of a relatively new invention, the printing press, Luther's theses circulated quickly through the German principalities and found a receptive audience among Christians disturbed by the corruption of the Church. They also caught the attention of the German nobles, many of whom regarded the Church as their main rival for earthly power. The resulting furor led Luther's superiors in the Church to command him to admit that he was mistaken and to submit to the authority of the Pope. But Luther refused, saying, as legend has it, "Here I stand. I can do no other." Thus began the Reformation.

The Church, in Luther's view, had vested too much authority in priests and too little in the Bible. In place of the Church's emphasis on tradition, rituals, and sacraments, Luther called for strict attention to Scripture, the word of God. And in place of the Church's emphasis on the authority of priests, bishops, and the Pope, Luther called for the "priesthood of all believers." All that matters is faith, he declared, and the only way to nurture faith is to read the Bible and do as God there commands us to do. With that in mind, Luther and his colleagues translated the Bible into German to make it accessible to those who could not read Latin.

Despite some early remarks defending freedom of conscience, Luther never meant to encourage people to believe and worship in whatever way they chose. Apparently he expected that everyone who read the Scriptures could not help but understand them as he did. But this was not what happened. To the contrary, Luther's proclamation of the priesthood of all believers, with its stress on individual conscience, opened the floodgates for a variety of interpretations of the Bible and a profusion of Protestant sects. Luther neither foresaw nor welcomed this development. Nor did he intend to separate church from state. Indeed, one reason why Luther's challenge to the supremacy of the Church succeeded where earlier challenges had failed is that Luther was able to win the protection of the German princes, many of whom saw in the controversy a welcome opportunity to gain wealth and power at the Church's expense. In any case, in Germany and elsewhere the immediate effect of the Reformation was to forge an alliance between a king or prince, on the one hand, and the leaders of a reformed or Protestant church, on the other. In this way various local or national churches began to challenge the authority of the universal church.

England soon provided the best example of a national church. There, King Henry VIII (reigned 1509–1547), angered by the Pope's refusal to grant him permission to divorce his first wife, declared the Church of England separate from Rome and, with the approval of the English Parliament, made himself its head. An example of a different sort emerged in Geneva. Now part of Switzerland, Geneva was an independent city-state when Jean Calvin (1509–1564), a French Protestant, became its leader in political as well as in religious matters. Like most of the other Protestants or reformers, in fact, Calvin was no more inclined to distinguish politics from religion, or church from state, than his Roman Catholic opponents were. The point of the Reformation was not to enable people to believe as they saw fit, but literally to *reform* the Church so that people could believe as, in the reformers' eyes, they should. Under Calvin's leadership, Geneva attempted to make the law of the city a direct reflection of God's will, to the extent that a pastor could enter a house at any hour of the day or night to make sure that no one was violating God's commandments.

Where the earthly authorities remained faithful to the Catholic church, they often tried to suppress the Protestants. In such cases Luther and Calvin usually counseled their followers not to resist their rulers, since God gave rulers their power to do His will. Later, however, some of Calvin's followers concluded not only that resistance is sometimes justified, but that the people have a right to overthrow any ruler who denies them the free exercise of their religion. By this they meant the exercise of their form of Calvinism, to be sure, because few of them wished to allow the free exercise of other religions. Yet their arguments for freedom of conscience, which rested in part on the claim that government receives its authority from the consent of the people, planted the seeds of the argument in favor of religious toleration.

Before these seeds could sprout, however, people had to be convinced that it was either wrong or simply impossible to replace enforced conformity to the Roman church with enforced conformity to one or another of the Protestant churches. This did not begin to happen until the seventeenth century, and then only after a series of bloody religious wars persuaded some, like John Locke, that it was better to tolerate some differences of religion than to try to win converts at the point of a sword.

Without ever quite intending to do so, then, the Protestant reformers prepared the way for liberalism. By teaching that salvation comes through faith alone, and not through the sacraments of the Church, Luther and the other reformers encouraged people to value the individual conscience above the preservation of unity and orthodoxy. From individual conscience to individual liberty was still a radical step for the time, but it was a step that the early liberals took. Thus liberalism began as an attempt to free individuals from the constraints of religious conformity and ascribed status in society. It also began, as most ideologies have begun, as an attempt to bring about a fundamental transformation of society. It was, in short, revolutionary. To see this more clearly, we need to look at the great revolutions of the seventeenth and eighteenth centuries.

LIBERALISM AND REVOLUTION

England

After defeating the Spanish Armada in 1588, England began the seventeenth century more secure and powerful than ever. Queen Elizabeth I was on the throne and William Shakespeare was writing plays. Then came contributions to literature by John Donne and John Milton, to philosophy by Thomas Hobbes and John Locke, and to science by Isaac Newton and William Harvey, the physician who discovered the circulation of blood. Commerce and exploration were thriving, too, as English colonies sprang up in North America and India.

But the seventeenth century was also a time of turmoil for England. Elizabeth was succeeded in 1603 by a distant cousin, James Stuart, King of Scotland. As the new king, James I soon found himself engaged in a contest for power with Parliament, a contest that grew more heated during the reign of his son, Charles I. Money was often at the root of the conflict, with Charles insisting that he had a right, as king, to gather revenue through taxes, while Parliament insisted that this was its right as the body representing the people of England. In 1642 the conflict erupted into civil war.

The war between Crown and Parliament was further fueled by religious, social, and economic elements. For many people the war was primarily a religious conflict. As king, Charles I was the official head of the Church of England, and all the English were expected to conform to the beliefs and practices of that Church. Those loyal to the Church of England tended to support the King, then, while the dissenting Puritans took the side of Parliament. The Puritans often disagreed with one another—some were Presbyterians, some Independents or Congregationalists, some Separatists—but all wanted to "purify" the Church of England of the traces of Catholicism they thought it had retained. Their hope, in general, was to enforce conformity to their religion, just as those who supported the established church sought to enforce conformity to theirs. The social and economic divisions are less clear, but it seems that the land-owning aristocracy supported the King while the middle class—the "gentlemen" landowners and the merchants—generally sided with Parliament.

In this war pen and ink played as great a part as bullets and swords. From every point of view came a vast outpouring of pamphlets, treatises, sermons, and even major works of political theory. In the previous chapter we noted the efforts of James Harrington, who argued for a republican form of government, and of the Levellers, who pressed the case for a more democratic form. Now we must take note of the first major work of political philosophy to bear the distinctive stamp of liberalism, Thomas Hobbes's *Leviathan*.

Hobbes (1588–1679) wrote *Leviathan* in France, where he had fled to avoid the war, and published it in 1651, two years after the beheading of Charles I brought the war to an end. There was nothing new in the conclusion he reached in *Leviathan*. Like St. Paul and many others, Hobbes maintained that the people of a country should obey those who have power over them. But he refused to base this conclusion on the simple claim that this was God's will. Even though Hobbes cited Scripture, his argument was fundamentally secular—and, he thought, scientific—as it was based on self-interest rather than divine commands.

According to Hobbes, the individual should obey whoever is in power, as long as the person or persons in power protect him or her. To provide protection or security is the only reason for government in the first place. And to prove his point, Hobbes asked his readers to imagine that they were in a state of nature with no one having any authority over them. In such a state, he said, all individuals are equal—no one is born to hold a higher rank or status than anyone else— and have a **natural right** to do as they wish. The problem is human nature: "I put for a general inclination of all mankind, a perpetuall and

Thomas Hobbes (1588–1679).

restlesse desire of Power after power, that ceaseth onely in Death."[1] This "restlesse desire" for power leads individuals into conflict with one another, according to Hobbes, and turns the state of nature into a "warre of every man against every man" where life can be nothing but "solitary, poore, nasty, brutish, and short."[2]

Nothing, in Hobbes's view, could be worse than this. So the individuals in the state of nature enter into a **social contract** to establish political authority. To provide for their security, they surrender all but one of their rights—the right to defend themselves—to those to whom they grant authority. In Hobbes's argument, then, government is founded in the consent of the people. But by their consent, the people authorize the sovereign—the person or persons in power—to do anything necessary to maintain order and peace. This includes the power to force everyone to worship as the sovereign requires, for Hobbes saw religious differences as one of the leading sources of conflict. For the sake of security, then, the people grant the sovereign absolute, unlimited power, retaining only the right to defend themselves when the sovereign directly threatens them.

Given this conclusion, the claim that *Leviathan* bears the distinctive stamp of liberalism may seem odd. Liberals certainly have not made a habit of supporting absolute rulers. What gives Hobbes's theory the stamp of liberalism is not his conclusion, however, but his premises. Individuals are equals, on Hobbes's account, and everyone has a natural right to be free. They create government through their consent in order to protect their interests. In these respects, Hobbes's position is very much that of a liberal or, as some prefer to say, a protoliberal; that is, one who articulated the main premises of an emerging liberal ideology. It remained for John Locke to use these premises to reach a conclusion that we may definitely regard as liberal.

Locke (1632–1704) was 16 years old when Charles I was beheaded and Parliament abolished the monarchy. Yet only eleven years later, Parliament invited the son of the late king to return from his exile in France—where Hobbes had been one of his tutors—to restore the monarchy. This Restoration brought a measure of relief from political turmoil, but it proved to be only temporary. As Charles II grew older, it became clear that he would leave no legitimate heir to the throne. This placed his brother James in position to be the next king and excited the suspicion that James, a Catholic, would try to take England back into the Catholic camp and become, like his cousin Louis XIV of France, an absolute ruler. To prevent this, an effort was mounted to exclude James from the throne. During the Exclusion Crisis of 1680–1683, Charles II suspended Parliament and his opponents responded with plots and uprisings against him. The effort failed and James became King James II upon Charles's death in 1685, but it did lead John Locke to begin writing his *Two Treatises of Government.*

Locke completed the *Two Treatises* while in exile in Holland, where he had fled for fear of his life in 1683. In Holland, then the most tolerant country in Europe, Locke also wrote his *Letter concerning Toleration.* Both works were published in England after the Glorious Revolution of 1688 forced James II to flee to France. James's daughter Mary and her husband William, Prince of Orange (in the Netherlands), became England's new monarchs. In assuming the throne, however, William and Mary accepted the Bill of Rights, which recognized the "true, ancient, and indubitable rights of the people of this realm"[3] and the supremacy of Parliament. From this time forward England would be a constitutional monarchy, with the king or queen clearly subject to the law of the land. In the Toleration Act, furthermore, Parliament granted freedom of worship to "dissenters," that is, those Protestants who refused to join the established Church of England.

These developments were very much to Locke's liking. In the *Letter concerning Toleration* he argued that it is wrong for governments to force their subjects to conform to a particular religion. Drawing a distinction between private and public matters, Locke said that religious belief is normally a private concern and not a proper subject for government interference. Governments

John Locke (1632–1704).

should tolerate diverse religious beliefs unless the practice of those beliefs directly threatens the public order. But Catholicism should *not* be tolerated for exactly this reason. Catholics owe their first loyalty to a foreign monarch, the Pope, so they cannot be trustworthy members of a commonwealth. Locke also denied toleration to atheists for a similar reason, claiming that anyone who denied the existence of God, salvation, and damnation could not be trusted at all. If these seem severe restrictions by our standards, they were nonetheless quite liberal, even radical, by the standards of Locke's time.

Important as his argument for toleration was, Locke's theory of political authority in the second of his *Two Treatises of Government* marked an even more important milestone in the development of liberalism. Locke's purpose in the *Second Treatise* was much the same as Hobbes's in *Leviathan*—to establish the true basis for political authority or government—and in several crucial respects his premises resemble Hobbes's. He began his argument, as Hobbes did, with the state of nature, where everyone is free and equal. There is no ascribed status in this state of nature, "there being nothing more evident, than that Creatures of the same species and rank promiscuously born to all the same advantages of Nature, and the use of the same faculties, should also be equal one amongst another without Subordination or Subjection. . . ."⁴ There are natural rights, though, which Locke usually referred to as "life, liberty, and property." These rights a person may choose to surrender or forfeit, but no one can simply take them away.

Unlike Hobbes's state of nature, Locke's is *not* a state of war. It is "inconvenient," however, largely because so many people are unwilling to respect the rights of others. Recognizing this difficulty, the residents of the state of nature enter into a social contract to establish a political society with a set of laws and a government to make, interpret, and enforce those laws. But we should remember, Locke said, that people create government to protect their natural rights. The government has authority, therefore, only insofar as it does what it needs to do to preserve the lives, liberty, and property of its subjects. If the government begins to violate these rights by depriving its subjects of life, liberty, and property, then the people have the right to overthrow the government and establish a new one in its place.

Proceeding from premises very similar to Hobbes's, in sum, Locke reached a very different conclusion. Both denied that social status was somehow fixed or ascribed by nature, and both believed that government is founded on the consent of the people; but Locke believed that people can only consent to create and obey a limited or constitutional government. To give anyone total and absolute power over our lives would be both irrational and contrary to the will of God. Both also believed that people have natural rights; but for Locke this included a right to worship as one chose, within limits, and a right of revolution—a right that would be invoked in the next century in the Declaration of Independence of the United States of America.

The American Revolution

Neither the American nor the French Revolution was the direct result of Locke's writings, of course. In both cases a variety of social, economic, and religious factors combined with philosophical and political issues to lead to revolution.

In the case of the thirteen British colonies that eventually became the United States, the first point to notice is that they were settled during England's turbulent seventeenth century. Perhaps because it was preoccupied with problems at home, the British government generally left the colonists to look after their own affairs during the 1600s. This continued throughout the first half of the eighteenth century, a relatively stable period in English politics. The colonies had governors appointed by the Crown, but they also had their own legislatures and raised their own taxes. The colonists consequently took it for granted that they enjoyed all the rights of Englishmen, including the right to constitutional self-government through elected representatives.

But in 1763, at the end of the French and Indian (or Seven Years) War, the British government began to levy taxes on the colonists in order to pay for the war and the defense of the colonies. The colonists objected that this violated their rights as Englishmen. Parliament had no right to tax the American colonists, they argued, as long as the colonists elected no representatives to Parliament. For Parliament to tax them when they had no voice in the matter was tantamount to taking their property without their consent. Indeed, the colonists' position was quite simple: "no taxation without representation!"

Parliament's response was to point out that the colonists were in the same situation as most of the people of England itself, where only a small minority enjoyed the right to vote at this time. Because of corruption and out-of-date electoral rules, whole cities were without representatives; yet all British subjects were "virtually represented" by the members of Parliament who looked after the interests of the entire commonwealth. To this argument the colonists replied by saying, in effect, that if the people of England were foolish enough to settle for "virtual" representation, so much the worse for them. As the colonists saw it, representation must be "actual," else it is not representation at all.

This, in brief, was the quarrel that led to armed rebellion in 1775. In the beginning the colonists maintained that they were loyal subjects of the Crown who fought only to restore their rights—rights the British government was supposed to protect, but had instead violated. Yet in little more than a year they abandoned this position to take the radical step of declaring themselves independent of Great Britain.

They took this step in part because of the arguments set out in *Common Sense*, a pamphlet written and published in February of 1776 by Thomas Paine (1737–1809). The arguments of *Common Sense* are quite similar to Locke's in the *Second Treatise*, but Paine expressed them in a highly charged and effective rhetoric. Society, Paine said, is always a blessing; but government, even the best government, is a "necessary evil." It is evil because it coerces us and controls our lives; but it is necessary because most of us, fallen creatures that we are, cannot be trusted to respect the natural rights of others. To protect our natural rights, then, we create government. If the government does its job, it deserves our obedience. But if it fails to protect our natural rights—if it turns against us and violates our rights—the government ceases to be a necessary evil and becomes an intolerable one. When this happens, Paine concluded, the people have every right to overthrow their government and replace it with one that will respect their rights.

The American colonies, said Paine, should sever their ties with Great Britain and establish themselves as an independent, self-governing state. If it is to be truly self-governing, though, the new state must be a republic. Paine took this to mean that there must be no king, for he believed monarchy to be absolutely incompatible with individual liberty. In this respect he went beyond Locke—who may have preferred to abolish monarchy, but did not say as much in the *Second Treatise*—in what was otherwise an essentially Lockean argument.

Within six months of the publication of *Common Sense* the Continental Congress did as Paine had urged and declared, on July 2, 1776, that "These United Colonies are, and of right ought to be, free and independent states." Two days later the Congress adopted the Declaration of Independence, a document written principally by Thomas Jefferson (1743–1826). The exact character of Jefferson's justification of the separation from Great Britain is a matter of some dispute among scholars, but there is no doubt that the argument of the Declaration, as well as some of its striking phrases, closely resembles Locke's.[5] Thus we are told that certain "truths" are "self-evident":

> that all men are created equal, that they are endowed by their Creator with certain unalienable Rights, that among these are Life, Liberty, and the pursuit of Happiness.—That to secure these rights, Governments are instituted among Men, deriving their just powers from the consent of the governed.—That whenever any Form of Government becomes destructive of these ends, it is the Right of the People to alter or to abolish it, and to institute new Government, laying its foundation on such principles, and organizing its powers in such form, as to them shall seem most likely to effect their Safety and Happiness.[6]

Following this preamble comes a list of specific grievances submitted as evidence that the British government had indeed become "destructive of these ends" for which governnment is created, thereby entitling the colonists "to alter or to abolish it, and to institute new Government, . . ."

In the Declaration of Independence, then, we have a compressed version of the argument made by Locke, Paine, and other early liberals. Two features of this argument deserve particular attention. The first is the claim that "all men are created equal, . . ." This caused some embarrassment when the Declaration was issued, for a number of colonists, "patriots" as well as "tories," pointed out that it was hypocritical for a slave-holding country to proclaim the equality of all mankind. In fact, Jefferson, a slave-owner himself, included a sharp attack on slavery in his original draft of the Declaration. This passage was removed by other members of Congress, however, while the claim that all men are created equal remained.

This embarrassment reveals a more general problem in the position of the early liberals. They spoke a democratic language when they proclaimed that all men are naturally free and equal and that government rests on the consent of the people; yet they never explained whom they counted as "men" or "the people." For instance, Locke's references to "men" and "the people" make him seem to be a democrat. But Locke did not clearly advocate an extension of voting rights beyond the property-holders who were allowed to vote in his day; he also held shares in a company engaged in the slave trade.[7] Locke and the other early liberals simply took it for granted, moreover, that natural equality and the right to self-government did not include women.[8] By making these claims, however, the early liberals at least provided an opening for those who could say, "If all men are created equal, why isn't this or that group of men or women being treated as equals?" By speaking the language of equality, that is, they contributed, perhaps unwittingly, to the growth of democracy and the expansion of the franchise.

The second feature of the Declaration that deserves particular attention is its defense of the rights and liberties of individuals against government. This, again, is typical of the early liberals, who saw government as a continuing threat to individual liberty. This concern may betray the influence of classical republicanism, with its constant warnings about the danger of corruption. Indeed, the republican and liberal traditions were so closely entwined at this point that it is difficult to separate them. But there were differences of emphasis. The republicans worried about the corruption of the people as much as the corruption of the government, while the early liberals were concerned almost exclusively with the abuse of power by government. Freedom, as republicans saw it, was largely a matter of governing oneself through political participation, and therefore closely connected with civic virtue; on the liberal view, freedom was more a matter of being free from interference by the government, and virtue something to be learned and practiced in private life.

Out of this combination of attitudes came the Constitution of the United States. The Constitution provides for a strong central government, but it also limits the government's powers in a number of ways. In this respect it is a republican as well as a liberal framework for government. But it makes no direct provision for the promotion of civic virtue. Some of the Founding Fathers urged the creation of a national university partly for this purpose, but their efforts failed. This lack of concern for civic virtue suggests the specifically liberal element of the Constitution—the attempt to prevent the government from meddling in those areas of life, such as religion and the cultivation of character, that belong to the domain of privacy.

Drafted in 1787 and ratified by the necessary states in 1788, the Constitution took effect in 1789. These were momentous years for the United States, yet every bit as momentous for the development of political ideologies world wide. For in these years a revolution began in France that was to prove at least as important in world affairs as the events taking shape in the United States.

The French Revolution

To understand the French Revolution and the part liberalism played in it, it is necessary to know something about the *ancien régime*—the *old order* of French society in the years before the Revolution. Three features of this order are particularly important: its religious conformity, aristocratic privilege, and political absolutism. In all three respects the condition of France before its revolution differed significantly from that of the American colonies before theirs.

First, **religious conformity.** In the years following the Reformation France suffered a series of bloody civil wars between Huguenots, as the French Protestants were called, and Catholics. Most of the violence ended in 1598 with the Edict of Nantes, a compromise that granted freedom of worship to the Huguenots while acknowledging Catholicism as the official religion. This lasted until 1685, when Louis XIV, the so-called Sun King, revoked the Edict and required all his subjects to conform to Catholic doctrine. From then until the eve of the Revolution, religious conformity remained government policy. This favored status, together with the wealth it enjoyed through its extensive landholdings, made the Catholic Church a bulwark of the *ancien régime,* and therefore a major obstacle for those who desired a more open society. The Church's chief opposition came from the thinkers of the **Enlightenment,** such as Voltaire, who believed that the light of reason would lead to a better understanding of the world and a freer, more rational society. For this to happen, however, reason would first have to overcome the forces of superstition—forces led, as they saw it, by the Catholic Church.

Aristocratic privilege, the second leading feature of the old order, was a vestige or remnant of feudalism. In this respect France was markedly different from the American colonies, where hereditary aristocracy had never taken root. In France the roots of the aristocracy were very deep indeed, and the aristocrats of the 1700s were generally anxious to preserve the special rights they enjoyed as nobles. One of these privileges was exemption from most taxes. This was troublesome for the French government, which was constantly in need of funds, and greatly resented by those who felt the burden of taxation most heavily—the middle class (bourgeoisie) and the peasants. Another important privilege the nobles enjoyed was the almost exclusive right to high positions in the government, military, and Church. Louis XVI, who was king when the Revolution began, chose almost all his advisors and administrators from the nobility, for instance, and required all candidates for officer's rank in the army to have at least four generations of noble blood.[9] Aristocratic privilege meant, then, that the *ancien régime* remained a society where ascribed status counted far more than ability or effort—something the bourgeoisie greatly resented.

Political absolutism, finally, placed the king above the law and concentrated political power in the throne. This was the legacy of Louis XIV, whose long reign (1643–1715) set the pattern for absolute monarchy. According to tradition, the king of France was responsible to the Estates General, which consisted of representatives of the three orders or "estates" of the country: the clergy, the nobility, and the bourgeoisie. But Louis XIV never convened the Estates General—it had last met in 1614—and found ways of appeasing and weakening the three estates. He secured the Church's support by suppressing the Huguenots; he drew the nobility to his extravagant court at Versailles, where they became dependent upon his favor; and he flattered the bourgeoisie by choosing some of his government ministers from their ranks. With no effective opposition to limit his power, Louis XIV was able to govern as he saw fit. As he supposedly said, *"L'état, c'est moi"* ("I am the state.")

Neither of his successors, Louis XV (r. 1715–1774) and Louis XVI (r. 1774–1792), was as adept as the Sun King at exercising absolute authority, but both followed his example. Neither summoned the Estates General, for instance, until a financial crisis finally forced Louis XVI to do so in 1788. This event sparked the Revolution.

When Louis XVI called for elections to the Estates General in the winter of 1788–1789, he and the nobles expected the representatives of the First and Second Estates—the clergy and the nobility—to prevent any drastic action by the Third Estate, or *le peuple* (the people). But the Third Estate insisted on double representation, and public pressure forced the King to concede. Then, with the support of some liberal nobles and parish priests, the deputies of the Third Estate declared themselves the National Assembly and began to draft a constitution for France. The French Revolution was underway.

Although the Revolution ended ten bloody years later with a new form of absolutism, the revolutionaries' original aim was to establish a limited government that would protect the natural rights of French citizens—rights that the French kings had refused to acknowledge. The revolutionaries wanted to overthrow the old order of society, replacing its religious conformity with tolerance, its aristocratic privilege with equality of opportunity, and its absolute monarchy with constitutional government. This is evident in their *Declaration of the Rights of Man and of the Citizen* of 1789. In the first of the Declaration's 17 articles, the National Assembly attacked aristocratic privilege and ascribed status: "Men are born, and always continue, free and equal in respect of their rights. Civil distinctions [i.e., hereditary ranks or estates], therefore, can be founded only on public utility." They aimed the second and third articles against political absolutism, proclaiming that government rests on the consent of the governed:

II. The end of all political associations, is the preservation of the natural and imprescriptible rights of man; and these rights are liberty, property, security, and resistance of oppression.

III. The nation is essentially the source of all sovereignty; nor can any individual, or any body of men, be entitled to any authority which is not expressly derived from it.

Nor did the National Assembly spare religious conformity. In the tenth article it declared, "No man ought to be molested on account of his opinions, not even on account of his *religious* opinions, provided his avowal of them does not disturb the public order established by the law."[10]

Liberalism was not the only current of thought in the French Revolution; others, especially republicanism with its emphasis on civic virtue, also played a part. "Liberty, Equality, Fraternity"—the famous slogan of the Revolution— suggests how liberalism and republicanism were entwined, as they had been in the American Revolution. Every man has a right to be free, the argument went, because all are born equal to one another and have a right to an equal opportunity to make their way in society. Yet liberty and equality were also prized, in republican terms, as the chief ingredients in a rich public life directed toward virtue. The cry for "fraternity" evoked republican themes, too. The demand for "fraternity" suggested that the civil distinctions of rank or estate that divided the people of France against each other should be replaced with a sense of their common citizenship. With this in mind, the revolutionaries abandoned the traditional titles or salutations of *monsieur* and *madame* and began to address everyone as *citoyen* or *citoyenne* (citizen). "Fraternity" suggested that there is more to life than being free to pursue one's private interests, just as a citizen has a responsibility to take a role in public life.[11] "Fraternity" implied an interest in solidarity, particularly in the form of putting the common good ahead of one's private desires. It also took on nationalistic overtones as the French thought of themselves less as subjects of a monarch than as members of a single nation.

As the Revolution continued, Church lands were confiscated and sold and, in 1791, the National Assembly completed a constitution that limited the powers of the king, abolished the three estates, and granted the right to vote to more than half the adult males. France had become a constitutional monarchy, with a government more limited and a franchise more nearly democratic than Great Britain's.

Once started, however, the Revolution could not be brought to a stop. The more radical revolutionaries demanded greater democracy, help for the poor, and less concern for the protection of property. War broke out when Prussia and Austria sent armies to the French borders to check the spread of revolution and restore the *ancien régime*. And one economic crisis followed another. Under the pressure of these circumstances, the revolutionaries abolished the monarchy and established the Republic of France on September 22, 1792; later revolutionaries proclaimed this the first day of the first month of the Year I, the beginning of a new era of history that required a new calendar. The events of the next year were just as dramatic, beginning with the execution of Louis XVI in January, followed by a new constitution that granted universal manhood suffrage. Then, from June 1793 until July 1794, came the Reign of Terror. During this period the guillotine became the chief symbol of the Revolution. Some 300,000 people were arrested on suspicion of betraying the Republic and more than 17,000 were executed. The Terror ended when its principal leader, Maximilien Robespierre, was himself beheaded, and in 1795 a measure of calm was restored under another constitution. Less democratic than its predecessor, the Constitution of 1795 restricted the vote to the property-owning bourgeoisie and created a five-member Directory to head the government. This arrangement survived until 1799, when Napoleon Bonaparte seized power, turning France into a military dictatorship and later a monarchy with himself as emperor.

LIBERALISM AND CAPITALISM

In both the Old World and the New, then, liberalism was a vigorous revolutionary force in the seventeenth and eighteenth centuries. In the name of natural rights and the rights of man, liberals struggled for individual liberty against the social, political, and religious arrangements that lingered from the Middle Ages. But there is one aspect of this struggle that we have yet to attend to, namely, the struggle for *economic liberty*.

By struggling against ascribed status, the early liberals sought wider opportunities for more people, not just the privileged few born into the nobility. One form of opportunity, economic opportunity, was particularly important to the merchants, bankers, and lawyers who came to make up the middle class or bourgeoisie. For them, acquiring wealth was the main avenue of social advancement. But in early modern Europe, numerous restrictions on manufacturing and commerce remained. These included the traditional Christian limits on usury—the practice of charging interest on loans—and a wide variety of local regulations concerning working conditions and the production, distribution, and sale of goods. And in the seventeenth and eighteenth centuries, there were the restrictions associated with the prevailing economic theory, **mercantilism.**

Mercantilism According to mercantilism, one country could improve its economic strength only at the expense of others. Acting on this theory, the European nation-states engaged in an economic warfare that frequently led to real combat. One tactic was to establish colonies, exploit their resources, and forbid the colonists to buy from or sell to anyone but the so-called mother country. Another was to set high tariffs, or taxes on imported goods, to discourage the sale of foreign goods and encourage the growth of domestic industries. A third tactic was the **monopoly,** the practice of granting exclusive control over a market to a single firm on the grounds that this was the most efficient way to handle the risks of trade between the far-flung colonies and the European homeland. Two leading examples of monopolies were the Dutch East India and the British East India companies, each of which received from its own government (but not from the native peoples) the exclusive right to govern as well as trade with vast colonial territories.

Mercantilism, then, attempted to promote the national interest directly through the use of restraints and monopolistic privileges. These attempts worked to the advantage of some—especially those who were able to secure the privileges—and the disadvantage of others. The middle class, which generally fell into this second camp, pressed for a wider and more nearly equal opportunity to compete for profits. Anything less, they believed, was an unjust obstacle in the way of individual liberty. This liberal belief found expression in the economic theory of **capitalism.**

Capitalism According to capitalism, economic exchanges are essentially a private matter between persons pursuing profits. This emphasis on private profit ran against the grain of much of the Christian and republican traditions, neither of which assigned great value to either privacy or profits. But the 1700s produced some forceful statements of the argument that people ought to be free to pursue their private interests, including their economic interests. One of the first was *The Fable of the Bees* (1714) by Bernard Mandeville (1670–1733). Mandeville's fable is the story of a hive where the bees, shocked by their own selfishness, decide to reform and act with the good of others in mind. But reform proves disastrous. Soldiers, servants, merchants and most of the other bees are thrown out of work because there is no demand for their services. The richness and variety of life is gone. Indeed, Mandeville suggests, the hive was much better off in the old, selfish days when the bees acted out of vanity and greed—a time when

> . . . every Part was full of Vice,
> Yet the whole Mass a Paradise;
>
> 　　　　. . .
>
> 　Such were the Blessings of that state;
> Their Crimes conspir'd to make them Great.

The moral of the story, captured in the subtitle of the *Fable*, is *Private Vices, Publick Benefits*.

The idea that the best way to promote the good of society as a whole is to let people pursue their private interests became the cornerstone of liberal economic thought in the eighteenth century. In the middle of the century a group of French thinkers known as the **Physiocrats** developed this idea into an economic theory. Arguing against mercantilism, the Physiocrats maintained that the true basis of wealth is neither trade nor manufactures, but agriculture. Furthermore, they claimed, the best way to cultivate wealth is not through regulations and restrictions, but through unrestrained, free enterprise. Remove regulations and leave people alone to compete in the marketplace was their advice to governments, summarized in the phrase, *"Laissez faire, laissez passer"* (or, let it be, leave it alone).

The most thorough and influential defense of laissez faire was to be found in Adam Smith's *Inquiry into the Nature and Causes of the Wealth of Nations* (1776). Smith (1723–1790), a Scottish philosopher, agreed with the Physiocrats' attack on mercantilism and monopoly. Far from serving the public interest, Smith said, restraints on economic competition serve only the interests of those few people who are able to take advantage of them. For most people, lack of competition simply means higher prices and scarcer goods.

To remedy this, Smith called for an economic policy that would allow individuals to compete freely in the marketplace. Not only will this be the fairest policy, since it gives everyone an equal opportunity, it will also be the most efficient. For there is nothing like self-interest—in this case, the desire for profits—to motivate people to provide the goods and services that others want. As Smith put it, "It is not from the benevolence of the butcher, the brewer, or the baker that we expect our dinner, but from their regard to their own interest. We address ourselves, not to their humanity but to their self-love, and never talk to them of our own necessities but of their advantage."[12]

Smith reasoned that removing economic restrictions and privileges will encourage people to produce and sell goods for a profit. In order to turn a profit, however, producers will have to be able either to produce a better or a cheaper good than their competitors; otherwise, people will not buy their products. Private interest, set free, will thus indirectly promote the public good by making available more and better and cheaper goods. It is, Smith said, as if an "invisible hand" were directing all these self-interested competitors to serve, through their competition, the interest of the whole society.

Smith also argued vigorously for free trade between countries. If people in some foreign land can sell us something we want for less than it costs to produce it ourselves, then let them do it. High taxes on foreign imports may encourage industry at home, Smith said, but it does so at great cost to the consumer, who has fewer and more expensive goods available. In the long run, peaceful and unrestricted trade between countries is better for everyone than the economic warfare of mercantilism.

From Smith's point of view, then, government should have as little as possible to do with economic exchanges. Government has only three proper functions, he said. First, it must defend the country against invasion. Second, it must promote justice—mostly by protecting property rights—and maintain order. Finally, it must provide certain public works and institutions that private enterprise will not provide, such as roads, bridges, canals, and harbors (what economists now refer to as the infrastructure necessary to the conduct of business), as well as public education. All other matters are best left to the private business of private individuals, who should be free to make their own way in the world as they see fit. In this respect, Smith and the other advocates of capitalism have taken a liberal position.

LIBERALISM IN THE NINETEENTH CENTURY

At the beginning of the 1800s, liberalism remained a revolutionary force throughout much of the world. In South America, liberal ideas helped to inspire struggles for independence in the Spanish colonies. Even in France the dictatorship of Napoleon did not mean a return to the *ancien régime*. In his revision of the French laws, the Napoleonic Code, Napoleon gave lasting approval to the principle of civil equality: the aristocrats kept their titles but lost most of their economic and political privileges. And though he reestablished Catholicism as the official religion of France, Napoleon also guaranteed freedom of worship to Protestants and Jews. Some Europeans even greeted Napoleon's conquests of their countries as liberation from the old aristocratic social order. Napoleon's defeat of the Prussian army in 1806 led Prussia (later part of Germany) to undertake many reforms, for instance, the abolition of serfdom among them.

On the European continent, however, Napoleon's defeat in 1815 marked the beginning of 30 years of reaction against these revolutionary changes, including the reassertion of the rights of hereditary monarchs and aristocrats. Ironically, the country most responsible for this defeat, England, was also the country in which liberalism had made its greatest gains.

At the beginning of the 1800s the British Empire was still expanding. The thirteen American colonies had gained their independence, but Britain continued to control India, Canada, and Australia, and in the course of the century it was to gain vast territories in Africa, too. England was also enjoying expansion in another form as the Industrial Revolution made it the world's first great industrial power. Beginning about 1750, the invention of new machinery, the discovery of steam power, and the development of assembly lines and other mass production techniques brought about a remarkable increase in productive power. These forces enabled English merchants to import raw materials, such as cotton, and to manufacture goods to be sold at home and abroad for handsome profits. With its combination of empire and industry, Great Britain became "the workshop of the world"—and the world's greatest imperial power—in the nineteenth century.

But power comes at a price, and in Britain the price was a society more sharply divided along class lines. Although the landed aristocracy was still the dominant force when the 1800s began, the merchants and professionals of the middle class made enormous social and economic gains during the first half of the century. The same cannot be said of the men, women, and children of the new working class. Poor and numerous, these people toiled in the mines, mills, and factories that sprang up during the Industrial Revolution, and their situation was bleak indeed. Without unemployment compensation, or regulation of working hours or safety conditions, or the legal right to form trade or labor unions, they worked under extremely harsh and insecure conditions. Just how harsh is suggested by a bill proposed in Parliament early in the century to *improve* the workers' position. The bill forbade factories to employ children under the age of ten, to put anyone under eighteen on night work (i.e., 9 P.M. through 5 A.M.), or to require anyone under eighteen to work more than $10\frac{1}{2}$ hours a day. Even this bill did not pass until, after years of debate, it had been so weakened as to be ineffective.

In economic status and in political power, too, the working class fell far behind the middle class in the first half of the nineteenth century. The Reform Bill of 1832 lowered property qualifications enough to give middle class males the right to vote, but most adult males and all women were still denied suffrage. This was a matter of some concern to the leading liberal writers of the day, who promoted the theory of **utilitarianism.**

Utilitarianism

Jeremy Bentham   The original leader of the Utilitarians (or Philosophic Radicals) was Jeremy Bentham (1748–1832). Society should be reformed along more rational lines, Bentham insisted, and the way to do this is to begin by asking why people do what they do. His answer, like Thomas Hobbes's in the seventeenth century, was that people act out of self-interest. As Bentham put it, "Nature has placed mankind under the governance of two sovereign masters, *pain* and *pleasure.* It is for them alone to point out what we ought to do, as well as to determine what we shall do."[13] This is simply a fact of human nature, he thought, and there is nothing we can do to change it. But once we understand that all people seek pleasure and avoid pain in everything they do, we can take steps to be better pleasure-seekers and pain-avoiders.

Bentham did not mean that we should look for pleasure in immediate gratification, as in getting drunk, because the pain we or others suffer later will probably outweigh the short-term pleasure drunkenness provides. What he did mean is that we should look for **utility.** Something has utility for someone—a hammer for a carpenter, for instance, or money for almost everyone—if it helps that person do what he or she wants to do. Since people want to be happy, utility promotes happiness. This led Bentham to argue that everyone should follow *the principle of utility:* do whatever will produce the greatest happiness of the greatest number.

Bentham recognized that people will sometimes fail to see what does and does not have utility for them—someone who drops out of school may not appreciate the utility of education, for example. He also admitted that, in pursuing our own pleasures, we may bring pain to others. But the purpose of government is to solve these problems. In Bentham's words, "The business of government is to promote the happiness of society, by punishing and rewarding."[14] By punishing those who cause pain to others and by rewarding those who give pleasure, in other words, government can and should act to produce the greatest happiness of the greatest number.

From this Bentham drew two general conclusions about government. The first was that government could best promote the greatest happiness of the greatest number, in most cases, by leaving people alone. The individual is usually the best judge of his or her own interests, he said, so government should usually let people pursue those interests as they see fit. In economic matters, this led Bentham to accept the laissez faire arguments of Adam Smith. His second conclusion was that government is not likely to promote the greatest happiness of the greatest number if it is open to only a small segment of society. In the pursuit of utility, Bentham declared, everyone is to count equally. The government must take everyone's utility or happiness into account, then, and it can only do this if almost everyone is allowed to vote. Although Bentham's views on voting are not altogether clear, he did support universal male suffrage, and he may have supported the vote for women, too.[15]

John Stuart Mill   The views of John Stuart Mill on this matter are not in doubt, for Mill was an ardent advocate of women's rights. The most important of the utilitarians, Mill (1806–1873) was probably the leading liberal philosopher of the nineteenth century. Whether he was supporting women's rights or arguing that the government should set minimum educational standards for everyone, Mill's great concern was to defend and extend individual liberty. This is most evident in his essay *On Liberty*.

When Mill published *On Liberty* in 1859, liberalism seemed to have triumphed, at least in England and the United States. The old enemies—ascribed status, religious conformity, and absolute government—were no longer the obstacles to individual liberty they had been. Yet Mill was alarmed by what he took to be a new threat to liberty in the growing power of public opinion. In the old days, Mill said, the chief enemy of freedom was the government; but now that we elect representatives, the government is more responsive to the desires of the people. It is responsive, however, to the majority of the people, or at least the majority of those who vote, and this allows them to use the government to take away the liberty of those who do not share the majority's views. More directly than this, the majority can bring social pressure to bear on those who do not conform to the ordinary, conventional ways of life. Without going through the government or the law, the "moral coercion of public opinion" can stifle freedom of thought and action by making social outcasts of individuals who do not conform to social customs and beliefs. Like Alexis de Tocqueville, whose *Democracy in America* he greatly admired, Mill was worried about "the tyranny of the majority."

On Liberty was Mill's attempt to deal with this new form of tyranny. In that essay he advanced "one very simple principle" that he hoped to persuade his readers to follow: "the only purpose for which power can be rightfully exercised over any member of a civilized community, against his will, is to prevent harm to others. His own good, either physical or moral, is not a sufficient warrant."[16] According to this principle—sometimes called the **harm principle**—every sane adult should be free to do whatever he or she wants as long as his or her actions do not harm or threaten to harm others. Government and society, then, should not interfere with an individual's activities unless that individual is somehow harming or threatening to harm others. Government has no business prohibiting the sale of alcohol, for instance, on the grounds that drinking harms the drinker; but government should certainly prohibit drunken driving on the grounds that this poses a serious threat of harm to others.

Mill defended his principle by appealing not to natural rights, as most of

John Stuart Mill (1806–1873).

the early liberals had done, but to utility. Freedom is a good thing, he argued, because it promotes "the permanent interests of man as a progressive being." He meant by this that both individuals and society as a whole will benefit if people are encouraged to think and act freely. For the individual, freedom is vital to personal development. Our mental and moral faculties are like muscles, Mill said. Without exercise, they weaken and shrivel. But people cannot exercise their minds and their powers of judgment when they are constantly being told, by government and public opinion, what they can and cannot do. To be fully human, then, the individual must be free to think and speak for himself or herself—as long as he or she neither harms nor threatens harm to others.

It is possible, of course, that people who speak and act freely will make others, perhaps even the majority of society, uncomfortable and unhappy. But in the long run, Mill argued, this works to the benefit of society. Progress is possible only when there is an open competition among different ideas, opinions, and beliefs. As in economics, competition between ideas, in a free marketplace of ideas, gives us a greater variety to choose from and allows us to distinguish the good ideas from the bad. Freedom of thought and action is necessary to social progress, therefore, because without it society, stuck in the rut of conformity, will never go forward.

Mill's desire to promote individual liberty also led him to recommend representative democracy as the best possible form of government. He did this, in *Considerations on Representative Government* (1861), because he believed that political participation was one of the best forms of exercise for the mental and moral faculties of men and women. This kind of exercise is only available to *all* citizens, moreover, in a democracy. Even so, Mill's fear of the tyranny of the majority kept him from embracing democracy wholeheartedly. Among other things, he favored a form of plural voting where every man and woman will have a vote, but some—those with higher levels of education, for instance—will have two, three, or more. In this way Mill thought that plural voting would enable everyone to enjoy the benefits of political participation, yet give enough power to the more enlightened and better informed members of society to protect individual liberty. Such a system was necessary, Mill believed, at least until the overall level of education was high enough to remove the threat of the tyranny of the majority.

As for economic matters, Mill began his career as a staunch defender of laissez faire capitalism. Toward the end of his life, however, he called himself a socialist. Indeed, the shift in his thinking on these matters was one of the first signs of an even greater shift on the part of many liberals in the latter part of the nineteenth century, a shift that divided liberalism into two rival camps.

LIBERALISM DIVIDED

The occasion for this split was the reaction of different liberals to the social effects of the Industrial Revolution. As the nineteenth century wore on, the misery of much of the working class in England became increasingly obvious, in part through the depiction of their plight in the popular novels of Charles Dickens. A number of reform movements were underway, and socialism was gaining support, especially on the European continent. One group of liberals began to argue that government should take steps to rescue people from poverty, ignorance, and illness. Because of their concern for the well-being or "well-faring" of the individual, this branch of liberalism has come to be called **welfare** (or **welfare-state) liberalism**. The other group of liberals maintained that any steps of this sort would invest too much power in the government, which they took to be a necessary evil and one of the main obstacles to individual liberty. Because their view is similar to the position of the early liberals, it has come to be called **neoclassical** (or new classical) **liberalism.**

Neoclassical Liberalism

Since the second half of the nineteenth century, neoclassical liberals have consistently argued that government should be as small as possible in order to leave as much room as possible for the exercise of individual freedom. The state or government, in their view, should be nothing more than a nightwatchman, for its only legitimate business is to protect the person and property of individuals against force and fraud. Some neoclassical liberals have based this argument on an appeal to natural rights, others on an appeal to utility. In the late 1800s, however, the most influential among them based their arguments on Darwin's theory of evolution.

In his *Origin of Species* (1859), Charles Darwin used the idea of "natural selection" to account for the evolution of life forms. Darwin held that individual creatures within every species experience random mutations, or accidental changes, in their biological make-up. Some mutations enhance a creature's ability to find food and survive, while others are either neutral or harmful to the chances of survival. Those lucky enough to have beneficial mutations are more likely to survive, and to pass these biological changes along to their offspring, than less fortunate members of their species. Thus nature "selected" certain creatures with certain mutations and thereby "directed" the path of evolution. But all this was accidental and unintentional. This biological good fortune also puts some species at an advantage over others in competition for food—for instance, giraffes are able to eat the leaves on the higher branches of trees which is a distinct advantage when food is scarce. Mutations can thus account not only for the evolution of species, but also for their survival or extinction.

Although Darwin did not draw any conclusions about the proper social and political arrangements for human beings from his theory of natural selection, others were quick to do so. Many who had stressed the importance of economic competition seized upon Darwin's theory as proof of the correctness of their claim that the struggle for survival is natural to human life and government should not "interfere" in that struggle. Two of the most important of these **Social Darwinists** were Herbert Spencer, an Englishman, and William Graham Sumner, an American.

Social Darwinism   Herbert Spencer (1820–1903), who had begun to think in evolutionary terms before Darwin's *Origin of Species* appeared, took Darwin's work to confirm the main lines of his own thought. Where Darwin stressed the competition between different species for survival, however, Spencer focused on competition between individual members of the same species. In particular, Spencer claimed that there is a struggle for survival *within* the human species. This struggle is entirely natural, moreover, and it is wrong to interfere with it. Individuals must be free to compete with one another. Those who are strongest, smartest, and most fit for this competition will succeed and prosper; those who are unfit will fail and suffer. But this is simply nature's way, Spencer said. Helping the poor and the weak is a threat to individual freedom and social progress because it holds the rest of society back. Indeed, it was Spencer who coined the phrase, "survival of the fittest." Given these views, it is hardly surprising that Spencer was one of the leading advocates of the nightwatchman state.

William Graham Sumner (1840–1910) advanced the Social Darwinist theory in the United States. A professor of social and political science at Yale, Sumner proclaimed that "there are two chief things with which government has to deal. They are, the property of men and the honor of women."[17] These are the *only* matters with which government should concern itself. In the competition for survival, government should simply see to it that everyone competes fairly and freely. Freedom, for Sumner, was freedom to compete, including the freedom of the victors to keep and enjoy the fruits of their victory without having to share them with anyone else—certainly not with the poor, who were poor precisely because they had lost in this life-and-death competition. In fact, Sumner and the Social Darwinists insisted that neither government nor even private charity should try to help anyone, no matter how weak or desperate he or she might be, except by providing protection against force and fraud. As Sumner put it, "A drunkard in the gutter is just where he ought to be, according to the fitness and tendency of things. Nature has set up on him the process of decline and dissolution by which she removes things which have [outlived] their usefulness."[18]

Most neoclassical liberals have not been as extreme in their views as the Social Darwinists; neoclassical liberals today do not base their arguments on evolutionary premises at all. But in the latter part of the nineteenth century the Social Darwinists were quite influential in England and the United States, especially among businessmen.

Welfare Liberalism

Like the classical and neoclassical liberals, welfare liberals believe in the value of individual liberty. But welfare liberals maintain that government is not just a necessary evil. On the contrary, if it is properly directed government can be a positive force for promoting individual liberty by seeing to it that everyone has an equal opportunity in life.

T. H. Green   One of the first to make the case for welfare liberalism was T. H. Green (1836–1882), a professor of philosophy at Oxford University. The heart of liberalism, Green said, has always been the desire to remove obstacles that block the free growth and development of individuals. In the past that meant limiting the powers of government so that people can be free to live, worship, and compete in the marketplace as they see fit. By the mid-1800s these aims had largely been accomplished in countries like England, and it was time to recognize and overcome still other obstacles to freedom and opportunity, such as poverty and illness, prejudice and ignorance. To overcome *these* obstacles, Green argued, it was necessary to enlist the power of the state.

Green based his argument on a distinction between two different ways of thinking about freedom, ways that he called **negative** and **positive freedom.** The early liberals regarded freedom as a negative thing, he said, for they thought of freedom as the *absence* of restraint. Someone who was restrained— tied up and locked in jail, for instance—was not free, whereas someone who was unrestrained was. But Green believed that there is more to freedom than this. Freedom is not merely being left alone; it is the positive power or ability to do something. Thus we may say that a child born into poverty, with no real opportunity to escape, is not truly free to grow and develop to the full extent of his or her abilities. Even if no one is intentionally keeping that child in poverty, and thereby restraining him or her, the child is still not free. But if we admit this, Green argued, anyone who values individual liberty will want to take steps to overcome those circumstances that are such formidable obstacles to freedom.

For Green and other welfare liberals, this meant that society, acting through government, should establish public schools and hospitals, provide aid for the needy, and regulate working conditions to promote the health and well-being of the workers. Only in these and similar ways would the poor and powerless members of society be truly free. Neoclassical liberals complained that these policies simply robbed some individuals of their freedom by forcing them to transfer their property, through taxes, to others. Green responded that everyone gained freedom when he or she served the common good. For *positive* freedom is the ability to realize or achieve our ideal or "higher" selves in cooperation with others. Human beings are not merely pleasure-seekers and pain-avoiders. We have higher ideals, including higher ideals of what we can and ought to be as persons. From Green's perspective, then, the laws and programs that help the unfortunate, smooth social relations, and restrict all-out competition are positive *aids* to liberty, not restraints that limit our freedom. They may restrict our "lower" selves, but laws and programs of this sort encourage our "higher" selves to realize our nobler and more generous ideals through social cooperation.

In the late nineteenth and early twentieth centuries Green's views were taken up and extended by a number of scholars and political figures. Like Green, these welfare liberals saw an active government as a useful, even necessary tool in the campaign to expand individual liberty. And like Green, they also emphasized that human beings are social creatures, not isolated individuals who owe nothing to anyone else. Gradually their ideas and arguments prevailed among liberals. By the middle of the twentieth century, in fact, welfare liberals were usually known simply as liberals, while their neoclassical rivals were often called conservatives.

The Welfare State   As we note in later chapters, socialists invoked similar sentiments in support of their own schemes for social reform. But it is important to distinguish welfare or welfare-state liberalism from socialism. Socialists want to do more than tame or reform capitalism; they want to replace it with a system of publicly owned and democratically controlled enterprises. Welfare liberals, by contrast, prefer private ownership and generally take a competitive capitalist system for granted. From the perspective of the welfare liberal, the role of government is to regulate economic competition in order to cure the social ills and redress the individual injuries wrought by capitalist competition. Unlike socialists, welfare liberals regard economic competition as a good thing—but only when it is not at the expense of individual welfare.

It is also important to note that the grandfather of the modern welfare state was neither a socialist nor a liberal of any sort. Otto von Bismarck, the ardently antisocialist "Iron Chancellor" who united Germany in the latter part of the nineteenth century, believed that the welfare state was the best way to oppose socialism. Through a state-sponsored system of taxing employers and employees to support ill, injured, and unemployed workers, the German state stole the thunder of the socialists, who had played upon the anxieties of workers subject to the up-and-down cycles of a capitalist economy.

The birth of the welfare state also coincided roughly with the expansion of voting rights throughout much of Europe. In England the reforms of 1867 and 1885 brought the franchise to almost all adult males and thus made the working class a more powerful political factor. The support of this class contributed not only to the growth of the welfare state, but to the dominance of welfare liberalism in the twentieth century.

LIBERALISM IN THE TWENTIETH CENTURY

Another factor also contributed to the dominance of welfare over neoclassical liberalism. By the beginning of the 1900s, the nature of economic competition looked quite different from the competition of a century before. In the industrialized parts of the world the entrepreneur—the person who ran his or her own business—seemed to have given way to the corporation, the trust, the syndicate, and conglomerate. Business was now "big business," and many people began to call for government intervention in the marketplace, not to restrict competition, but to keep the large corporations from stifling it.

Historical Developments

In one form or another, however, the neoclassical liberals' faith in individual competition and achievement survived into the twentieth century, most notably in the United States. This faith was severely tested by the Great Depression of the 1930s. Individuals, no matter how rugged, seemed no match for this devastating economic collapse. The effects, political as well as economic, were felt throughout the world, as ideologists of all varieties sought ways to account for and take advantage of the situation. Many blamed the Depression on capitalism and turned to socialism or communism, on the one hand, or to fascism, on the other. In the English-speaking world, the main response to the Depression was to turn to the welfare state.

The liberal case for an active government gained support in the 1930s from the theory formulated by the English economist John Maynard Keynes (1883–1946). In his *General Theory of Employment, Interest and Money* (1936) Keynes argued that governments should use their taxing and spending powers to prevent depressions and maintain a healthy economy. Put simply, Keynes's theory holds that governments should try to manage or "fine tune" the economy. When prices are rising, that is, the government should raise taxes in order to reduce consumer spending and prevent inflation. Then, when inflation is no longer a threat, government should lower taxes, or increase spending on social programs, or both, in order to stimulate the economy and maintain high levels of employment. Whatever the strategy at any particular time, Keynes's approach calls for active government management of economic matters—an approach adopted by welfare liberals.

World War II brought an end to the Depression. But the welfare state remained, with its supporting ideology, welfare liberalism, the dominant ideology of the Western world—or at least its noncommunist parts. Welfare liberals usually reached some sort of accommodation with their socialist and conservative rivals, as most parties accepted the desirability of the welfare state. Indeed, this consensus seemed so broad and firm that some political observers began to speak in the late 1950s of "the end of ideology." That hope was soon dashed in the turmoil of the 1960s.

For one thing, there were controversies within liberalism. In the United States Martin Luther King, Jr., and other leaders of the civil rights movement pointed out that liberal promises of liberty and equality were still unfulfilled for blacks. This was a painful truth that all liberals had to acknowledge, however reluctantly. When King and others protested against the segregation laws that made blacks second-class citizens, neoclassical and welfare liberals alike could join in support. But King went on to call for government action not only to eliminate legal discrimination against blacks and other minorities, but to provide social and economic opportunities as well. This was acceptable to welfare liberals, but not their neoclassical cousins. The neoclassical wing formed a distinct minority among liberals, however, as their losing battle against President Lyndon Johnson's Great Society programs of the 1960s testifies. These programs, which sought to end discrimination against racial minorities, to fight a

War on Poverty, and to use the powers of government in various ways to provide equality of opportunity in American society, were largely the product of the welfare liberal's belief that government can and should be used to foster individual liberty.

The turmoil of the 1960s also presented another challenge to welfare liberalism, this time in the form of the New Left. Vaguely socialist in its orientation, the New Left rejected both the "obsolete communism" of the Soviet Union and the "consumer-capitalism" of the liberal countries. Most new-leftists accepted the liberal emphasis on individual rights and liberties, and most also supported government programs to promote equality of opportunity. But they complained that liberal governments worked first and foremost to protect the economic interests of capitalist corporations. Although they agreed that these governments did take steps to improve the material circumstances of their people, the new-leftists charged that the people were reduced to mere consumers when they ought to be encouraged to be active citizens. This led to the call for "participatory democracy," a society in which average people would be able to exercise greater control over the decisions that most closely affected their lives.

If welfare liberalism remains the dominant ideology and the dominant form of liberalism in the Western world—and from the perspective of the 1990s it seems that it does—it has clearly not gone unchallenged. A particularly strong challenge, in the form of a mixture of neoclassical liberalism and conservatism, appeared in the 1970s and '80s, as first Margaret Thatcher in Great Britain and then Ronald Reagan in the United States became heads of government. Neither leader has dismantled the welfare state, although both have moved in this direction. But dismantle it is just what we should do, the neoclassical liberals continue to insist. So the contest within liberalism continues, with neoclassical and welfare liberals engaging in ongoing disputes at the philosophical as well as political level.

Philosophical Considerations

The ongoing debate within liberalism is captured nicely in books by two philosophers: John Rawls's *A Theory of Justice* (1971) and Robert Nozick's *Anarchy, State, and Utopia* (1974).[19]

Rawls and Justice   According to Rawls (1921–), the old liberal device of the social contract can help us discover the principles of social justice. Rawls begins by asking the reader to imagine a group of people who enter into a contract that will set out the rules under which they will all have to live as members of the same society. Imagine too that all these people are behind a "veil of ignorance"—a veil that prevents anyone from knowing his or her identity, age, gender, race, or abilities or disabilities. Although all act out of self-interest, no one will be able to stack the deck, or fashion rules that lead to his or her personal advantage, because no one will know what is to his or her personal advantage. Thus the veil of ignorance insures impartiality.

What rules will emerge from such an impartial situation? Rawls believes that the people behind the veil of ignorance will unanimously choose two fundamental principles to govern their society—the two principles of justice. According to the first principle, everyone is to be equally free. Everyone is to have as much liberty as possible. That is, as long as every person in society has the same amount. According to the second principle, everyone is to enjoy equality of opportunity. To help insure this, each person is to have an equal share of wealth and power unless it can be shown that an unequal distribution will work to the benefit of the worst-off persons. If an equal distribution means that each gets $10, say, it is more just than a distribution where half the people get $18 and the other half only $2. But if an unequal distribution would give everyone, even the worst-off person, *at least* $11, perhaps because of incentives that encourage people to work harder and produce more, then justice requires the unequal distribution, not the equal distribution where each receives only $10.

Why does justice require this? Isn't it just to pay or reward people according to their efforts and abilities, not on their position at the bottom of the social scale? Rawls's response is to say that the people who make the greatest efforts and display the highest abilities do not really *deserve* a larger reward than anyone else. This is because effort and ability are generally characteristics that people come by through heredity and environment. Someone may be an outstanding surgeon, for instance, because she was born with superior mental and physical potential that she worked hard to develop. But this person cannot take credit for talent she was born with, nor even for her hard work if her family instilled in her the desire to work and achieve. If justice requires us to give greater rewards to some people than to others, Rawls concludes, it is not because they deserve more, but because this is the best way to promote the interests of the worst-off people in society. If justice requires us to pay physicians more than coal miners or barbers or secretaries, then it can only be because this is the best way to provide good medical care and thus promote everyone's vital interest in health—including the vital interests of society's worst-off.

The significance of Rawls's second principle is that it takes welfare liberalism in a more egalitarian direction. An equal distribution of wealth and resources is the benchmark for Rawls, and an unequal distribution is justified only if it proves superior from the point of view of those at the bottom of society. If the wealth and power of those at the top of the social scale do not truly work to the benefit of those at the bottom, then Rawls's theory calls for a redistribution of that wealth and power in a more nearly equal manner. For people can enjoy neither equal liberty nor equal opportunity when there are great and unjustified inequalities of wealth.

Nozick and the Minimal State   Three years after Rawls's *Theory of Justice* appeared, Robert Nozick (1938–) published *Anarchy, State, and Utopia*. In this book Nozick asserts that all individuals have rights that it is wrong to violate. But if this is true, he asks, can there ever be a legitimate government or state, one that does not violate the rights of its people? To answer this question,

Nozick draws on another old liberal idea—the state of nature. Like Hobbes and Locke, Nozick wants the reader to suppose that there is no government, no state, no political or legal authority of any sort. In this state of nature, individuals have rights, but they lack protection. Some sharp-eyed entrepreneurs will notice this and go into the business of providing protection, much as security guards and insurance agencies now do. Those who want protection may sign on with a private protective agency—for a fee, of course. But the choice is strictly theirs, unlike the citizens who must pay the government for protection whether they want it or not.

When people subscribe to a private protective agency, in other words, no one violates their rights by forcing them to do something they do not want to do. But out of a large number of competing protective agencies, Nozick says, one will grow and prosper until it absorbs the rest. This single protective agency, so large that it serves almost everyone in an area the size of a modern nation-state, will become for all practical purposes a state itself. And it will do so, Nozick claims, without violating anyone's rights.

This new state, however, performs only the functions of the protective agency. It is what Nozick calls "the minimal state," although it might also be called the nightwatchman state. It is a legitimate or just state, according to Nozick, because no one's rights are violated by its creation. But it is also the *only* legitimate state. Any state or government that does more than merely protect the people *must* violate someone's rights and therefore must be unjust. The policy of using taxation to take money from some people for the benefit of others, for instance, is "on a par with forced labor."[20] Someone who earns $100 and has $20 taken in taxes probably has no complaint if that $20 goes to provide him or her with protection; but if, say, $10 goes to provide benefits for others— health care, education, unemployment compensation—then the worker is effectively forced to spend 10 percent of his or her working time working for others. This is the equivalent of forced labor, according to Nozick, and therefore a violation of individual rights.

In general, Nozick's argument is that government should protect us and otherwise leave us alone. Like other neoclassical liberals, he insists on an unrestricted, free market economy. Government should not forbid capitalist acts between consenting adults, as he puts it. Like other neoclassical liberals, Nozick also insists on the individual's right to think and say and do whatever he or she pleases—as long as no one else's rights are violated. But the individual can be free to enjoy these rights only if the state is a "minimal" one.

Nozick's philosophical defense of neoclassical liberalism has extended the arguments of a number of contemporary theorists, notably Friedrich Hayek (1899–) and Milton Friedman (1912–). In the last 20 years, in fact, neoclassical liberalism has enjoyed a revival in both philosophy and politics under the name of **libertarianism,** playing an important part in the "conservative" economic policies of Margaret Thatcher and Ronald Reagan. In the United States, moreover, it has given rise to a political party, the Libertarian party, that sponsors candidates who want to move the country in the direction of the minimal state. But for some libertarians, even the minimal state is too much. In their view, true devotion to liberty demands that government be abolished.

Libertarian Anarchism

In many respects libertarian anarchism is simply the most extreme version of liberalism. Libertarian anarchists share the liberal belief in the value of individual liberty and equal opportunity. They also agree with the classical and neoclassical liberals' attitudes toward the state, which all take to be a major threat to individual freedom. But the libertarian anarchists go beyond other liberals to argue that the state is an altogether unnecessary evil. Since the state or government is both evil and unnecessary, they conclude, it ought to be eliminated. In their view, then, true liberalism leads to anarchy.

Although this position has never had broad popular support, it has had some articulate defenders. Perhaps the best known today is Murray Rothbard (1926–), an American economist. Rothbard and other libertarian anarchists maintain that free market anarchism is both desirable and practical. It is desirable because, when there is no coercion from government, every individual will be free to live as he or she chooses. And it is practical, according to the libertarian anarchists, because anything governments do can be done better by private enterprise. Education, police protection, defense, traffic regulation—these and all other public functions can be performed more efficiently by private companies competing with one another for customers. Someone who wants police protection, for instance, can "shop around" to find the company that provides the right level of protection at the best price, just as consumers nowadays can shop for a car, house, or insurance policy. Roads can be privately owned and operated, just as parking lots are now; all schools can be private, just as some are now; even currency can be provided by private enterprise, just as credit cards are now. There is, in short, no good reason to retain the state. Once enough people recognize this, the libertarian anarchists say, we will be on the way to a truly free and truly liberal society.[21]

LIBERALISM TODAY

Now that we have traced liberalism from its beginnings to the present, what can we say about its current state? There are three conclusions we want to stress here. The first is that liberalism is not the revolutionary force it once was—at least not in the West. But there are other parts of the world where the liberal attack on ascribed status or religious conformity or political absolutism still strikes against the foundations of society. This is most evident in Iran and other countries of the Middle East, where liberalism may have provoked a radical response from Islamic fundamentalists. In Eastern Europe and Asia, moreover, various protests against communist forms of ascribed status and political absolutism claim *liberalization* as their goal. In the Western world, however, the aims of the early liberals are now deeply entrenched in public policy and public opinion. In these places liberalism is no longer a revolutionary ideology, but an ideology defending a revolution already won.

The second conclusion is that liberals remain divided among themselves. Despite their agreement on fundamental points, especially the importance of individual liberty, liberals disagree sharply on how best to define and promote their goals. Welfare liberals believe that we need an active government to give everyone an equal chance to be free; neoclassical liberals (or libertarians) believe that we need to limit government to keep it from robbing us of freedom; libertarian anarchists believe that we should abolish government altogether.

Finally, we can also conclude that liberals are now wrestling with two very difficult problems that stem from their basic commitments to individual liberty and equality of opportunity. The first problem is, how far should individuals be able to go in exercising their freedom? Most liberals, welfare and neoclassical alike, accept some version of Mill's harm principle—people should be free to do as they wish unless they harm (or violate the rights of) others. When it comes time to apply this principle, however, the difficulty of deciding what harms someone becomes clear. Many liberals say that so-called victimless crimes like prostitution, gambling, and the sale of pornography should not be considered crimes at all. If one person wants to be a prostitute, the argument goes, and another wants to pay for his or her services, no one is being harmed, except perhaps the persons who have agreed to take part—the prostitute and the client. And if no one else is harmed, government has no business outlawing prostitution. To this argument some other liberals respond that victimless crimes are not as victimless as they appear. Pimps force women into prostitution, they say, and loan sharks take unfair advantage of people who borrow money from them at very high rates of interest. Those who favor abolishing penalties for victimless crimes counter this claim by arguing that these activities can be carefully regulated by the government if they are made legal, as prostitution is in the Netherlands and parts of Nevada, for example. But the argument continues without a clear-cut resolution. Despite their desire to separate the area of private freedom from the area of public control, liberals have found the boundary between private and public quite difficult to draw.

The second problem grows out of the liberal commitment to equal opportunity. For the libertarian, this means simply that everyone ought to be free to make his or her way in the world without unfair discrimination. The only kind of discrimination that is justified is discrimination on the basis of ability and effort. The liberal state should then see to it that discrimination on the basis of race, religion, gender, or any other irrelevant factor is illegal. By contrast, most welfare liberals maintain that government ought to take steps to help disadvantaged people enjoy an equal opportunity in life. Thus they have supported public schools, medical care, and even financial assistance for those in need. But how far should this go? Should we try to bring about a more nearly equal distribution of wealth and resources, as Rawls suggests, in order to promote true equality of opportunity? Is this fair to those who have earned their wealth without violating the rights of others?

Faced with a legacy of discrimination against women and members of racial minority groups, furthermore, many welfare liberals have endorsed **affirmative action** programs. These programs are supposed to assist members of groups that have suffered from discrimination by giving them special consideration in employment and education. But how is this to be done? By providing special training? By setting aside a certain number of jobs or places in colleges and professional schools for women and minorities? Aren't these ways of discriminating *against* some people—white males—by discriminating in favor of others? Can this be justified in the name of equality of opportunity?

These are difficult questions for anyone, but they are especially difficult for liberals because they are the kind of questions that liberalism leads people to raise. And there is, as yet, no obviously correct answer to these questions from the liberal position. Some critics see this as a serious or even fatal weakness—a sign that liberalism is either lost or at the end of its rope. A more sympathetic response might be to say that liberalism is still doing what it has always done, that is, searching for ways to advance the cause of individual liberty and opportunity. Certainly anyone who agrees with Mill's claim that flexing our mental and moral muscles is vital to individual growth will find plenty of room for exercise in contemporary liberalism—which is just as Mill would want it.

CONCLUSION

Liberalism as an Ideology

What can we conclude, then, about liberalism as an ideology? Given the rift between welfare liberals and libertarians, or neoclassical liberals, does it even make sense to speak of liberalism as a single ideology? We think it does, although the division between the two camps is deep and the gap between them may be widening. For the present, however, the differences are largely matters of emphasis and a fundamental disagreement about means, not ends. A quick look at how liberalism performs the four functions that all ideologies perform should make this clear.

Explanation   First, all ideologies explain why things are the way they are, with particular attention to social, economic, and political conditions. For liberals, these explanations are typically individualistic. Social conditions are the way they are at any particular time and place, they say, because individual choices and actions made them that way. Liberals recognize that the choices open to individuals are often limited, and they also acknowledge that actions frequently have consequences that no one intended or desired. Yet within the limits available to them, including the limits on their foresight and understanding, individuals make choices that, taken together, explain why things are the way they are at any particular place and time.

Why, for example, do economic depressions occur? Liberals generally believe that they are the wholly unintended results of decisions made by rational individuals responding to the circumstances in which they compete—or in some cases, are prevented from competing—in the marketplace. Welfare liberals generally follow Keynes's economic views and argue that the job of the government is to shape these choices, perhaps by lowering or raising taxes to give people more or less disposable income, in order to prevent or lessen economic distress. The neoclassical position is that the competitive marketplace will correct itself if left alone, and it is wrong for government to interfere. Despite these different views of what should be done, however, both sides share the fundamental premise that individual choices ultimately explain why things are as they are.

Evaluation   When it comes to *evaluating* conditions, liberalism turns again to the individual. Conditions are good, as a rule, if the individual is free to do as he or she wishes, as long as he or she does not harm or violate the rights of others. The more freedom people have, liberals say, the better things are; the less freedom, the worse they are. And what freedom there is must be enjoyed as equally as possible. If the law grants a wide range of liberty to some people, but strictly limits the liberty of others, then the law must be changed—unless those whose liberty is restricted have harmed or violated the rights of others, in which case their loss of liberty is a fitting penalty for their misdeeds.

So the liberal view of freedom requires that individuals have an equal opportunity to make their way in the world. On this point all liberals agree. Where they disagree, with welfare liberals going in one direction and libertarians another, is on the question of how best to provide equality of opportunity. For both sides, however, a society in which individuals enjoy an equal opportunity to make a wide range of free choices is clearly better than a society in which freedom is restricted and opportunity unequal.

Orientation   Political ideologies also provide people with some sense of orientation, of where and how they fit into the great scheme of things. Liberalism pictures people as rational individuals who have interests to pursue and choices to make. Liberals direct our attention to the characteristics they believe all people share, not toward the differences separating people from one another. Some liberals push this view much farther than others, and Bentham and the Social Darwinists perhaps farthest of all, but there is a tendency among liberals to believe that deep down all women and men are fundamentally the same. Differences of culture, race, religion, gender, or nationality are ultimately superficial differences. At bottom, almost all people are rational, self-interested individuals who want to be free to choose how to live. Once we understand this, liberals believe, we will then be better able to see how we should act toward others in order for all to live as freely as possible.

Program   With regard to the programmatic function, it is clear that liberals have tried and continue to try to do what they believe will promote individual liberty and opportunity. Historically this has meant that liberals have opposed religious conformity, ascribed status, economic privileges, political absolutism, and the tyranny of majority opinion. With these obstacles removed, individuals are free to worship (or not) as they see fit, to rise or fall in society according to their efforts and ability, to compete on an equal footing in the marketplace, to exercise some control over the government, and to think, speak, and live in unconventional ways. On these points liberals seldom disagree. When some liberals began to say that freedom is not merely a matter of being left alone, however, but a positive power or ability to do what one chooses, the disagreements began. Welfare liberals insist that the government must be enlisted in the struggle against illness, ignorance, prejudice, poverty, and any other condition that threatens liberty and equality of opportunity, whereas neoclassical liberals insist that government "meddling" is itself the chief threat to this liberty and equality.

These two groups now offer rival political programs not because their goals are different, but because they disagree on how best to achieve those goals. The dispute is over means, not ends. Hence our view that liberalism, divided as it is by the intramural dispute between its neoclassical and welfare camps, remains a single ideology.

Liberalism and the Democratic Ideal

At the end of the twentieth century liberals are firmly committed to democracy, but this has not always been the case. Throughout most of its history, in fact, liberalism has been more concerned with protecting people from their rulers than with establishing rule by the people. From its beginning, liberalism has fought to remove those obstacles that stand in the way of the individual's freedom to live as he or she sees fit, and in the beginning most of those obstacles—religious conformity, ascribed status, political absolutism, monopolies and other restraints on economic competition—were either provided or supported by government. Rather than strive to enable people to rule themselves *through* government, then, the classical liberals struggled to free people *from* government. They tried, in other words, to constrict the areas of life that were considered public matters in order to expand the realm of the private.

From the beginning, however, liberalism also displayed several democratic tendencies, the most notable being its premise of basic equality among human beings. Whether couched in terms of natural rights or the Utilitarians' claim that everybody is to count for one and nobody for more than one, liberals have always argued from the premise that every person's rights or interests should count as much as everyone else's. They have often defined *person* in very narrow terms, beginning with the view that the only true person was a free adult male who owned substantial property. But as they spoke and argued in terms of natural equality, liberals opened the door for those—including later liberals—who demanded that slavery be abolished and that women and the propertyless should be accounted equal to property-owning males.

This liberal tendency did not lead in an openly democratic direction until the 1800s, when Bentham and the Utilitarians began to argue that democracy gave every citizen the chance to protect his—and later her—interests. If the business of government is to promote the greatest good of the greatest number, they reasoned, then the only way to determine the greatest good is to allow every citizen to say what is good for him or her. Earlier liberals had proclaimed that government must rest on the consent of the people, and they had devised constitutions and bills of rights to limit the powers of government, but it was not until the 1800s that liberals began to regard the vote as a way to give everyone an equal chance at protecting and promoting his or her interests.

For the most part, liberals have continued to regard democracy as good because it enables people to hold government accountable, thus enabling them to protect their personal interests. Some, like John Stuart Mill, have gone further to argue that democracy is good because it encourages widespread political participation, which in turn enriches people's lives by developing their intellectual and moral capacities. Yet most liberals have attached no particular value to political activity, seeing it as simply one possible good among many. The state should be neutral, they say, leaving people free to pursue whatever they consider good—as long as they respect others' freedom to do the same. If people find pleasure or satisfaction in public life, well and good; but if they derive more pleasure from private pursuits, then they should be free to follow that path.

As a rule, **liberal democracy** emphasizes the importance of individual rights and liberty. Everyone is supposed to be free to participate in public life in a liberal democracy, but the greater concern is with protecting people from undue interference in their private affairs. There is much attention devoted, as a result, to determining what counts as a private matter and how far an individual's right to privacy extends. For the liberal, democracy is good so long as it serves to protect these rights and interests in privacy and free action. It does this primarily by making the government responsive to the needs and interests of the people, thus preventing government from being arbitrary and tyrannical. But if rule by the people begins to threaten individual rights and liberties, then one can expect liberals to demand that it be curbed. In liberal democracy, in short, democracy is defined mainly in terms of the individual's right to be free to do as he or she thinks best.

NOTES

1. Thomas Hobbes, *Leviathan*, chap. 11; also in Terence Ball and Richard Dagger, eds., *Ideals and Ideologies: A Reader* (New York: HarperCollins, 1991), selection 11.
2. Ibid., chap. 13; *Ideals and Ideologies*, selection 11.
3. Quoted in Herbert Muller, *Freedom in the Western World: From the Dark Ages to the Rise of Democracy* (New York: Harper & Row, 1963), p. 307. The English Bill of Rights, of course, should not be confused with the United States Bill of Rights, which comprises the first ten amendments to the U.S. Constitution.
4. John Locke, *Second Treatise of Government*, par. 4; also in Ball and Dagger, eds., *Ideals and Ideologies*, selection 12.
5. On the background and meaning of the Declaration, see Carl Becker, *The Declaration of Independence* (New York: Random House, 1942); Garry Wills, *Inventing America: Jefferson's Declaration of Independence* (Garden City, N.Y.: Doubleday, 1978); Morton White, *The Philosophy of the American Revolution* (New York: Oxford University Press, 1978); and Richard Matthews, *The Radical Politics of Thomas Jefferson* (Lawrence, Kans.: University Press of Kansas, 1984).

6. The full text of the Declaration is printed in Ball and Dagger, eds., *Ideals and Ideologies*, selection 14.
7. See James Farr, " 'So Vile and Miserable an Estate': The Problem of Slavery in Locke's Political Thought," *Political Theory*, 14 (1986): 263–289.
8. For a debate on Locke's "feminism," see Melissa Butler, "Early Liberal Roots of Feminism: John Locke and the Attack on Patriarchy," *American Political Science Review*, 72 (1978): 135–150; also Terence Ball, "Comment on Butler," ibid., 73 (1979): 549–550, followed by Butler's "Reply," ibid., 550–551.
9. Muller, *Freedom in the Western World*, p. 382.
10. As translated in Thomas Paine, *The Rights of Man* (1972); emphasis in original. For the full text of the Declaration of Rights, see Ball and Dagger, eds., *Ideals and Ideologies*, selection 15.
11. Michael Walzer, "Citizenship," in Terence Ball, James Farr, and Russell L. Hanson, eds., *Political Innovation and Conceptual Change* (Cambridge: Cambridge University Press, 1989), pp. 211–219, provides an insightful account of the notion of citizenship in the French Revolution.
12. Adam Smith, *The Wealth of Nations*, book 1, chap. 2; also in Ball and Dagger, eds., *Ideals and Ideologies*, selection 16.
13. Jeremy Bentham, *Introduction to the Principles of Morals and Legislation* (New York: Hafner, 1948), p. 1.
14. Ibid., p. 70.
15. For Bentham's views on voting, see Terence Ball, "Utilitarianism, Feminism and the Franchise," *History of Political Thought*, 1 (1980): 91–115.
16. John Stuart Mill, *On Liberty*, chap. 1; also in Ball and Dagger, eds., *Ideals and Ideologies*, selection 18.
17. William Graham Sumner, *What Social Classes Owe to Each Other* (Caldwell, Idaho: Caxton, 1970), p. 88; also in Ball and Dagger, eds., *Ideals and Ideologies*, selection 19.
18. Ibid., p. 114; see *Ideals and Ideologies*, selection 19.
19. John Rawls, *A Theory of Justice* (Cambridge, Mass.: Harvard University Press, 1971); Robert Nozick, *Anarchy, State, and Utopia* (New York: Basic Books, 1974).
20. *Anarchy, State, and Utopia*, p. 169.
21. For an elaboration of the libertarian anarchist position, see Murray Rothbard, *For a New Liberty* (New York: Macmillan, 1973); also Ball and Dagger, eds., *Ideals and Ideologies*, selection 22.

FOR FURTHER READING

Ashcraft, Richard. *Revolutionary Politics and Locke's Two Treatises of Government* (Princeton: Princeton University Press, 1986).

Berlin, Isaiah. *Four Essays on Liberty* (Oxford: Oxford University Press, 1969).

Dagger, Richard. "Rights," in Terence Ball, James Farr, and Russell L. Hanson, eds., *Political Innovation and Conceptual Change* (Cambridge: Cambridge University Press, 1989), pp. 292–308.

Dworkin, Ronald. *Taking Rights Seriously* (Cambridge, Mass.: Harvard University Press, 1977).

Elton, G. R. *Reformation Europe, 1517–1559* (New York: Harper & Row, 1963).

Friedman, Milton, and Rose Friedman. *Free to Choose* (New York: Avon Books, 1981).

Gray, John. *Liberalism* (Minneapolis: University of Minnesota Press, 1986).

Halevy, Elie. *The Growth of Philosophic Radicalism* (London: Faber & Faber, 1928).

Hall, John. *Liberalism: Politics, Technology, and the Market* (Chapel Hill, N.C.: University of North Carolina Press, 1987).

Hayek, Friedrich. *The Road to Serfdom* (Chicago: University of Chicago Press, 1976).

Manning, D. J. *Liberalism* (New York: St. Martin's Press, 1976).

Ruggiero, Guido de. *The History of European Liberalism,* trans. R. G. Collingwood (Boston: Beacon Press, 1959).

Skinner, Quentin. *The Foundations of Modern Political Thought,* 2 vols. (Cambridge: Cambridge University Press, 1978).

Chapter
4

Conservatism

Perilous is sweeping change, all chance unsound.

William Wordsworth

*I*n one sense conservatism is easy to define, in another quite difficult. It is easy because all conservatives share a desire to *conserve* or preserve something—usually the traditional or customary way of life of their societies. But these traditions or customs are likely to vary considerably from one society to another. Even where they do not, different conservatives are likely to have different ideas about what elements or parts of their established way of life are worth preserving. Conservatives may all want to conserve something, then, but they do not all want to conserve the same things. And that is what makes conservatism so difficult to define.

This difficulty is evident in two ways. First, the word "conservative" is often applied to anyone who resists change. There is nothing wrong with this, except that it means that two people who are bitterly opposed to one another's position can both be described as conservative. As many communist countries move toward free market economies, for instance, the hard-line communists who resist this change are sometimes called conservatives. Yet these so-called conservative communists are the old and bitter enemies of those who are known as conservatives in the English-speaking world. Indeed, *anti*communism has been one of the defining marks of conservatism in the West since at least the Russian Revolution of 1917, and most American-style conservatives advocate a free market economy. If a conservative is simply anyone who wants to preserve some important feature of his or her society, however, both the hard-line communist in the Soviet Union and the diehard anticommunist in the United States are conservatives, if not allies. And that is plainly absurd.

If conservatism is a distinctive political position, as we believe it to be, it must entail more than the simple desire to resist change. There must be some underlying principles or ideals that conservatives share, or some general agreement on what is worth preserving. But here we encounter the second difficulty in defining the term *conservative*. This difficulty is evident in the contrast between the early conservatives and the most prominent self-proclaimed conservatives of recent years. Early **classical** (or **traditional**) **conservatives** were in large part trying to preserve or restore an aristocratic society that was under attack from liberalism in general and the French Revolution in particular. They defended the traditional social hierarchy; they insisted on the need for a government strong enough to restrain the passions of the people; and they were often skeptical of attempts to promote individual freedom and equality of opportunity in a competitive society. By contrast, the best known conservatives of the late twentieth century—British Prime Minister Margaret Thatcher and former U.S. President Ronald Reagan—are **individualist conservatives** who advocate reducing the size and scope of government to free individuals to compete for profits.[1] With its enthusiasm for laissez faire capitalism, in fact, their brand of conservatism is remarkably similar to classical and neoclassical liberalism. What early conservatives resisted, many self-proclaimed conservatives now embrace.

Many, but not all. Conservatism nowadays is a house often divided against itself. The divisions run deep enough for one conservative to declare that "what popularly passes for 'conservative' in America is often only a petrified right-wing of atomistic *laisser-faire* liberalism."[2] Later in this chapter we will explore the different forms of conservatism. But first, we must begin with a point on which the house of conservatism was built and upon which it still stands—a shared conception of human nature.

THE POLITICS OF IMPERFECTION

In Chapter 1 we noted that every political ideology rests on a conception of human nature. In the case of conservatism, the fundamental conviction is that human beings are, and always will be, deeply flawed. This is why some scholars call conservatism the political philosophy of imperfection.[3]

What does it mean to say that human beings are imperfect? According to conservatives, it means that we are neither as intelligent nor as good as we like to think we are. We may believe ourselves capable of governing solely by the light of reason, but we are wrong. The light of reason does not shine far enough or bright enough to enable most of us to see and avoid all the problems that beset people and societies, conservatives say, and even the smartest among us can never foresee all the consequences of our actions and policies. That is why the boldest attempts to do good often do the greatest harm.

In the face of our passions and desires, moreover, human reason is weak, even impotent. When we want something that we know is not good for us, for instance, or when we want to do something that we know may harm others, we often find ways to rationalize our conduct, or to invent "reasons" for following our desires. Human beings are not only intellectually imperfect, then, but morally imperfect too. We tend to be selfish, to put our desires and interests above those of others, to reach for more power and wealth than is good either for us or for social peace and stability. Indeed, most conservatives have believed that in some sense, either theological or psychological, human beings are marked by **original sin.** They believe, that is, that the story of Adam and Eve's defiance of God in the Old Testament Book of Genesis conveys a basic truth, whether literal or symbolic, about human nature. Just as Adam and Eve in the Garden of Eden could not resist the temptation to reach for something more—something they knew they were not meant to have—so men and women continue in their pride and greed to risk the destruction of all they have in their desire for something more.

This, conservatives say, is an immutable fact of human life. To hope for some radical change in human nature—to hope that our intellectual and moral imperfections can be removed—is vain and foolish. More than that, it is dangerous. Any attempt to remake human beings by remaking their societies is likely to end in disaster. The best we can do, as they see it, is to restrain the passions and instincts that lead to conflict. This we can do through government, which imposes restraints on us, or through education—whether in schools, churches, families, or other groups—which teaches us self-restraint. As one conservative puts it,

> the function of education is conservative: not to deify the child's "glorious self-expression" but to limit his instincts and behavior by unbreakable ethical habits. In his natural instincts, every modern baby is still born a caveman baby. What prevents today's baby from remaining a cave man is the conservative force of law and tradition, that slow accumulation of civilized habits separating us from the cave.[4]

This view of human nature leads directly to the conservative warning against bold attempts to improve society. Radical proponents of other ideologies hold out visions of utopian societies; they call for revolutions to create perfect societies; or they promise at least to bring about great progress. Conservatives are skeptical of these ideological claims—so skeptical, indeed, that conservatism has been called an "anti-ideology."[5] In their view, all these grandiose attempts to transform human life and society are doomed to end not only in failure, but in catastrophe. We do much better, conservatives argue, to proceed slowly and cautiously in our attempts to improve society; and we are much wiser to cherish a peaceful and stable society than to risk its loss in the futile quest for perfection. This has been the fundamental conviction of conservatism from its beginning, 200 years ago, in the writings of Edmund Burke.

THE CONSERVATISM OF EDMUND BURKE

Because conservatism is largely a matter of temperament, of a disposition to preserve the tried and true ways of life, it is easy to find many people at any period in history who might reasonably be called conservatives. Yet there is widespread agreement that the true founder of conservatism was Edmund

Burke (1729–1797), an Irishman who moved to England and served for nearly 30 years in the House of Commons of the British Parliament. Burke never called himself a conservative—the words *conservatism* and *liberalism* did not enter the vocabulary of politics until the 1800s—but in his speeches and writings he defined a distinctively conservative political position.

Burke developed and expounded his views in the heat of political controversies, particularly in reaction to the French Revolution. When the Revolution began in 1788 and 1789, many observers in England hailed it as a great step forward for both France and the cause of liberty. But Burke saw the French Revolution, from the beginning, as a foolhardy attempt to create a new society from the ground up. Nearly three years before the Revolution's Reign of Terror, Burke issued his condemnation and warning in his *Reflections on the Revolution in France* (1790). In particular, Burke took exception to the revolutionaries' view of human nature and government, which he thought mistaken, and their conception of freedom, which he thought misguided.

Human Nature and Society

Burke's objection to the French Revolution rests largely on the claim that the revolutionaries misunderstood human nature. By concentrating on the rights, interests, and choices of the individual, he charged, the revolutionaries had come to think of society as nothing more than a loose collection of self-contained atoms who are no more connected to one another than marbles on a tray. From Burke's point of view, this **atomistic conception of society,** as later conservatives called it, is simply wrong. It loses sight of the many important ways in which individuals are connected to and depend upon one another. Political society is no mere heap of individuals, but a living and changing organism, a whole that is greater than the sum of its parts. In this **organic conception of society,** individuals are related to society in the same way that the heart, eyes, and arms are related to the body—not as separate and isolated units, but as interdependent members of a living organism. Or, to use one of Burke's favorite metaphors, society is like a fabric—the "social fabric"—and its individual members are like the interwoven threads. Far from being artificial institutions that individuals choose to create, then, society and government are outgrowths of human nature that are necessary to human life.

This is why Burke rejected the claim that civil society is brought into existence—and can just as easily be dissolved—by consenting individuals who enter a **social contract.** If civil or political society rests on a contract, he said, it is no ordinary contract between individuals, but a sacred covenant that binds whole generations together. To recognize that "society is indeed a contract," does not mean that it is

> nothing better than a partnership agreement in a trade of pepper and coffee, calico or tobacco, or some other such low concern, to be taken up for a little temporary interest, and to be dissolved by the fancy of the parties [to the contract]. . . . It is a partnership in all science; a partnership in all art; a partnership in every virtue, and in all perfection. As the ends of such a partnership cannot be obtained in many

Edmund Burke (1729–1797).

generations, it becomes a partnership not only between those who are living, but between those who are living, those who are dead, and those who are to be born.[6]

To preserve this partnership, Burke believed that both government and customs are necessary. People tend to be self-interested (a view Burke shared with the early liberals), so they need the power of government to restrain them and keep their passions in check. But government is not something that can be taken apart and reassembled whenever and however people want. It is a complex and delicate organism that must be rooted in the customs and traditions of the people, who must acquire the habit of obeying, respecting, and even revering it.

Freedom

Burke also believed that the French revolutionaries' conception of freedom was misguided. From his point of view, freedom is not necessarily good. It *can* be; but it does not *have* to be. Like fire, freedom is good if it is kept under control and put to good use. Used wisely and with restraint, freedom is valuable indeed. But the destructive power of people freed from all legal and traditional restraints is truly terrifying. In Burke's words, "The effect of liberty to individuals is, that they may do what they please; we ought to see what it will please

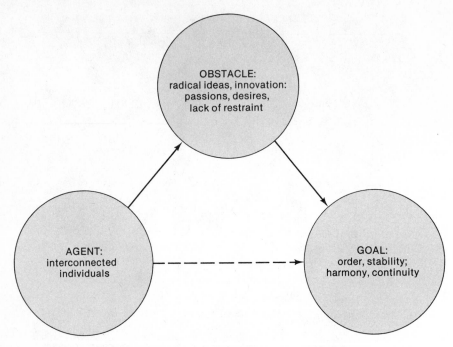

Figure 4.1 The classical conservative view of freedom.

them to do, before we risk congratulations, which may be soon turned into complaints."[7]

For Burke and classical conservatives, liberty is worthwhile only when it is properly ordered. In other words, individuals should be free from obstacles to pursue their goals, but only when their goals do not threaten the social order; if they do, then their freedom must be restricted. Unlike the early liberals, furthermore, Burke did not regard government as a major obstacle to freedom, and therefore as a necessary evil. In Burke's eyes, government makes ordered liberty possible by preventing people from doing just anything they happen to desire. Without government restraints, more people would do more things that endanger both themselves and social peace (See Figure 4.1). Burke would surely agree with the observation of a more recent conservative:

> Freedom is comprehensible as a social goal only when subordinate to something else, to an organization or arrangement which defines the individual aim. Hence the aim of freedom is at the same time to aim at the constraint which is its precondition. . . . One major difference between conservatism and liberalism consists, therefore, in the fact that, for the conservative, the value of individual liberty is not absolute, but stands subject to another and higher value, the authority of established government.[8]

Revolution and Reform

Burke was not opposed to all **revolutions.** He looked back with approval to England's Glorious Revolution of 1688, and as a member of Parliament he was sympathetic to the American colonies in their struggle with the British government. But in Burke's view these were revolutions in the old-fashioned sense. As noted in Chapter 1, "revolution" referred originally to a return or restoration—a revolving or coming full circle. According to Burke, then, the English and Americans had fought to restore their rights, to revolve back to a condition they had previously enjoyed. But the French were engaged in a revolution of a new and much more radical sort. They sought to uproot the settled order of their society and government in order to replace it with something new and untried—and therefore certain, Burke believed, to end in disaster.

Burke never claimed that French government and society were perfect, nor did he flatly oppose any and all attempts at change. On the contrary, he regarded change as a necessary feature of human life and society. But change should be brought about carefully and gradually—the kind of change that Burke called **reform**—and not through **innovation.** As he saw it, innovation is the attempt to do something new or novel on the grounds that the new must be better than the old. Innovation is therefore change for the sake of change, based on abstract reason. It abandons the old ways, the habits that have stood the test of time, in order to launch drastic and dangerous experiments.

Burke believed that the French revolutionaries were like people who lived in a house with a leaky roof and broken windows. Rather than make the necessary repairs, they decided that the house that had sheltered them all their lives must be torn down to make way for a new, glorious, rational structure. Drawing their plans with no experience of architecture or carpentry, they would soon find themselves homeless and unprotected. The revolutionaries had forsaken the tried and true way of reform for the path of innovation, and were now following it to their ruin.

So Burke preferred reform to innovation because it was safer and surer. After all, a successful reform will do some good, and an unsuccessful one will do little harm. He also claimed that reform grew out of **prejudice,** which he thought superior to reason. But prejudice for Burke is not so much a matter of prejudging people as it is a disposition to prefer the familiar habits and traditions of one's own society. In this sense, Burke claimed, prejudice is stored-up or "latent wisdom." Customs and traditions have gradually taken form over the generations, so they reflect the lessons people and societies have learned, bit by bit, in the course of their lives. The fact that traditions have lasted so long is evidence that they have withstood the test of time. They embody the wisdom not just of one or two people, but of generations. If we seldom appreciate that wisdom, it is because we take our customs for granted as they become second nature to us.

Burke on Government

With prejudice as our guide, then, we can reform government and preserve society without exposing ourselves to the dangers of innovation. But what sort of government and society did Burke have in mind? What was his idea of a sound body politic? Burke's response to questions of this sort was that there is no one best form of government. Government must reflect the history, habits, and "prejudices" of a people. A form of government that serves the needs of one country could fail completely in another. Even so, Burke's speeches and writings suggest that there were certain features of government and society that he thought especially desirable, at least in countries like Great Britain. These features include representative government, a "true natural aristocracy," private property, and the distribution of power among the "little platoons" that compose society.

Representative Government   It is scarcely surprising that Burke, a member of Parliament, should favor representative government. But we should not take this to mean that he also favored democracy. In Burke's day only a small minority of the British population, principally the large landholders, could vote or stand for election, and Burke saw no need to expand the electorate significantly. The interests of the people should be represented in government, according to Burke, but one did not have to vote to have his or her interests well represented. What matters more than the right to vote is having the right kind of person in office—a wise, prudent, and well-informed person to whom we can entrust our interests. In his "Speech to the Electors of Bristol" in 1774, Burke stated his case in this way:

> Certainly, Gentlemen, it ought to be the happiness and glory of a representative to live in the strictest union, the closest correspondence, and the most unreserved communication with his constituents. Their wishes ought to have great weight with him; their opinions high respect; their business unremitted attention. It is his duty to sacrifice his repose, his pleasure, his satisfactions, to theirs—and above all . . . to prefer their interest to his own.
>
> But his unbiased opinion, his mature judgment, his enlightened conscience, he ought not to sacrifice to you, to any man, or to any set of men living. . . . Your representative owes you not his industry only, but his judgment; and he betrays, instead of serving you, if he sacrifices it to your opinion.[9]

Like many conservatives, Burke thought that democracy would seriously threaten the health of representative government. As the masses of people gain the franchise, they will vote for candidates who pander to their passions and desires. They will thus elect representatives who will respond to their momentary whims instead of promoting the society's long-term interests. So it is best, Burke thought, not to broaden the franchise—at least not until the people as a whole have given some sign that they are ready and willing to cast their votes responsibly.

The Natural Aristocracy   But even under a restricted franchise, where are these unbiased, mature, and enlightened trustees to be found? Burke's answer is to look to what he called a *true natural aristocracy*. These are the people, the rare few, who have the ability, the experience, and the inclination to govern wisely in the interest of the whole society. These are the people who are natural leaders; who learn from an early age that others look to them for direction. These are the people who have the leisure as children to study, to gain knowledge of politics and society, and to develop their abilities. These are the people, Burke thought, who are most likely to come from the hereditary aristocracy.

Burke did not say that the true natural aristocracy and the hereditary aristocracy are one and the same. But he did believe that a person could not achieve a place in the natural aristocracy without both the ability *and* the necessary opportunity. In Burke's day the people who were most likely to have the opportunity were those who came from the hereditary aristocracy. Society was accustomed to looking to the nobility for leadership, and the nobles were accustomed to providing it. Perhaps even more important was the opportunity the hereditary aristocracy enjoyed as the largest landholders in a society where wealth came primarily from the land. Because they had wealth, the sons of the aristocracy enjoyed leisure; because they enjoyed leisure, they had time for education; because they were educated, they could gain the knowledge and develop the abilities necessary to play a leading part in politics. For all these reasons, Burke thought that they were bound to form the core of the true natural aristocracy. There was room for others, to be sure, but a society deprived of its hereditary aristocracy was deprived of many of its best and brightest members. Those who attacked aristocratic privilege in the name of freedom— the French revolutionaries, for instance—were guilty of the worst kind of folly, for the destruction of the hereditary aristocracy will surely set off a mad scramble for power among men whose only claim to leadership is their ability to rouse the rabble.

Private Property   Burke's own respect for **aristocratic privilege** was due in part to the connection he saw between aristocracy and property. In general, he took private property to be a stabilizing and conservative force in society. People who own property, especially property in land, will identify their interests, and even themselves, with their property, thus strengthening their attachment to the society and government that surround and protect their property. This is especially likely to happen, according to Burke, when property is passed down, generation after generation, within a family, so that attachment to land, family, and country become practically indistinguishable from one another. And this is most likely to happen among the hereditary aristocracy.[10]

The Little Platoons   Burke's notion of a good government, then, is one that will enlist enlightened representatives, drawn from the natural aristocracy, in the defense of private property and the common good. To do this job properly, the government must be strong. Yet its strength should not be concentrated in one person or in one place, lest this tempt those in power to abuse it. This is why Burke stressed the importance of the little platoons that make up a society. Without setting out a specific scheme for its distribution, Burke argued that power should be spread throughout society. Local concerns should be dealt with at the local level, not the national; and instead of placing all power in the government itself, the traditional authority of churches, families, and other groups should be respected. In this way government will be strong enough to protect society, but not strong enough to smother the little platoons that make ordered liberty possible.

Burke's Legacy

In all four of the preceding respects, many conservatives continue to share Burke's views. Although many have come to accept democracy, they still prefer a representative government that is not directly responsive to the will of the people. Few conservatives defend hereditary aristocracy nowadays, but most still believe that some form of natural aristocracy is necessary if society is to be stable, strong, and healthy. All contemporary conservatives, moreover, share both Burke's faith in the value of private property and his desire to defeat the concentration of power by maintaining the strength of society's little platoons. Despite the differences that divide them, twentieth century conservatives owe enough to Burke to make it clear why he is so often called the father of conservatism.

CONSERVATISM IN THE NINETEENTH CENTURY

Edmund Burke died in 1797, two years before Napoleon Bonaparte seized power and halted the Revolution Burke so feared and despised. Yet in some respects the Revolution continued until Napoleon's final defeat in 1815 at the battle of Waterloo. For Napoleon's regime preserved many of the changes the Revolutionaries had fought for—including the abolition of feudalism with its privileges for the aristocracy. Many aristocrats resisted these changes throughout both the Revolution and the Napoleonic era. Some even saw the Revolution as the enemy of all that was good and worthwhile in life. Their reaction against it was so fierce and uncompromising that they became known as the Reactionaries.

Conservatism and Reaction

When scholars and journalists say that someone is a **reactionary,** they mean that he or she wants to return to an earlier form of society. Unlike Burkean or classical conservatives, whose concern is to preserve the traditional features of existing society through cautious reform, reactionaries want to turn back the clock. Society as it is, they charge, is a perversion of society as it used to be. Their task, then, is to overthrow the current social and political arrangements in order to return to the ways of the past. This is precisely what the European Reactionaries proposed to do.

Perhaps the most important of the Reactionaries was Count Joseph de Maistre (1753–1821). De Maistre was born in Savoy, now a part of France but then a French-speaking province of the Kingdom of Piedmont-Sardinia. De Maistre soon reacted vehemently against the Revolutionaries' attacks on monarchy, aristocracy, and religion. As he saw it, the Revolution was primarily an assault on "throne and altar," king and church. But without these two institutions to provide the subjects with a sense of majesty and unity, no society could long survive. Once throne and altar were gone and people were left with nothing to rely on but their own wits and reason, chaos and catastrophe were sure to result. That, de Maistre said, is precisely what happened during the Revolution. How could people be surprised at the bloodshed of the Reign of Terror when the Revolutionaries had uprooted the old society, the work of God, to replace it with the work of man? Indeed, de Maistre went so far as to reject the notion that a people is capable of drafting and establishing a suitable constitution for its society. A written constitution is downright dangerous, he declared, because it exposes the weakness of government.

> The more that is written, the weaker is the institution, the reason being clear. Laws are only declarations of rights, and rights are not declared except when they are attacked, so that the multiplicity of written constitutional laws shows only the multiplicity of conflicts and the danger of destruction.[11]

De Maistre's quarrel with the French Revolution was part of his larger struggle against the spirit of the eighteenth century. The French *philosophes* had proclaimed this the time of **Enlightenment,** the period when human reason was beginning at last to rout the forces of superstition, prejudice, and ignorance. But de Maistre saw the Enlightenment as an age of arrogance that led to the downfall of the most sacred and necessary social institutions, namely, throne and altar. So not only the Revolution, but the eighteenth century mentality must be defeated in order to return society and government to their proper conditions.

De Maistre lived long enough to see the Reaction, as it was called, take effect in the years after Napoleon's defeat. The chief architect of this attempt to restore the old aristocratic order was a German noble, Clemens von Metternich (1773–1859). As Foreign Minister of the Hapsburg (or Austrian) Empire, Metternich presided over the Congress of Vienna in 1815. This Congress brought together representatives of the forces at war with Napoleonic France—chiefly Britain, Russia, and Austria—to find some basis for preserving peace and stability in Europe. With Metternich's guidance, the Congress settled on hereditary monarchy as the only legitimate form of rule and aimed to restore to the throne the European kings who had been ousted from power after 1789. For more than 30 years Metternich's reactionary work held up. In 1848, however, a series of liberal uprisings swept through Europe, and Metternich himself was forced from office, a victim of the forces he had sought to turn back.

Throughout this period and well into the second half of the 1800s the leadership of the Catholic church also played a conservative, and often reactionary, role in Europe. Given the church's privileged position in the old aristocratic order—as the First Estate in France's Estates-General, for instance—this is hardly surprising. When early liberals attacked the church as an enemy of reason and freedom, the church counterattacked at every opportunity. Thus in 1864 Pope Pius IX issued his *Syllabus of Errors*, in which he sharply criticized liberalism for undermining religion and the traditional order. Among the errors of liberalism, Pius IX included the following beliefs:

> 3. Human reason, without any regard to God, is the sole arbiter of truth and falsehood, of good and evil; it is a law to itself, and by its natural force it suffices to secure the welfare of men and nations.

. . .

77. In the present day, it is no longer expedient that the Catholic religion shall be held as the only religion of the State, to the exclusion of all other modes of worship.[12]

But reaction was not the only form that conservatism took in the nineteenth century. There were more moderate forms, too, particularly those that emerged in Great Britain: **cultural conservatism** and **Tory democracy.**

Cultural Conservatism

When the French Revolution began, many people in England greeted it as the dawn of a glorious new age. As William Wordsworth (1770–1850) put it in his poem, "French Revolution as It Appeared to Enthusiasts at Its Commencement,"

> Bliss was it in that dawn to be alive,
> But to be young was very heaven.

But Burke's *Reflections on the Revolution in France* soon helped to quell this early enthusiasm for the Revolution. Then came war between England and France, beginning in 1793 and continuing almost without interruption until 1815. Compared to the countries of the European continent, England survived the Revolutionary era with relatively little social upheaval, leaving English conservatives little reason to become reactionary.

English conservatives did oppose the Revolution and the changes it wrought, to be sure. Even Wordsworth turned against it, arguing that the Revolutionaries placed too much faith in reason and too little in people's emotional or spiritual tie to nature. But for Wordsworth, his friend and fellow poet Samuel Taylor Coleridge (1772–1834), and other English conservatives of the early 1800s, the greatest threat to English society came not from the French Revolution, but from the Industrial Revolution that was reshaping English society. In particular, English conservatism after Burke defended the traditional agricultural society against the ravages of industry and commerce. Commerce and capitalism were the enemies of the spirit and culture, they argued. The new creed of production in pursuit of profit simply fostered crass materialism. All the old virtues, all loyalties, all ties to persons and places were vanishing in the pursuit of money—a pursuit that would end with men and women out of touch with themselves, with one another, and with Nature. As Wordsworth complained in 1806,

> The world is too much with us; late and soon,
> Getting and spending, we lay waste our powers:
> Little we see in Nature that is ours;
> We have given our hearts away, a sordid boon!

With its suspicion of commerce and its hatred of materialism, cultural conservatism has proved to be an enduring theme, not only in England, but in the United States and elsewhere. In England more than other countries, however, cultural conservatism found an ally in a political party that made conservatism an effective political force.

Tory Democracy

Throughout the eighteenth century the Tory and Whig parties had vied for power. This division continued into the 1800s, with the Tories generally defending the interests of the land-owning aristocracy and the Whigs urging a more commercial and competitive society. The differences between the two gradually focused on their attitudes toward the expansion of the electorate. Tories typically opposed any expansion of voting rights beyond the small minority who already enjoyed them. But the Whigs campaigned to win the vote for middle-class males—merchants, industrialists, and professional men for the most part—until they succeeded in 1832 in passing the Great Reform Bill. With the influx of new voters eager to support their cause, the Whigs looked forward to a long period of political dominance.

The Tories, on the other hand, could look forward only to losing elections unless they could find some way to attract new voters to their cause. The man who found the way was Benjamin Disraeli (1804–1881). Disraeli's solution was to form an alliance between the aristocratic upper class and the working class. This would enable his party, which he began to call the Conservative party, to compete against the Liberals, as the Whigs had come to be called. To accomplish this, Disraeli pursued the policies of *Tory democracy*.

Tory democracy attempted to address the needs of the working class while instilling in the workers a respect for the traditional order of English life—including a respect for the monarchy, the aristocracy, and the established Church of England. In Disraeli's words,

> Instead of falling under . . . the thraldom of capital—under those who, while they boast of their intelligence, are more proud of their wealth—if we must find a new force to maintain the ancient throne and monarchy of England, I, for one, hope that we may find that novel power in the invigorating energies of an educated and enfranchised people.[13]

So Disraeli set out both to include the workers in the electorate and to improve their condition in life. His support of the Reform Bill of 1867 helped to bring the vote to the working-class males of the cities, and in his second stint as prime minister (1874–1880) he made trade unions legal and recognized the workers' right to strike against their employers. With these and other measures, Disraeli extended the cultural conservatives' dislike of the commercial middle class into a political alliance between the conservative aristocracy and the potentially revolutionary working class. Hence the term, Tory democracy. This was to be the dominant form of British conservatism, under the leadership of Winston Churchill (1874–1965) and others, until the shift to individualist conservatism when Margaret Thatcher became Prime Minister in 1979.

But Tory democracy remained a distinctly British form of conservatism. The Prussian Prime Minister Otto von Bismarck (1815–1898) did accomplish something similar in Germany with his provision of state-supported insurance and benefits for workers. But Bismarck was no democrat. Nor was he much of a conservative, since he was more interested in consolidating the various provinces of Germany into a united and powerful nation-state than he was in preserving the traditional way of life. Elsewhere, especially in the United States, what came to be called conservatism was a far cry from Tory democracy.

Conservatism in the United States

Conservatism in the United States followed a different course in the nineteenth century. When the Constitution was drafted in 1787, the free population of the United States comprised about three million people, almost all Protestants. Lacking a history of feudalism and hereditary aristocracy, having no monarch, no aristocracy, and no established national church, conservatives in the United States were hardly likely to follow the path either of Burke, or of de Maistre's reactionary appeal to throne and altar, or of Tory democracy. In a country founded on the principles of liberalism—or perhaps more accurately, as we noted in Chapter 3, on a mixture of liberal and republican principles—conservatives were much more likely to be engaged in the preservation of liberalism.

Two members of the founding generation, John Adams (1735–1826) and Alexander Hamilton (1757–1804), are sometimes taken to be conservatives in the Burkean mold. There are similarities between them and Burke, certainly, but the differences are telling. Like Burke, Adams often spoke favorably of the "natural aristocracy"; but Adams could not look to the nobility, as Burke did, to provide the core of this group of natural leaders, for there was no hereditary nobility in the United States. The closest Adams could come was men of property, and this was a much broader group in the United States than in Burke's England. As for Hamilton, his claim to the credentials of a classical conservative rests largely on his defense of constitutional monarchy at the time of the founding. But the plan he drafted as Secretary of the Treasury—a plan to make the United States a great commercial power—hardly displayed a classical conservative's suspicion of commerce and reverence for the settled forms of social life.

In the early and middle 1800s, several American authors held views that could be linked to cultural conservatism. Perhaps the most important of these, at least in retrospect, were two friends who stand as giants of American literature, Nathaniel Hawthorne (1804–1864) and Herman Melville (1819–1891). In various stories and novels, both authors criticized what they saw as the foolishly optimistic temper of their times. Hawthorne depicted the vanity and futility of the quest for perfection in his story "Earth's Holocaust," for instance, then portrayed the tragic consequences of such a quest in stories like "The Birthmark." For his part, Melville heaped scorn on those who preached the doctrine of faith in human nature in his bitterly ironic novel, *The Confidence Man;* and his "Bartleby the Scrivener: A Story of Wall Street" can be read as an attack on the dehumanizing consequences of capitalism.

As in England, cultural conservatism has remained an important thread in the fabric of American conservatism. More characteristic, however, was the shift in the direction of laissez faire capitalism that took place in the late nineteenth century. This was the period when the title of conservative began to fall upon the businessmen and industrialists who had previously been seen as the enemies of tradition. What people in other countries called liberalism, in other words, the people of the United States began to think of as conservatism. How did this happen? Two principal factors seem to have been at work.

First, businessmen and industrialists stressed the importance of private property—a point on which conservatives and liberals agree—and individualism. Both these ideals had long been important in the United States, so the captains of industry could in a sense appeal to traditional values of their country when they defended laissez faire capitalism. The United States had been founded on the belief in the individual's natural rights to life, liberty, and the pursuit of happiness, after all. Once the business leaders interpreted these words to mean that every individual should be free to pursue profits in the competitive marketplace, they could then be regarded as conservatives.

The second factor was the development of welfare liberalism in the late nineteenth century. The rise of this new form of liberalism, with its call for government action to promote individual liberty and equality of opportunity, meant that those who clung to the views of early or classical liberalism were now in danger of being left behind. As explained in Chapter 3, this produced a split between welfare and neoclassical liberalism. Because the neoclassical liberals remained true to the faith of the early liberals—the faith in what men and women can do when they are freed from the restraints of that "necessary evil," government, they came to seem old fashioned and therefore conservative.

For both these reasons, classical liberalism came to be called conservatism in the United States. Even the Social Darwinists, whom we described in Chapter 3 as neoclassical liberals, were included. Herbert Spencer and William Graham Sumner advanced a vision of society that was thoroughly atomistic, with every person locked in a struggle for survival with every other. No classical or cultural conservative could accept such an unorganic vision. But in the United States the Social Darwinists' defense of private property and competitive individualism, coupled with their attack on government regulations, placed them squarely, but uncomfortably, in the conservative camp.

For the last century, conservatism in the United States has suffered from the continuing tension between traditional conservatives, on the one hand, and individualist conservatives—those who see conservatism as primarily the defense of laissez faire capitalism—on the other. There are points on which the two sides agree, such as the value of private property and the folly of abstract social planning—especially in the form of socialism or communism. But there are so many points on which they disagree that the two sides seem to be enemies as often as allies. Certainly it is difficult to see how anyone with a Burkean distrust of innovation can join comfortably with someone who, in the name of competition and progress, is constantly seeking new products to sell to more people in hopes of a better, and more profitable, life.

CONSERVATISM IN THE TWENTIETH CENTURY

In recent years the tension between traditional and individualist conservatism has spread beyond the United States, leading most notably to a division in the ranks of conservatives in Great Britain. In the early years of this century, however, conservatives in Europe and traditional conservatives in the United States were united in their attacks on what they called **mass society.**

Conservatism Versus Mass Society

According to conservative commentators, and to other social analysts as well, the nineteenth century had seen the rise of democracy. This was true in terms of voting rights, of course, for the franchise had been greatly extended throughout the Western world during the century. But it was true in terms of social relations, too. The power of the old aristocracy had been broken in the course of the century, and the spread of public education meant that many of the barriers to social mobility and advancement were falling. At the beginning of the twentieth century, moreover, the rapid development of mass production in industry made it seem as if economic barriers, too, were collapsing. Items that once would have been available only to the wealthy few—the automobile, for instance—were now being built for and sold to the masses.

Some social analysts welcomed these developments enthusiastically. Not so the conservatives. From their point of view, this new mass society posed the same threat democracy had always posed—the threat that the masses would throw society first into chaos, then into despotism. In arguments similar to those of Plato, Aristotle, and more recently Alexis de Tocqueville, traditional conservatives maintained that the common people were too weak and too ignorant to take charge of government. Too weak to curb their appetites or restrain their desires, the people will want more and more—more wealth, more property, more power—like gluttons who ruin their health because they cannot stop eating. And they are too ignorant, too short sighted, to see the disaster they are bringing upon their society and themselves. Once their unchecked demands have taken society to the brink of anarchy, the masses will then cry out for a ruler, a strong and decisive leader who will restore law and order—even at the expense of liberty.

This conservative argument against mass society gained credence in the 1920s and 1930s as fascism and nazism came to power in Italy, Spain, and Germany. To the conservative eye, these brutal movements were the logical result of the democratic excesses of mass society. All the hard-won accomplishments of European civilization, particularly representative government in parliaments, were in danger of being ground under the bootheels of the fascist "blackshirts" and the nazi "stormtroopers" and their dictatorial leaders. Even defenders of liberal democracy like the Spanish philosopher José Ortega y Gasset (1883–1955) adopted a conservative stance in the face of fascism. In *The Revolt of the Masses*, Ortega asserted:

> Nothing indicates more clearly the characteristics of the day than the fact that there are so few countries where an opposition exists. In almost all, a homogeneous mass weighs on public authority and crushes down, annihilates every opposing group. The mass . . . does not wish to share life with those who are not of it. It has a deadly hatred of all that is not itself.[14]

In response to this threat, conservative critics of mass society maintained that the masses needed to learn, or be taught, self-restraint. This means that the masses must learn either to curb their appetites and respect the traditional ways or, more likely, to recognize that it is better to entrust their government to the aristocracy or elite—to those with superior wisdom, experience, and foresight. This argument is, of course, similar to that made by Burke on behalf of his true natural aristocracy. The difference is that, by the twentieth century, relatively few conservatives looked to the hereditary aristocracy to form the core of this natural governing elite. Still, conservatives believed—and classical conservatives continue to believe—that in every society there will be some small number of men and women who are suited by ability, experience, and temperament to govern, while the great majority are utterly unsuited in one or more of these respects. If we must live in mass society, conservatives say, we should at least be prudent enough to put a substantial share of power in the hands of those who rise above the mass.

Levelling

This fear of mass society is why so many conservatives, from Burke to the present, have opposed efforts to diminish or eliminate the gap between the rich and poor, or what they call **levelling.** Conservatives have typically been suspicious of attempts to achieve greater democracy or equality because they believe these will equalize or "level" society. As conservatives point out, attempts to make the people at the bottom of society better-off usually involve taking something away from those at the top—as in so-called soak-the-rich tax policies. The problem with such schemes, according to the conservative argument, is that they raise the people at the bottom very little, lower the people at the top a great deal, and in the long run reduce everyone in society to the same low level. In the name of equality, conservatives claim, levelling programs simply promote economic and social stagnation.

Levelling is culturally pernicious, too, according to conservatives. In this age of equality everyone is taught that his or her opinions or beliefs are just as good as anyone else's. Thus we find ourselves in an age of fads and fancies, with fashions changing constantly and the only standards of worth being novelty and popularity. Serious literature, music, and art are overwhelmed by the levelling tendencies of mass society. The quantity of sales counts for more than the quality of the work in this age of "best-selling" books and "blockbuster" movies, all produced according to formulae that appeal to a mass audience. Even in colleges and universities, students forsake philosophy, literature, and history to study advertising and marketing—two "disciplines" that are concerned not with truth, but with increasing the sales of dubious products.

Conservatives have often seen levelling as a threat to society in another way as well. In addition to its harmful effects in economic and cultural matters, they see it as the enemy of social variety and diversity. Drawing on arguments similar to Burke's praise of society's little platoons, conservatives frequently defend the neighborhood, the town, or the region as centers of local variety—

centers that are always in danger of being flattened by the levelling forces of mass society. Within a society, conservatives say, it is healthy to have diverse communities. Diversity, in fact, is a sign of health, for it shows that people at the local level are able to muster the resources they need to meet the challenges of life—challenges that will vary considerably from one community to another. We should especially hope to preserve communities where people are disposed to follow the customs and habits of their ancestors. Such a disposition, or prejudice in the Burkean sense, inclines people not only to follow the time-tested ways, but to remain loyal to a community that they see themselves sharing with their ancestors, their children, and generations yet to come.

This is the kind of argument offered, for instance, in *I'll Take My Stand*, a collection of essays published in 1930 by a group of writers known as the Southern Agrarians.[15] In these essays the Agrarians defended the traditional agricultural society of the southern United States against the invasion of industrialism from the northern states. An agricultural society will necessarily be traditional, they argued, for it will necessarily be concerned with property and family. Literally and figuratively, an agricultural society is concerned with roots. Industrial society, however, is rootless, and all traditional loyalties and affections give way in face of the demands for production and consumption that characterize mass society.

From early in the twentieth century, then, conservatives have issued warnings against the excesses of mass society. Mass society threatens to degenerate into anarchy and despotism, at worst, and to level society into a rootless crowd that relentlessly seeks new commodities to consume, at best. It gives us mindless consumerism, it gives us fascism and nazism, and it also gives us communism.

Conservatives and Communism

One of the pervasive themes of conservatism in the twentieth century is its fear and hatred of **communism.** This theme, indeed, is one of the few on which all conservatives agree. There are some, like historian and journalist Garry Wills, who think that conservatives have been so obsessively anticommunist that they have made the mistake of seeing everything in the world as part of a fight-to-the-death between communism and Western civilization.[16] But even those who share Wills's concern believe that communism and conservatism are incompatible, and most conservatives will go further and say that the two ideologies are implacable enemies. From the Russian Revolution of 1917 to the present, conservatives have been among the most outspoken opponents of communism.

Why are conservatives so united, and generally so vehement, in their opposition to communism? At bottom, the answer lies in their contrasting views of human nature and freedom. For conservatives, as we have seen, human beings are fundamentally imperfect creatures who are as likely to abuse freedom by turning to savagery as they are to use it peacefully to grow and develop. But communists, as we observe in Chapters 5 and 6, usually take a more optimistic view. Communists typically argue that the source of social problems is not human nature, but social conditions—especially the division of society into social and economic classes based on the ownership and control of property. Once people are freed from these crippling conditions, communists say, they will grow and flourish. This view, of course, is directly opposed to that held by conservatives.

Out of this general opposition emerge three more particular issues on which conservatives are fundamentally at odds with communism: progress, perfectibility, and planning. In all three cases conservatives reject the communist position. First, conservatives deny that great progress can be brought about through efforts to change society. Following Burke, most conservatives continue to argue that faith in progress is unreasonable. Social change is not necessarily change for the better, they say. Every change carries with it a certain risk, and the kind of revolutionary changes communists call for are far too risky—and unrealistic—to be taken.

Second, the communists' faith in progress rests on their unjustified faith in the perfectibility of human nature and society. This, according to conservatives, runs counter to all human experience. Indeed, some conservatives suggest that belief in perfectibility is a heresy—a view that contradicts certain religious truths. When communists claim that men and women must free themselves from oppressive social conditions in order to live rich and full lives, they deny original sin and human imperfection. The fact that many communists have been atheists, including Karl Marx, has only fueled the hostility of religiously minded conservatives. And those conservatives who are not themselves religious attack the communist belief in perfectibility as a dangerous illusion, if not a heresy.

Third, most conservatives dislike the communists' emphasis on planning. Like neoclassical liberals, some conservatives believe that social planning is always inefficient; instead of planning, they say, we should leave matters to competition on the open market. Burkean or classical conservatives believe that some planning is necessary and desirable, but only planning on a small scale for gradual, piecemeal social change. Communists, however, have often called for social planning of the broadest, most comprehensive kind. They want to survey all aspects of society, according to their conservative critics, to try to anticipate all social needs, to estimate the resources available to meet those needs, and to take action to solve all social problems. Planning on such a grand scale places entirely too much faith in human reason, conservatives say. It encourages grandiose social schemes that are almost certain to collapse in failure, thereby sinking people deeper in the misery from which the communists planned to rescue them.

Moreover, planning of this sort requires that power be concentrated in the hands of a few at the center of society. There is no room for diversity or variety—no room for freedom—at the local level. The "little platoons" of society are incorporated into the homogeneous mass as everyone in society is "levelled" to a similar condition—everyone, that is, but the few who hold power. The price of grand social planning, in short, is neither progress nor perfection, but misery, brutality, and despotism. Instead of freeing people from oppressive social conditions, conservatives charge, communist planning sacrifices freedom to the oppression of communist planners.

In view of the differences between them, it is hardly surprising that conservatives have been so bitterly opposed to communism. This opposition was particularly strong in the years following the end of World War II in 1945. As communist regimes came to power in Eastern Europe, Asia, and elsewhere, communism became the chief cause of conservative concern. As the principal representative of international communism, the Soviet Union appeared to many conservatives to be an "evil empire," as President Ronald Reagan called it in the early 1980s. With the introduction of Soviet Premier Mikhail Gorbachev's policies of *glasnost* (openness) and *perestroika* (restructuring) in the 1980s, followed by the apparent collapse of communism in Eastern Europe and its possible demise in the Soviet Union itself, matters have become more complicated. Some conservatives are delighted by these changes; some suspect that the changes are designed to lull the West into complacency; others do not know how to react. The question is whether communist regimes are really backing away from communism or merely changing their tactics. Conservatives are divided in their answers to this question. But they remain very much united in their opposition to communist ideology. In many other respects, however, conservatives are now often at odds with one another.

CONSERVATISM TODAY: A HOUSE DIVIDED

In the last decade of the twentieth century conservatism seems to have given way to a variety of conservat*isms*. There are points on which conservatives continue to agree, of course, such as a general respect for private property and an opposition to communism. But there are so many differences of opinion and emphasis that we can now identify four distinct strands of thought in what now passes for conservatism. Two of these, *traditional* (or *classical*) and *individualist conservatism*, are familiar from our discussion of the split in conservatism in the United States in the 1800s. The remaining two, *neoconservatism* and the *New Christian Right*, have emerged into prominence in the last quarter-century or so. Each of these four deserves a closer look, with special attention to the two most recent forms of conservatism.

Traditional Conservatism

The heirs of Edmund Burke, those who cling closely to the positions of the classical and cultural conservatives, are now often called traditional conservatives. Like Burke, they think of society as a delicate fabric in which individual lives are woven together. In this view, a society of self-seeking individuals, each of whom is essentially independent of the others and therefore free to pursue his or her own self-interest, is deranged and disordered; it is a threadbare fabric that hardly deserves to be called a society. Society should promote freedom, to be sure, but traditional conservatives share Burke's conviction that this must be ordered liberty. Society does not consist of isolated or atomistic individuals, but of people involved in interdependent and mutual relationships. Each person has a particular station or status and a stake in the larger society into which he or she is born, lives, and dies. The purpose of political activity, then, is to preserve the social fabric within which these vital human activities are carried on from generation to generation. Because this fabric is easily torn, it requires our constant care and respect. Hence politics, as the British conservative philosopher Michael Oakeshott puts it, is nothing more than attending to the arrangements of one's society.[17]

Like Burke, again, the traditional conservatives see private property as essential to social stability. But they do not equate private property with capitalism, which they continue to regard with some suspicion. According to conservative columnist George Will, capitalism is a "solvent" that can dissolve the web of traditional relationships.[18] Government must therefore take care to see that the economic competition of capitalism is kept within bounds—a point on which traditional conservatives sharply disagree with the individualists.

Individualist Conservatism

In the nineteenth century, as we noted earlier, businessmen, industrialists, and others who held to the views of the early liberals came to be called conservatives in the United States. This trend has continued into the present century, and in recent years, especially, it has spread beyond the United States. For these individualist or free-market conservatives, society is not a delicate fabric, but a rough-and-tumble competitive marketplace. Rather than talk about how individuals are inevitably situated in a web of interdependency and connected across generations with their ancestors and their unborn successors, as traditional conservatives do, individualist conservatives prefer to talk about "rugged individualists" pulling themselves up by their bootstraps. For the individualist, furthermore, freedom is not ordered liberty, but the freedom of individuals to compete with one another, particularly in the economic arena of the free market.

Individualist conservatism is the conservatism identified with former Senator Barry Goldwater and former President Ronald Reagan in the United States and of Prime Minister Margaret Thatcher of Great Britain. Contrary to the traditional conservatives, who stress the intricacy of society and the complexity of its problems, individualist conservatives are inclined to claim that social problems and solutions are simple. Most problems stem from "too much government," as they see it, by which they usually mean too much government interference in the operations of the free market. The solution then is correspondingly simple: "get government off our backs!" Reduce government spending, particularly for social welfare, and give the free market a free rein, in economic if not in moral matters. Some traditional conservatives have criticized these individualist schemes to cut spending for health services, education, and social welfare, complaining that these amount to cuts or tears in the social fabric of civility and stability. But Prime Minister Thatcher has been scornful, in turn, of these "wet hanky" conservatives, or "wets" for short. Let the free market do its work, she and the other individualist conservatives say, and everyone will eventually benefit. So the tension between traditionalists and individualists continues within conservatism.

Neoconservatism

To complicate matters further, other forms of conservatism have emerged in the last generation. One of these, **neoconservatism,** occupies a position some-where between the traditional and individualist conservatives. Neoconserva-tism has taken its bearings from a group of prominent academics and public figures, including sociologists Daniel Bell, Nathan Glazer, and Senator Daniel Patrick Moynihan, and political scientist and former U.N. Ambassador Jeane Kirkpatrick.

Neoconservatives are often described as disenchanted welfare liberals. Once enthusiastic supporters of President Lyndon Johnson's Great Society pro-grams in the 1960s, these neoconservatives became disillusioned with these programs and with the general direction of welfare liberalism. Government is trying to do too much, they concluded, and it is making things worse, not better. The time has come for government to do less for people so that they may be encouraged to do more for themselves.

Like the traditional conservatives, neoconservatives regard capitalism with a mixture of admiration and suspicion. They acknowledge its merits as an eco-nomic system capable of generating great wealth, but they also are aware of the social disruption and dislocations brought about by a free-wheeling market economy—labor unrest, unemployment, and an apparently permanent "un-derclass" of the uneducated and unemployed, for instance. As one neoconser-vative, Irving Kristol, once said, capitalism deserves two cheers, but not three.[19]

According to Daniel Bell, capitalism harbors a number of "cultural contra-dictions" through which it undermines its own moral and intellectual founda-tions.[20] On the one hand, capitalism rests on people's willingness to defer plea-sures and gratifications—to save and invest in the present in order to receive a greater return in the future. On the other hand, capitalism creates such abun-dance that people tend to think that there are no limits, that anything is possi-ble, and that one can have it all, here and now. So capitalism is, in a sense, at odds with itself.

Nor is this attitude confined to economic matters. It spills over into other areas as well, the neoconservatives say. It is especially dangerous insofar as it shapes attitudes about government. As the neoconservatives complain, too many people now expect too much, too quickly from all their institutions, in-cluding their government. Many want lower taxes and, at the same time, in-creased government spending for their pet projects. They want to buy now and pay later, to live on their lines of credit in politics as they do in their personal finances. These attitudes on which contemporary capitalism relies have poten-tially disastrous social and political consequences. This is particularly true in modern democracies, where every interest group clamors for an ever-larger share of the public pie. The consequences, neoconservatives say, are too obvious to miss—runaway debt, budget deficits too large to comprehend, and, worst of all, a citizenry incapable of checking its appetites and demands. And as these problems mount, demands on government increase; thus government loses its capacity to govern.

In domestic matters, then, neoconservatives tend to be skeptical liberals. They support government-sponsored welfare programs, for instance, but they insist that these programs should help people become independent, not make them evermore dependent upon the government. In foreign affairs, they have taken a hard-line anticommunist stance, generally calling for economic and military assistance for anticommunist regimes and rebel movements around the world. They also take a strong interest in the political implications of artistic, literary, educational, and other broadly cultural issues.

Like all cultural conservatives, neoconservatives believe that a people defines who they are, or aspire to be, through their culture. In too many aspects of our culture—in our music, our literature, our theater, our art, our schools— we are defining ourselves, they argue, as ill-mannered, amoral drifters and degenerates who are undermining or discarding what remains of a once great and vibrant Western culture. Indeed, neoconservatives sometimes suggest that an "adversary culture" of left-leaning intellectuals, feminists, and assorted malcontents poses a greater threat to our values and way of life than do any real or imagined threats to the free market. So the political struggle "true" conservatives wage must be, in their view, a cultural and intellectual struggle against this adversary culture. So-called highbrow culture and university education may initially influence the outlooks and attitudes of only a relatively small segment of society, but these attitudes and values eventually trickle down to the masses—just as the long hair and drug-dabbling of college radicals in the 1960s gradually spread throughout American society.

Neoconservatives, like other cultural conservatives, see politics and culture as two sides of the same coin. Anyone who wants to preserve existing social and political arrangements will have to attend to cultural changes—and perhaps even try to stem the cultural tide. On this point, if few others, neoconservatives agree with the so-called New Christian Right.

The New Christian Right

In the years after World War II, a number of evangelical Protestant ministers led campaigns against the dangers of what they called "Godless, atheistic communism." These campaigns grew into a larger movement in the 1970s, the movement known as the **New Christian Right,** because of a reaction against the changes many saw, and deplored, in the United States during the 1960s. High crime rates, urban decay and riots, growing welfare rolls, the decline of patriotism, widespread drug use, and legalized abortion—all these were signs that the United States had lost its way. The time was ripe for a movement that would restore the country to its traditional ways. The time had come, according to the New Right, for a return to morality in government and society.

Leaders of the New Christian Right tend to equate morality with the moral code of Christian fundamentalism. Christian fundamentalists believe that the Bible is to be read literally, not symbolically, with every word expressing the will of God. This is why they protest against the teaching of evolutionary theory in public schools, for instance, and why they generally decry the growth of liberal or secular humanism. In their view, the United States was founded and prospered as a Christian nation, and must now return to its roots. It comes as no surprise that the leaders of the New Right have so often been ministers of evangelical churches—Jerry Falwell, Pat Robertson, and Jimmy Swaggart perhaps foremost among them.

The New Right also claims to be democratic, by which it means that society should follow the lead of a righteous or *moral majority* of Christians. Where will this moral majority lead? To less government intervention in the economy, as the individualist conservatives wish, but to a large and active government in other respects. The New Right wants a strong defense to check and turn back the threat of communism, to begin with. It also wants increased government intervention in activities and areas of life that others, including many other conservatives, deem to be private. They want the government to ban abortions, to set aside time for prayer in public schools, to restrict or outlaw certain sexual activities, and to purge schools and public libraries of materials that they regard as morally offensive. In these and other respects, the New Christian Right would greatly expand the powers of government. And in that respect, their views stand in sharp contrast to the professed views of other conservatives.

CONCLUSION

What, then, is the condition of conservatism today? Two points stand out. First, different kinds of conservatives coexist in uneasy tension. They can agree and cooperate on some matters, but on others they are apt to disagree. This was especially clear during the Reagan administration, when conservatives of all four kinds disagreed, sometimes vehemently, over the direction the administration should take. In the end, the individualist conservatives seemed to emerge as the leading, if not dominant, group.

Second, such disputes may well be a sign of conservatism's vitality. That people find it stimulating to argue about what "true" conservatism is and what direction "proper" conservatism should take suggests that conservatism remains a powerful force in the politics of the English-speaking world. Here and elsewhere there are apparently many people who are unhappy with the fruits of liberalism and unsympathetic to the aims of socialism. For these people, conservatism remains an attractive ideology.

Conservatism as an Ideology

With all the division and diversity within the conservative camp, does it still make sense to speak of conservatism as a single ideology? In our view it does.

For one thing, conservatives are no more divided among themselves than the followers of other ideologies. For another, the differences that distinguish the several varieties of conservatism from one another should not obscure certain shared family resemblances. These may be best clarified by considering how conservatism performs the four functions of all ideologies: the explanatory, evaluative, orientative, and programmatic functions.

Explanation   For most conservatives, the basis for explaining why social conditions are the way they are is human imperfection. Conservatives do refer to other factors—historical circumstances and economic conditions, for instance, and certainly government policies and cultural trends—but they ultimately trace all these to the frailty of imperfect human nature. If things have gone wrong, it is probably because men and women, acting through government, have tried to do more than men and women are capable of doing. If things have gone well, it is because they have kept their hopes and expectations within reason and proceeded slowly and cautiously.

Evaluation   Conservatives typically evaluate social conditions by appealing to social peace and stability. If the relations between the different classes or levels of society are harmonious, so that the leaders display a sense of responsibility to the followers and the followers a sense of loyalty to the leaders, then the social fabric is in good condition. If it is torn by conflict, strife, and bitterness, however, action must be taken to repair the social fabric.

Orientation   Conservatism tells the individual that he or she is not simply an individual. Each of us is part of a greater whole, and each should realize that he or she must act with the good of the whole society in mind. The best way to do this is usually to play our part in society—to be a good parent or teacher or engineer or plumber—and to recognize how each part must blend with all others to provide social harmony. Individualist conservatives sharply differ from the others on this point, for they favor competitive individualism. But in this respect they are simply closer to the liberal tradition than the conservative.

Program   The political program that conservatives pursue will vary from one time and place to another, of course. Nevertheless, the general message of conservatives is to take things slowly, proceed carefully, on the grounds that it is better to do a little good than a lot of harm. In gazing toward the possibilities of a glorious future, conservatives point out, it is all too easy to lose sight of the good things we already enjoy. We should take our eyes off distant horizons in order to appreciate the scenery that surrounds us. Once we see this clearly, conservatives say, we will cherish and conserve what we already have.

Conservatism and Democracy

This desire to preserve the good things a society presently enjoys helps us to see how conservatism, which began with a distinctly antidemocratic attitude, has in the last century come to terms with the democratic ideal. In societies where representative democracy has become part of the social fabric, the traditional and customary way of life, conservatives generally support it. Many conservatives continue to stress the importance of a natural aristocracy, to be sure, but they believe that these natural leaders must be accountable to the people at election time.

The conservative view of human nature, then, leads to a modest view of what is possible in any political society, including a democracy. Given the weakness of human reason and the strong tendency toward selfishness, conservatives will expect any pure democracy to degenerate into anarchy, followed shortly by dictatorship or despotism. Democracy is acceptable to conservatives, therefore, when the people generally have limited power and make limited demands. The people must learn self-restraint, or learn at least to place sufficient power to restrain them in the hands of those prudent and virtuous women and men who form the natural aristocracy of any society. Instead of turning to demagogues, or rabble-rousers, the people must elect cautious, conservative leaders who will perform their duties with great care for the needs of the people and the delicacy of the social fabric. To do more might be democratic, but it could not be conservative.

NOTES

1. Given the growth in government spending and deficits during their administrations, due largely to increased military expenditures, critics charge that neither has made good on this claim.
2. Peter Viereck, *Conservatism: From John Adams to Churchill* (New York: Van Nostrand Reinhold, 1956), p. 19.
3. Anthony Quinton, *The Politics of Imperfection* (London: Faber & Faber, 1978); N. K. O'Sullivan, *Conservatism* (New York: St. Martin's Press, 1976), chap. 1.
4. Peter Viereck, *Conservatism Revisited* (New York: Collier Books, 1962), p. 35. See also William Golding's novel, *Lord of the Flies.*
5. Isaac Kramnick and Frederick Watkins, *The Age of Ideology: 1750 to the Present,* 2nd ed. (Englewood Cliffs, N.J.: Prentice-Hall, 1979), p. 27.
6. *Reflections on the Revolution in France,* ed. Conor Cruise O'Brien (Harmondsworth: Penguin, 1968), pp. 194–195; see also Terence Ball and Richard Dagger, eds., *Ideals and Ideologies: A Reader* (New York: HarperCollins, 1991), selection 23.
7. Ibid., p. 91.
8. Roger Scruton, *The Meaning of Conservatism* (London: Macmillan, 1984), p. 19.
9. In Hanna Pitkin, ed., *Representation* (New York: Atherton, 1969), pp. 174–175.
10. For an ironic comment by a twentieth century conservative on this claim, see Evelyn Waugh's novel, *A Handful of Dust.*
11. *Considerations on France,* in Jack Lively, ed., *The Works of Joseph de Maistre* (New York: Macmillan, 1965), p. 78; also Ball and Dagger, eds., *Ideals and Ideologies,* selection 24.
12. In Viereck, *Conservatism,* pp. 165–166.
13. Ibid., p. 44.

14. José Ortega y Gasset, *The Revolt of the Masses* (New York: W. W. Norton, 1932), p. 77; also in Ball and Dagger, eds., *Ideals and Ideologies*, selection 26.

15. *I'll Take My Stand*, by Twelve Southerners (New York: Harper & Brothers, 1930).

16. Garry Wills, *Confessions of a Conservative* (Garden City, N.Y.: Doubleday, 1979).

17. See the essays in Michael Oakeshott's *Rationalism in Politics* (London: Methuen, 1962), especially "Political Education" and "On Being Conservative." Most of the latter essay is included in Ball and Dagger, eds., *Ideals and Ideologies*, selection 27.

18. George Will, *Statecraft as Soulcraft: What Government Does* (New York: Simon & Schuster, 1983), p. 120.

19. Irving Kristol, *Two Cheers for Capitalism* (New York: Basic Books, 1978).

20. Daniel Bell, *The Cultural Contradictions of Capitalism* (New York: Basic Books, 1976).

FOR FURTHER READING

Hogg, Quintin. *The Case for Conservatism* (Harmondsworth: Penguin, 1947).

Kirk, Russell. *The Conservative Mind: From Burke to Eliot*, 4th ed. (New York: Avon Books, 1968).

——, ed., *The Portable Conservative Reader* (Harmondsworth: Penguin, 1982).

Kirkpatrick, Jeane. "Dictatorships and Double Standards," *Commentary*, 68 (1979): 34–45.

Nash, George H. *The Conservative Intellectual Movement in America: Since 1945* (New York: Basic Books, 1979).

O'Gorman, Frank. *Edmund Burke: His Political Philosophy* (London: Allen & Unwin, 1973).

O'Sullivan, Noel K. *Conservatism* (New York: St. Martin's Press, 1976).

Rossiter, Clinton. *Conservatism in America: The Thankless Persuasion*, 2nd ed. (New York: Random House, 1962).

Scruton, Roger. *The Meaning of Conservatism* (London: Macmillan, 1984).

Steinfels, Peter. *The Neoconservatives* (New York: Simon & Schuster, 1979).

Wills, Garry. *Nixon Agonistes: The Crisis of the Self-Made Man* (New York: New American Library, 1971).

Chapter
5

Socialism and Communism: More to Marx

> *Wherever men have private property and money is the measure of everything, there it is hardly possible for the commonwealth to be governed justly or to flourish in prosperity.*
>
> Thomas More, Utopia

Modern socialism, like classical conservatism, began in part as a response to the liberalism of the late eighteenth and early nineteenth centuries. Like the conservatives, socialists objected to the liberal emphasis on competition and individual liberty. For socialists believed then, as now, that human beings are by nature social or communal creatures. Individuals do not live or work or reproduce the species in isolation, that is, but in cooperation with one another. It is cooperation among individuals, then, not competition between them, that socialists see as the foundation of a society in which everyone can enjoy a decent measure of liberty, justice, and prosperity.

Yet socialists, unlike classical conservatives, assign no particular value to tradition or custom. Nor do they share the conservative's affection for private property. From the socialist viewpoint, in fact, private property is the source of the class divisions that establish some people in positions of power and privilege while condemning others to poverty and powerlessness. Indeed, socialists usually call for programs that will distribute wealth and power more evenly throughout society—programs that conservatives typically deplore as "levelling." Everything that people produce, socialists say, is in some sense a social product, and everyone who participates in producing a good is entitled to a share in it. This means that society as a whole, and not private individuals, should own and control property for the benefit of all. This is the fundamental conviction that all socialists share.

But what exactly does this mean? How much property is society to own and control? Socialists answer these questions in very different ways. Some suggest that most goods should be regarded as public property; others maintain that only the major means of production, such as rivers and forests, large factories and mines, should be publicly owned and controlled. Most socialists fall somewhere between these two positions, with no clear point of agreement except on the general principle that anything that contributes significantly to the production, distribution, and delivery of socially necessary goods must be socially controlled for the benefit of all.

To advocate the social control of property is, however, to raise a second question: How is society to exercise this control? It is one thing to say that society as a whole should own and control a power plant, but quite another to say just *how* society is to operate this plant. Is *everyone* to take a turn working in the plant, or to have a say in its daily operations? No socialist goes this far. Instead, they have generally argued for either **centralized** or **decentralized control** of public property. Those who favor centralized control want the state or government to assume the responsibility for managing property and resources in the name of the whole society. This was, until recently, the approach followed in the Soviet Union. Centralization promotes efficiency, its proponents say, because it makes it possible for the state to plan, coordinate, and manage the whole economy in the interests of every member of society. Other socialists dispute this claim by pointing to the top-heavy and sluggish bureaucracies that dominate centrally planned economies. As they see it, the best way to exercise control over public property is to decentralize it—to vest this control in groups at the local level, especially the workers who labor in the factories, fields, and shops, and the consumers who purchase and use the workers' products. Because these people feel most directly the effects of the use of social property, they should decide how the property is to be used.

Like conservatives and liberals, then, socialists differ among themselves on important issues. But socialists are united in their opposition to unrestricted **capitalism**, which they believe determines the distribution of power in every society in which it is the dominant form of economic exchange. Poor people have a good deal less power than the rich—less power because they have less ability to control and direct their own lives and to choose where and how to live. In a capitalist society, socialists charge, terms like "freedom" and slogans such as "equality of opportunity" ring hollow for many working people. To see why socialists object to capitalism, therefore, we next examine their conception of freedom. With that as background, we then explore the history of socialism.

HUMAN NATURE AND FREEDOM

It is often said, especially in the United States, that socialism is "opposed to freedom." Yet this claim requires clarification and qualification. Socialists are, to be sure, opposed to the liberal-individualist understanding of freedom that we discussed in Chapter 3 and to the conservative's notion of "ordered liberty" described in Chapter 4. This is not because socialists consider freedom undesirable or unimportant, but because they propose an alternative conception of freedom. Their alternative view can be most readily understood by referring once again to our triadic model. For socialists, the *agent* who is to be free is not the abstract or isolated individual, but individuals-in-relations. Human beings are social or communal creatures, socialists say, so we should think of an agent as someone who is connected to and dependent upon other people in various ways. In particular, we should think of agents as individuals engaged in relations of production, distribution, and exchange with others. The agent, in other words, is the producer, or worker, viewed not as an isolated individual but as a member of a **class**—the working class. Members of the working class share several common *goals*, furthermore, including but not restricted to the following: fulfilling work, a fair share of the product they produce (or the profits thereof), a voice in the management of their affairs, and an equal opportunity for everyone to develop and use his or her talents to their full extent. In pursuing these goals, finally, workers find that the system of capitalist production thwarts their aspirations by throwing various *obstacles* in their way.

These obstacles or barriers include the division of society into a wealthy class of owners and a poorer class of producers who are forced to sell their labor to eke out a subsistence living. Those who must devote most of their time and energy merely to making a living can scarcely hope to develop fully their talents. The division of society into classes of unequal political power and economic wealth also results in the sharpening and hardening of class differences that perpetuate these inequalities from one generation to the next. "The rich get richer," the old saying goes, "and the poor get poorer." And to the extent that the rich own or at any rate control the system of education and information (radio and television stations, newspapers, etc.), they are able to raise and maintain still other obstacles. They can, for example, ensure that the poor remain ignorant of radical alternatives to the status quo. In this way the members of the poorer classes may be kept in ignorance of their "true" or "real" interests and of the alternative political visions and economic arrangements that might better serve those interests.

True freedom, then, is freedom from such obstacles and freedom to pursue one's aims and aspirations—so long as such pursuits are not detrimental or harmful to others. Thus one should not be free to make a private profit by exploiting the labor of another. Since we are social or communal creatures it makes no sense to speak of one person's being free and another's not being so. Either all are truly free or none is. Karl Marx and Friedrich Engels made this point in *The Manifesto of the Communist Party* when they proclaimed that in a socialist society, "the condition for the free development of each is the free development of all." This conception of freedom, quite different from the liberal view examined earlier, is summarized in Figure 5.1.

SOCIALISM: THE PRECURSORS

The first name one associates with the ideology of socialism, or at least with its communist variant, is probably that of Karl Marx. Yet socialism predated Marx by many centuries.[1] Plato's *Republic* (ca. 380 B.C.) presents one early version, although Plato restricted the communal sharing of goods and spouses in his ideal society to a particular class, the Guardians.[2] Early Christians espoused

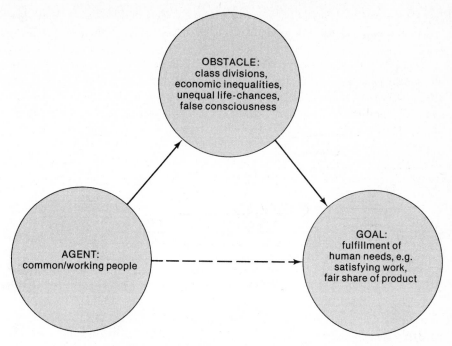

Figure 5.1 The socialist conception of freedom.

another and rather different version of socialism in the first and second centuries A.D. They believed that Christians had a duty to share their labor and their worldly goods with one another. This simple form of communism continued in the practices of certain monastic orders up through the Middle Ages and still survives in some monasteries today.

Utopian thinkers such as Sir Thomas More (1478–1535), the Catholic saint and martyr of the early sixteenth century, advocated communal ownership as an antidote to the sins of pride, envy, and greed that he saw flourishing in his day. Policies that encouraged competition for profits also encouraged these sins, More charged. As a result, most people were poor and powerless, while a few became rich and powerful. And even these few who gained material wealth paid a price, as their pursuit of money and position left them morally and spiritually impoverished. "Wherever men have private property and money is the measure of everything," the principal character of More's *Utopia* (1516) says, "there it is hardly possible for the commonwealth to be governed justly or to flourish in prosperity. . . . I am fully persuaded that no equal and just distribution of goods can be made, and that there can be no true well-being in human affairs, unless private property is outlawed and banished."[3] And in *Utopia* it is. Money is abolished. Every household contributes some good or service to the community and is entitled to withdraw what it needs, free of charge, from common storehouses of grains and other staples. Once the fears of poverty and hunger and homelessness are banished, the foundations of greed and envy disappear.[4] The society that results is indeed, as the punning name **utopia** (from the Greek *eu-* and *ou topos*) suggests, either a "good and happy place" or "no place."

Utopias like More's remained, of course, literary constructs—tributes to the fertile imagination that conceived them, but castles in the air nonetheless. In the aftermath of the English civil war of the 1640s, however, the real world seemed for a time to be a more hospitable place for radical dreams and utopian schemes. Several communist or socialist sects sprang up during this period. One of them, the Diggers, claimed that God had created the earth for all people to share in common; private property was therefore forbidden by Him and ought to be abolished. "The earth," wrote Gerrard Winstanley, is "a common treasury" from which all are entitled to draw what they need.[5] Proceeding from that premise, the Diggers established communes and began digging the earth to plant crops. But because some of them dug land that was not legally theirs, they soon ran afoul of the law and their communes were forcibly disbanded by the authorities.

These and other early views of communist or socialist society were, in the main, agrarian visions. The workers were to be agricultural laborers tilling the land together and sharing in the harvest. But this older agrarian vision was rendered quaint by the coming of the Industrial Revolution. In the late eighteenth and early nineteenth centuries peasant farmers by the tens of thousands left, or in some cases were forced off, the land to work in factories, mills, and mines. Steam power replaced horse power. The steamship replaced the sailing ship, the locomotive the stagecoach, and the power loom the spinning jenny. Workers were no longer tied to the seasonal rhythms of the land, but to the harsher and more insistent rhythms of the factory. Entire families—fathers, mothers, and small children—worked 70 to 80 hours a week in dirty and dangerous conditions. Ill-housed, often hungry, and sometimes homeless, they led lives of misery and squalor.

Some accepted as inevitable the social disruptions and dislocations brought about by early capitalism, but others rejected them as inhumane and unnecessary evils. The English poet William Blake lamented the "dark satanic mills" that polluted the air and poisoned the workers within them, and the novelist Charles Dickens embodied in the character of Ebeneezer Scrooge the evils of a system that rewarded greed and selfishness. Moral outrage over the excesses of early capitalism led some to become reformers and others to become radicals and revolutionaries. Reform-minded liberals wished to improve working conditions and, if possible, to raise wages. More radical critics of capitalism advocated abolishing a system that produced such vast inequalities of opportunity, freedom, and wealth.

Many, though not all, of these critics were socialists of one stripe or another. In their assault on capitalism, they sounded one or both of two basic themes. One, already noted, was sheer moral outrage; the other, an appeal to science and history, with some socialists claiming that there were half-hidden historical processes at work that were undermining capitalism and paving the way for a future socialist society.

Saint-Simon

One of the first to try to set socialism on a "scientific" basis was the French aristocrat, Count Claude-Henri de Saint-Simon (1760–1825). Human history, he held, is divided into successive stages or periods. As an older form of society disappears, a new one necessarily arises to take its place. Each is marked by the presence of particular classes and depends upon certain beliefs. As these beliefs lose credibility, so too does the social and economic system that rests upon them. Thus, said Saint-Simon, feudal society was marked by the presence of a landed nobility and a clergy who articulated the religious assumptions and beliefs upon which feudalism rested. These were in turn undermined and eventually replaced by the **Enlightenment** and the coming of industrial society, with its emphasis on science and technology. A new class of scientists, engineers, and industrialists was becoming increasingly important, said Saint-Simon, because, without them, there could be no industrial society. This new form of society was enormously complex, depending as it did on the coordinated knowledge and skills of many different types of technicians and experts. In such a society it made no sense to speak, as liberals did, of "the individual." The isolated individual is a fiction. In the real world of the industrial society individuals are reduced to their social roles and productive functions. In Saint-Simon's version, socialism involves the recognition and appreciation of social complexity and interdependence, leading to the application of "positive" scientific knowledge to social and economic planning by an elite of experts.[6]

Saint-Simon did not expressly call for the transfer of property from private to public control, but he did argue that laissez faire capitalism was inefficient because it led to gluts and waste, as people competing for profits produced too much of one good and too little of another. Through planning, Saint-Simon declared, experts could anticipate and thus meet social needs, providing an economic system that was both more efficient and more just than capitalism.

Carrying this idea further still, Saint-Simon's disciple Auguste Comte (1798–1857) called himself a Positivist and emphasized the importance of scientific planning, prediction, and social control. "From science," he said, "comes prevision; from prevision comes control."[7] With its emphasis on social control, Comte's "positivist" version of socialism was characterized by a deep aversion to democracy and a fondness for technocracy, or rule by experts. Like Saint-Simon, Comte equated socialism with systematic "scientific" social planning, which was in turn to be justified by a new "religion of humanity" in which scientists were to be the high priests and Comte the pope.[8]

Although Saint-Simon and Comte favored centralized control of social production, other socialists in the early 1800s took the opposite position. Two prominent proponents of a decentralist version of socialism were Charles Fourier and Robert Owen, both of whom inspired disciples to establish short-lived utopian communities in the United States. Fourier and Owen devised schemes for a socialist society that were as visionary as Saint-Simon's and Comte's, but their visions were of small, self-sufficient, self-governing communities in which decisions were made not by experts, but by all the members of the community.

Fourier

Charles Fourier (1772–1837) was a French socialist whose vision of utopia derived from a mixture of mysticism, numerology, and a crude psychological theory. Modern society, he said, is not so far from barbarism as its inhabitants are inclined to believe. It is afflicted with the evils of commerce, selfishness, and deception, among many others (144 of them, to be exact). We not only deceive others, we also deceive ourselves by holding false or mistaken beliefs—especially the belief that wealth will bring happiness. The evils of commercial society, with its mad pursuit of wealth, are embodied in its institutions. The institutions of marriage, the male-dominated family, and the competitive market prevent the satisfaction of the basic passions, which are 12 in number. These include the passions of the five senses, along with those of familism, friendship, love, and ambition; to these are added the "butterfly" passion that leads us to look for variety, the "cabalistic" passion for plotting and intrigue, and the "composite" passion for combining physical and mental pleasures. There is also a thirteenth, the passion for "harmony" that comes from the proper balance of the basic passions. But a competitive commercial society frustrates our desire for harmony, Fourier insisted. We can never satisfy this passion when we are divided against each other—and against ourselves—by competition for jobs and profits. Only when the evils of this society are overcome will humanity reach its highest stage, "Harmonism," in which human beings will cooperate freely for the common good.

Fourier's vision of a harmonious society was captured in his account of the "phalanstery," a community of about sixteen hundred—1610 is the ideal population, he said—in which the residents would produce all they needed and all the passions would be fully satisfied. The phalanstery was based on the principle of "attractive labor," which held that people will work voluntarily if only they find an occupation that engages their talents and interests. Those who like to grow things will be the gardeners. Those who like children will provide day care. And children, who like to play in the dirt, will sweep the streets and collect the garbage. Because people will work freely and spontaneously in these circumstances, the coercive apparatus of the state—laws, police, courts, prisons—will not be needed.[9] Socialist society, as Fourier envisioned it, will be productive, prosperous, and free.

Owen

Robert Owen (1771–1858) was a British capitalist who, appalled by the effects of early capitalism, became an ardent socialist. Drunkenness, debauchery, theft, and other evils were, he held, the result not of original sin or of individual character defects, but of a deformed social system. By rewarding the greed and selfishness of the capitalist, the capitalist system sent the wrong message to young people. Little wonder, then, that so many people try to advance themselves at other people's expense. The cure for the evils of capitalism can be found not only in a new system of production—cooperative production for public profit—but in a new system of education as well. Owen believed that de-formed character was the result of defective education—where education is understood in the broadest possible sense as the sum of all the formative influences in one's life.

In 1800 in New Lanark, Scotland, Owen established a model textile factory that was radical by the standards of the day. The factory was clean, and working conditions were relatively safe. The work week was reduced. Children under ten were not only not allowed to work, but were educated at the owner's expense. Besides learning the three Rs, children learned the value and necessity of cooperation in all aspects of life.

These and other practices Owen described and defended in A New View of Society (1814). Over the next ten years he labored tirelessly to persuade his fellow capitalists of the merits of his scheme. He also appealed to workers to share his vision of a network of small, self-sufficient communities that would spread around the globe. He was more successful in convincing the latter than the former group, who were understandably worried by Owen's attacks on private property and religion and by his growing popularity among the working class. In 1824 Owen took his ideas to North America. On 30,000 acres he had purchased in southwest Indiana, he established the socialist community of New Harmony, which he intended as a model of social organization. Within four years, however, New Harmony had failed, and Owen lost most of his fortune in the venture. He spent the remainder of his life promoting trade unionism and advocating the establishment of worker-owned cooperatives as the nucleus from which a larger and more comprehensive socialist society might grow.[10]

Many other thinkers also dreamed dreams and fashioned schemes for a socialist society. Important though these proponents of **utopian socialism** were, however, none of their efforts proved to be as long-lived and influential as those of Karl Marx. By the middle of the twentieth century, in fact, roughly one-third of the world's population lived in regimes that claimed to be Marxist. Marx, then, is not only the most important thinker in the history of socialism, but one of the most important in all history. And that is reason enough to study his views closely and carefully.

THE SOCIALISM OF KARL MARX

The Young Marx

Karl Marx was born in Trier, in the German Rhineland, in 1818, the son of a lawyer who had abandoned the Jewish faith and converted to Christianity because the government had decreed that Jews could no longer practice law. Comfortable though not wealthy, the Marx family was able to send their son Karl to the University of Bonn. There he studied law and engaged in the pursuits common to university students, including frequenting the local beer hall, talking politics, and fighting a duel with another student. Alarmed by their son's "wild rampagings" and lack of scholarly seriousness, Marx's parents made him transfer to the more demanding University of Berlin. Marx went on to earn his doctorate in philosophy in 1841, expecting to take up an academic post. But, being a political liberal of Jewish descent in a conservative and anti-Semitic society, Marx's academic aspirations went unfulfilled. He turned to journalism, first as a reporter and then as editor of the liberal *Rheinische Zeitung (Rhenish Times)* in 1842. In the following year Marx married his childhood sweetheart and moved to Paris to edit the *Deutsch-Französische Jahrbucher (German-French Yearbook)*. While in Paris, Marx and Friedrich Engels became friends and collaborators, forming a philosophical and political partnership that lasted almost forty years.

Marx's early career as a muckraking journalist brought about two important changes in his outlook. First, he came to appreciate the central social and political importance of economic matters—of property ownership, of market forces, of the state's systematically favoring the rich over the poor. Second, he ceased to be a liberal and became a radical who believed that the political and economic system of his day was so rotten that it could not be reformed from within. Marx's move toward political radicalism was further hastened by his experience with the Prussian police, who censored, confiscated, and finally closed both publications for which he worked and issued a warrant for his arrest. Unable to return to Germany for fear of imprisonment, Marx went into a "temporary" exile that was to last until his death in 1883.[11]

Joking that the German authorities had "given me back my freedom," Marx returned to his philosophical pursuits, plunging into a serious and systematic study of the philosophy of G. W. F. Hegel (1770–1831). The result of these labors, the *Economic and Philosophical Manuscripts* of 1844, remained unpublished during Marx's lifetime. But they reveal quite clearly the enduring influence of Hegel on the main outline and themes of Marx's later work. Since it is nearly impossible to understand Marx's economic and political theory without knowing something about Hegel's philosophy, we need to consider briefly several of its main features.

The Influence of Hegel

During his lifetime and for some two decades after his death, Hegel had a virtual stranglehold on the German philosophical imagination. It was largely within the framework of his philosophy that educated Germans, especially the young, discussed history, politics, and culture. Hegel's philosophy of history proved to be particularly influential. Human history, Hegel maintained, moves in a particular direction and according to a pattern that can be discerned, at least in hindsight. History is the story of the unfolding or evolution of mind or spirit *(Geist)*. There is nothing necessarily mystical or spiritual about *spirit*— any more than there is in our expression "the human spirit" (as, for example, when we say that the first ascent of Mt. Everest represented a triumph of the human spirit). Spirit, one might say, is a set of potentials waiting to be actualized or developed. The most important of these potentials is the capacity for freedom. As Hegel saw it, history is the story of spirit's struggle to overcome obstacles in its search for freedom or self-emancipation. In the course of these struggles, spirit itself changes, becoming ever more mature and expansive.

Karl Marx (1818–1883).

At this point another key concept in Hegel's philosophy—"estrangement" or **alienation** *(Entfremdung)*—comes into play. Spirit evolves into its higher and more inclusive forms through a succession of separations or "alienations." Spirit undertakes a journey, in other words, that resembles the spiritual or psychological development of individual human beings. A newborn baby is at first unable to distinguish itself from its mother. Over time, however, it becomes aware of itself as a separate creature with wants and needs distinct from those of its parents. This transition from infancy to childhood is the first of several alienations through which the individual develops his or her own distinctive personality. And, as is the case with individual biography, so too it is with human history: the human species develops its distinctive characteristics through a series of struggles and successive alienations. Although wrenching and sometimes acutely painful, these changes are necessary if spirit is to grow and develop into new and higher forms.

The various stages through which spirit passes reveal what Hegel called the **cunning of reason** (*List der Vernunft*) and the operation of the **dialectic.** Individual human beings, even whole nations, are characters in a vast unfolding drama whose plot—the progress of spirit and the growth of freedom—is unknown to them. Each plays his or her part, unaware of how that part fits into the greater whole. The story unfolds "dialectically," through the clash of opposing ideas and ideals. Out of this conflict emerge new and more comprehensive ideas and ideals. Foremost among these is the idea of freedom. In ancient and medieval times, to be free was to enjoy a particular legal status, that of free man, from which most people, including slaves and women, were excluded. Through the dialectic of reason, however, freedom becomes, over time, an ever more inclusive idea that old institutions and customs can no longer contain. In its quest for freedom, spirit breaks down old social forms and helps to create new ones.

To show how this dialectical process works to promote human freedom, Hegel invites us to imagine the kind of conflict that might develop between a master and slave,[12] or what he terms the **master-slave dialectic.** According to Hegel's account, the master becomes master by physically conquering another, whom he then enslaves. At first the slave is grateful for having his life spared, and fearful that the master might yet take it from him. He sees himself through his master's eyes, as inferior, degraded, and dependent. The master, likewise, sees himself through the slave's eyes as superior, ennobled, and independent. Yet each needs the other in order to be what he is: the master must have a slave if he is to be master; and the slave must have a master in order to be a slave. But their relationship is unstable. The slave chafes under his chains and dreams of freedom. He longs to lose his identity as slave and to take on (or to recover) his identity as a free human being. The slave, in other words, wants the master to recognize and acknowledge his humanity, which would in turn require the master to treat the slave as an equal, that is, to free him. Yet the master cannot free the slave without ceasing to be who he is, socially speaking—namely, a master. The master wants the slave to recognize and affirm his rank as master. And the slave wants the master to recognize him as an equally worthy human being. Clearly their wants are contradictory, in that they are incompatible and cannot both be satisfied. The stage is set for a showdown.

The master at first appears to have the upper hand. He has all the power. He holds the keys. He has a monopoly on the means of coercion—the chains, the whips, and other instruments of torture. And yet, when the slave refuses to recognize the master's moral or social superiority, *he* gains the upper hand. He withholds from the master the one thing that the master wants but cannot compel. From the moment of the slave's refusal, their positions are effectively reversed. The master is shown to have been dependent upon the slave all along. Not only did he depend for his livelihood on the slave's labor; but his very identity depended upon the presence and continued subservience of the slave—since, without a slave, he could not even be master. So, appearances aside, the master was in fact no more free than the slave, since his social role was in its own way restrictive and confining, keeping the master morally stunted and cut off from the humanity that he shares with the slave. Once they both recognize this, they cease to be master and slave, and the institution of slavery is superseded or surpassed. Stripped at last of their "particularity" (their historically specific social roles), the former master and the former slave confront each other in their "universality" or common humanity, as free and equal human beings. In freeing himself, the slave has freed his master as well.

Hegel tells this story to show how the dialectic operates so as to allow the idea of freedom to burst through the confines of a seemingly invulnerable institution. Although Marx changes the characters and modifies the story, the essential dialectical logic of Hegel's tale remains unchanged.

Marx's Theory of History

After his death, Hegel's followers split into two main camps. On one side were the conservative Right Hegelians, who interpreted Hegel's philosophy of history in theological terms. For them, *spirit* meant God or the Holy Spirit, and human history is the unfolding of His plan. On the other side were the Young or Left Hegelians, Karl Marx among them. They held that Hegel's philosophy was open to a more radical interpretation than Hegel had perhaps realized. So with the hope of revealing "the rational kernel within the mystical shell" of Hegel's philosophy, Marx renewed his study of Hegel in 1843–1844.[13]

Like Hegel, Marx saw history as the story of human labor and struggle. But history, for Marx, is the story not of the struggle of disembodied spirit, but of the human species' struggles in and against a hostile world. Humans have had to struggle to survive heat and cold and the ever-present threat of starvation in order to wrest a living from a recalcitrant nature. But human beings have also struggled against each other. Historically, the most important of these conflicts are to be found in the struggle of one class against another. "The history of all hitherto existing society," wrote Marx and Engels in the *Communist Manifesto*, "is the history of class struggles."[14] Different classes—masters and slaves in slave societies, lords and serfs in feudal society, and later, capitalists and workers in capitalist society—have different, if not diametrically opposed, interests, aims, and aspirations. So long as societies are divided into different classes, class conflict is inevitable.

To understand Marx's position here, we need to examine what he meant by "class," how he thought different classes come into being and into conflict, and how he expected a classless communist society to arise. We need, in short, to look closely at Marx's **materialist conception** (or **interpretation**) **of history,** which he called the "leading thread in my studies."

Marx called his interpretation of history *materialist* to distinguish it from Hegel's "idealist" interpretation. Where Hegel had seen history as the story of spirit's self-realization, Marx saw history as the story of class struggles over opposing material, or economic, interests and resources. This does not mean that Marx was, as has sometimes been charged, an "economic determinist" who wished to "reduce everything to economics." He did, however, emphasize the primary importance of material production. "Before men do anything else," he said, "they must first produce the means of their subsistence"—the food they eat, the clothing they wear, the houses they live in, and so on. Everything else, Marx held, follows from the necessity to produce the means of our subsistence.[15]

Material production requires two things. First, it requires what Marx called the **material forces of production**. These will vary from one kind of society to another. In a primitive hunting society, for example, the forces of production include the wild game, the hunter's bow, arrows, knives, and other tools. In a somewhat more sophisticated agrarian society, the forces of production include the seeds to be planted, the hoes or other implements used in planting and harvesting the crops, and the tools employed in separating the wheat from the chaff, milling the grain, baking the bread, and so on. And in a still more sophisticated industrial society, the productive forces include raw materials (metallic ores, coal, wood, petroleum, etc.), machinery for extracting these materials from their natural state, the factories in which these materials are turned into commodities, the freight cars and trucks for transporting raw materials to the factories and finished products to market, and the like.

In addition to raw materials and machinery—the forces of production—material production requires a second factor that Marx called the **social relations of production**. Human beings organize themselves in order to extract the raw materials, to invent, make, operate, and repair the machinery, to build and staff the factories, and so on. However primitive or sophisticated, material production requires a degree of specialization—what Adam Smith called the "division of labor" and Marx the social relations of production (or sometimes, for short, "social relations"). Different kinds of societies—or "social formations," as Marx sometimes says—have very different social relations of production. A hunting society, for example, will have hunters—almost always the younger males—who are organized into hunting parties, the females who bear and raise the children and transform the hides into clothing, blankets and other useful items, and others with still other tasks to perform. In an agricultural society, the social relations of production include those who make the tools, who shoe and harness the horses, who plant the seeds and harvest the crop, who winnow the grain, who grind or mill it, and who bake the bread. The social relations of production in an industrial society are even more complex. They include the miners who extract the ore, the lumberjacks who fell the trees, the railway workers who transport raw materials to the factory, the people who invent, build, operate and repair the machines, the bankers and brokers who raise the capital and the investors who invest it, and many others.

Out of these social relations of production the different classes arise. Marx suggests that for purposes of "scientific" social analysis, we can simplify somewhat by imagining any society to contain two antagonistic classes, one of which dominates the other. A slave society has a dominant class of masters and a subservient class of slaves. In feudal society the two contending classes are the feudal lords and their serfs. And in an industrial capitalist society these classes are the capitalists—the **bourgeoisie,** Marx calls them—and the wage-laborers, or **proletariat**. Which class you belong to depends upon your relation to the forces of production. Very roughly: you belong to the subservient class if you are merely a means or a force of production, much as a pit-pony or a piece of machinery is. And if you own or control the forces of production—including the human forces—then you belong to the dominant class. Less roughly and more precisely: you belong to the subservient or working class if you do' not own but are in fact forced to transfer your labor or "labor power" to another for his or her pleasure or profit.

In every class-divided society, Marx notes, the dominant class tends to be much smaller than the dominated class. Slaves outnumber masters, serfs outnumber feudal lords, and workers outnumber capitalists. What the ruling class lacks in numbers, however, it more than makes up for in two other ways. First, the ruling class controls the agents and agencies of coercion—the police, courts, prisons, and other institutions of the state. The modern state in capitalist society is, as Marx puts it, merely the executive "committee for managing the common affairs of the bourgeoisie."[16]

Marx emphasizes, however, that the ruling class does not rule by brute force alone. If it did, it would not rule for long. The longevity and stability of the ruling class dominance is due to a second and arguably more important factor: it controls the thoughts, the beliefs and ideas—the "consciousness"—of the working class. The material-economic **base** of every society is capped by an **ideological superstructure**—a set of ideas, ideals, and beliefs that legitimizes and justifies the arrangements and institutions of that society. These ideas characteristically take a number of forms—political, theological, legal, economic—but their function, in the final analysis, is the same: to explain, justify, and legitimize the division of labor, class differences, and vast disparities of wealth, status, and power that exist within a particular society. In a class-divided society, says Marx, we will always see "ideology" operating for the benefit of the dominant class and to the detriment of the subservient class. (See Figure 5.2.)

"The ideas of the ruling class," wrote Marx, "are in every epoch the ruling ideas."[17] By this Marx meant that the acceptable "mainstream" ideas in any society tend to serve the interests of the ruling class. Individual members of the ruling class may have their differences—personal, political, or other—but as a class they share an overriding interest in maintaining the social and economic dominance of their class. To do this, the ruling class must be able to portray their dominance as normal, natural, and perhaps even necessary. In ancient Greek society, for example, Aristotle and others said that some people are "slaves by nature"—that is, naturally fitted for no other role than that of slave or servant. Similarly, in the pre–Civil War American South, slaves and potential critics of slavery were taught from the pulpit that the institution of slavery had been ordained and blessed by God and should not be questioned or criticized. In modern capitalist societies, Marx claims, people internalize the ideas that serve the interests of the ruling capitalist class. These include religious ideas, such as that this world is a "vale of tears," that God loves the poor and the meek, who, if they walk humbly with their God in this life, will go to heaven in the next. Marx called religion the **opiate of the people** because it dulls their minds and makes them uncritical of the wretched conditions in

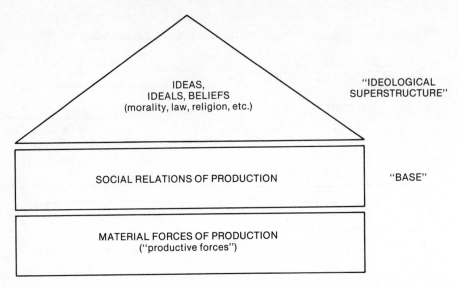

Figure 5.2 Marx's materialism.

which they live. People living in a capitalist society are also taught that it is "human nature" to be self-interested, acquisitive, and competitive. Moreover, Marx says, they learn to equate freedom with "the only unconscionable freedom—free trade," the freedom to compete, to make a profit without interference from the government, and to enjoy the unequal blessings bestowed by the so-called free enterprise system. The entire educational system, from kindergarten through college, hammers these lessons home. College professors, no less than lawyers and priests, are unwitting participants in this process of ideological indoctrination. And finally, the mainstream and mass-circulation media in capitalist societies portray capitalist relations of production as normal, natural, and necessary, and noncapitalist alternatives, such as socialism or communism, as unnatural, abnormal, aberrant, and unworkable.

In all these ways, Marx maintained, the working class is kept from forming a true picture of its real situation. It mistakenly takes the ideas of the ruling class as its own. The working class suffers, in short, from false consciousness. As long as it does it will be a class "in itself" but not yet "for itself"—that is, a class as yet unaware of its own interests and revolutionary political possibilities. To understand how the working class might overcome its false consciousness, and in the process become a class for itself ready to make a revolution against the ruling class, we need to examine Marx's critique of capitalism and his theory of revolution.

Marx's Critique of Capitalism

Although an outspoken critic of capitalism, Marx admitted that capitalism was at one time a progressive and even radical force. "The bourgeoisie, historically, has played a most revolutionary part."[18] In its early phase, he said, capitalism had performed three important and historically progressive functions.

First, in the late feudal period merchant capitalists hastened the demise of feudalism by breaking down trade barriers and opening new trade routes to Africa and the Orient. They were also instrumental in the discovery of the New World: Columbus, after all, was looking not for America but for a shorter trade route by which to bring back tea, silk, and spices from the East Indies. Kings and aristocrats often found themselves in debt to newly wealthy merchant capitalists, who frequently forced legal and political concessions from them. In short:

> The bourgeoisie, wherever it has got the upper hand, has put an end to all feudal, patriarchal, idyllic relations. It has pitilessly torn asunder the motley feudal ties that bound man to his 'natural superiors,' and has left remaining no other nexus [i.e., connection] between man and man than naked self-interest, than callous 'cash payment.' It has drowned the most heavenly ecstasies of religious fervor, of chivalrous enthusiasm, of Philistine sentimentalism in the icy water of egotistical calculation. It has resolved personal worth into exchange value, and in place of the numberless indefeasible chartered freedoms [of feudalism], has set up that single, unconscionable freedom—free trade. In one word, for exploitation, veiled by religious and political illusions, it has substituted naked, shameless, direct, brutal exploitation.[19]

Strange as it may seem, Marx views these as progressive moves—painful but necessary steps that will lead eventually to a more just and nonexploitative society.

Capitalism has been a progressive force in a second respect. It has made human beings masters over nature. Capitalism "has been the first [economic system] to show what man's activity can bring about. It has accomplished wonders far surpassing Egyptian pyramids, Roman aqueducts, and Gothic cathedrals; it has conducted expeditions that put in the shade all former exoduses of nations and crusades." In sum:

> The bourgeoisie, during its rule of scarce one hundred years, has created more massive and more colossal productive forces than have all preceding generations together. Subjection of nature's forces to man, machinery, application of chemistry to industry and agriculture, steam navigation, railways, electric telegraphs, clearing of whole continents for cultivation, canalization of rivers, whole populations conjured out of the ground—what earlier century had even a presentiment that such productive forces slumbered in the lap of social labor?[20]

A third and closely related respect in which capitalism has proved to be a progressive force resides in its need for innovation and change. To remain profitable, industry must have new and more efficient machinery. These changes in the material forces of production bring about changes in the social relations of production, and thereby in the wider society.

> The bourgeoisie cannot exist without constantly revolutionizing the forces of production, and thereby the relations of production, and with them the whole relations of society. . . . Constant revolutionizing of production, uninterrupted disturbance

of all social conditions, everlasting uncertainty and agitation distinguish the bourgeois epoch from all earlier ones. All fixed, fast-frozen relations, with their train of
ancient and venerable prejudices and opinions, are swept away, all new-formed
ones become antiquated before they can ossify. All that is solid melts into air, all
that is holy is profaned, and man is at last compelled to face with sober senses his
real conditions of life and his relations with his kind.[21]

In all these respects, Marx contends, capitalism has been a progressive force
for the good.

But if capitalism has been beneficial, why is Marx so critical of it? And why
does he think that capitalism should be overthrown and replaced? Of the many
reasons Marx gives for doing so, the following three are of special importance.

First, Marx claims that capitalism is outmoded. Although it was once progressive, capitalism has outlived its usefulness and now needs to be superseded. Just because capitalism represents an improvement over feudalism, that
does not mean that no further advance is desirable or necessary. Just as adoles-
cence prepares the way for adulthood, so, Marx maintains, capitalism has prepared the way for an even higher and freer form of society—communist society.

Second, Marx contends that capitalism creates alienation. As we noted earlier, the concept of alienation or estrangement loomed large in Hegel's philosophy of history. Marx also makes the concept of alienation central to his critique
of capitalism. But Marx has a somewhat different understanding of alienation.
In his view, it is not "spirit" that is alienated from itself, but people who are
alienated from their work and from each other. The sense of alienation felt by
the working class will eventually help to bring about the downfall of capitalism
and the coming of communism.

Under capitalism, Marx maintains, workers are alienated in four distinct
but related ways. (1) Because they are forced to sell their labor and do not own
what they produce, they are alienated from the product of their labor. (2) Because the capitalist system of mass production kills the creative spirit, workers
cannot find satisfaction in their labor and are therefore alienated from the activity of production itself. The worker becomes "an appendage of the machine."[22]
(3) Workers are alienated from their distinctively and uniquely human potentials or "powers"—particularly the power to create and enjoy beauty—which
are dulled or remain undeveloped in capitalist society. (4) Capitalism alienates
workers from each other, inasmuch as it makes them compete with one another
for jobs and wages.

But the workers are not the only ones who are alienated. Marx suggests
that the capitalists, like the master in Hegel's tale, also suffer from alienation.
With all their material comforts, they think themselves free and fulfilled; but
in fact they are not. They are, according to Marx, mere "appendages" to capital.
They are not its master but its slave. The capitalists bow to their master, the
market, and tailor their actions accordingly. Far from being free, then, their
actions are determined by forces outside their control.

Third, Marx maintains that capitalism is self-subverting. The operation of
the capitalist system has an iron logic that holds everyone—even the capitalist—in its grip. It keeps the capitalist from being a fully developed, kind, and

caring human being and makes him or her instead a cold and callous calculating machine. Yet Marx insists repeatedly that he is not criticizing capitalism on moral grounds, nor is he questioning the moral character of capitalists as individuals or even as a class. His supposedly "scientific" critique of capitalism aims to show how the logic of capitalism constrains the actions of everyone, including the capitalists themselves. This is especially evident, for example, in the way in which the system operates to keep workers' wages to a minimum subsistence level. "The average price of wage labor is the minimum wage, i.e., that quantum of the means of subsistence which is absolutely requisite to keep the laborer in bare existence as a laborer."[23] Capitalists keep wages low not because they are immoral or cruel, but because the logic of the system requires them to do so.

We can illustrate Marx's point by imagining two factories owned by competing capitalists. Both produce the same product—steel, say. One day, one of the capitalists takes pity on his workers. He raises their wages, shortens the working day, improves working conditions, installs safety equipment, adds a clinic and a day-care center. His competitor does none of these things. The result? The kindly capitalist goes out of business, his workers lose their jobs, and his heartless competitor flourishes. Why? Because to pay for these improvements he must either raise the cost of his product, thereby driving away consumers, or he must reduce his profit margin, driving away investors, who want the largest possible return on their investment. The kindly capitalist, now bankrupt, is forced into the ranks of the workers. His competitor, by contrast, grows even richer. He and others like him corner ever larger shares of their respective markets, resulting in reduced competition and a tendency toward monopoly. Such, according to Marx, is the logic of capitalism.

The point of this imaginary tale is that, under capitalism, worker and capitalist alike are alienated from the full and free development of their human powers. Yet they are prevented from seeing this because, under capitalism, nothing is what it appears to be; everything is "inverted."[24] Fair seems foul and foul seems fair. In this topsy-turvy world the market is free but individuals are not. "In bourgeois society," says Marx, "capital is independent and has individuality, while the living person is dependent and has no individuality."[25] The workers appear to exchange their labor voluntarily for a daily wage; in reality, they are forced by fear of unemployment and eventual starvation to work for a subsistence wage. Capitalists appear to be free to act as they please; in fact, they are in the grip of forces beyond their control. Like the sorcerer's apprentice, the capitalists have grabbed hold of a broom that will soon sweep them away.[26]

Marx contends that capitalism has created conditions and unleashed forces that will one day destroy it. In particular, capitalism has created its own "grave diggers" by creating a class—the proletariat—with interests implacably opposed to its own; a class with everything to gain and nothing to lose by revolting against the ruling bourgeoisie. And yet, ironically, it is the bourgeoisie who are responsible for their own downfall. For it was they who brought the workers together in the first place and then taught them to combine and cooperate in the production of commodities. The workers eventually come to think of themselves as a unified class with common interests and a common class enemy, the bourgeoisie. They will then make the revolution that will overthrow capitalism and lead eventually to the creation of a classless communist society.

Before examining the goal—the coming of a communist society—we need to look more closely at the process by which Marx believed that it would be achieved. Let us first examine the bare essentials of Marx's "dialectical" storyline, and then go on to fill in the more concrete social, economic, and political factors that lead to the revolutionary sequence in which capitalism is abolished and society radically transformed.

The Dialectic of Change

How, exactly, did Marx view the process that would bring about the momentous change from a competitive capitalist society to a cooperative communist society? Here we need to remember Marx's debt to Hegel, and particularly to Hegel's notion that history, in moving dialectically, exhibits the "cunning of reason." Capitalists and proletarians are characters enmeshed in a drama whose plot and ending they do not know. And, as we noted earlier, the plot of this drama resembles that of Hegel's parable of the master and the slave. Once again, of course, the actors are not individuals but two great contending classes, the bourgeoisie and the proletariat.

In Marx's retelling of Hegel's parable, the capitalist replaces the master and the worker the slave. The worker is in fact enslaved, though at first he or she does not know that. Grateful to the capitalist for a job, and fearful of losing it, the worker feels indebted to, and dependent upon, the capitalist. The worker also accepts the capitalist's view of the world and their respective places in it. In this view, the capitalist is credited with "creating" a job that he or she then "gives" to the lucky worker. Since the capitalist pays a wage in exchange for the worker's labor, the relationship looks like a reciprocal one. But the appearance is misleading. The capitalist exploits the worker by paying less than his or her labor is worth. By "extracting surplus-value"—Marx's phrase for making a profit—the capitalist is able to live luxuriously, while the worker barely ekes out a living. Their relationship, though ostensibly reciprocal, is far from equal. The worker is impoverished, even as the capitalist is enriched. The poorer the proletariat, the richer is the capitalist class, the bourgeoisie.

Under these conditions the worker feels a sense of unease. Often hungry and always insecure, the laborer begins to ask why his or her lot in life is so inferior to the capitalist's. The capitalists' stock answer—that they are rich because they have worked harder and saved more, and anyone who does so can become a capitalist, too—begins to ring hollow. For, after all, it would be impossible, that is, logically impossible, for everyone to become a capitalist, no matter how hard he or she worked or how much he or she saved. Some people (most, in fact) must be workers if capitalism is to survive as a system. Reflecting on this, the worker eventually realizes that the fault lies not in himself or herself, nor in the "stars" or "nature" or "fate," but in capitalism itself—a system that enriches the capitalist even as it stunts the mental and moral development of the worker. The worker, who had begun by believing that he or she needed the capitalist, now realizes, on reflection, that capitalists need the workers without whose labor no wealth can be created—and without which they would lose their very identity as capitalists. The capitalist is therefore dependent upon the worker.

The obverse is, of course, equally true: without the capitalist class there would be no working class. The capitalist, understandably, wishes to maintain this state of affairs. The worker, by contrast, comes to realize that gaining freedom and overcoming alienation require the abolition of the two contending classes—bourgeoisie and proletariat. This does not mean that their members must be killed, but that the conditions that create and maintain class differences must be eliminated. One class must cease to exploit and profit from the labor of the other. But this, Marx notes, means that classes will cease to exist. Class divisions are by their very nature exploitative; eliminate exploitation and you eliminate classes, and vice versa.

The proletariat is unique, Marx says, because it is the only class in modern society that has an interest in abolishing itself. Instead of seeking to preserve itself as a class—as the bourgeoisie does—the proletariat seeks to abolish class rule by abolishing all class distinctions. The proletariat is in Marx's view the "universal class" because, in serving its interests, it serves the interests of all humanity.[27] It is in the workers' interest to abolish the working class—one that is impoverished, despised, and degraded—and to become free and equal human beings. In freeing themselves, moreover, they free their former masters as well. They achieve at last "the full and free development of all."[28]

For Marx, then, true freedom—freedom from exploitation and alienation, the freedom to develop one's human powers to their fullest—can flourish only in a classless society. It is just this kind of society that workers have an interest in bringing about. But how, according to Marx's account, are they able to overcome their false consciousness and to discover what their true interests are? How does the proletariat come to be a class for itself, equipped with a revolutionary class consciousness? What, in short, are the actual stages in the revolutionary sequence that leads to the overthrow of capitalism and the creation of a classless communist society? And, not least, what will communist society look like?

The Revolutionary Sequence

Marx predicted that proletarian revolution, though eventually spreading worldwide, would begin in the more advanced capitalist countries and proceed in a fairly definite order. The stages in the revolutionary sequence can be briefly outlined in the following way. (See Figure 5.3.)

Economic Crises Capitalism, as Marx was by no means the first to observe, is beset by periodic economic downturns—recessions and depressions. "Bourgeois" economists refer to these as fluctuations in the business cycle that will, in time, correct themselves. Marx, by contrast, believed that these crises were due to the "anarchy in production" that characterizes capitalist society.[29] The more mature or advanced a capitalist society becomes, the more frequent and severe these crises will be—and the less likely they are to correct themselves.

Immiseration of the Proletariat   The capitalists, being wealthier, are better able to weather these crises than are the workers. Recessions and depressions deprive workers of their jobs, their income, and finally their food and shelter. Unable through no fault of their own to find work, some resort to begging, others to petty thievery for which they risk imprisonment or even death, and still others die of starvation. However miserable their lot as workers, they become even more miserable when they lose their jobs. This process, the **immiseration of the proletariat,** is inescapable in capitalist society, according to Marx.

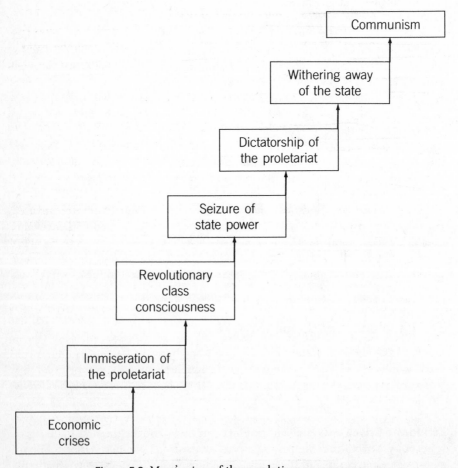

Figure 5.3 Marx's view of the revolutionary sequence.

Revolutionary Class Consciousness   The workers in their misery begin to realize that the fault lies not with them but with the system—a system beset by "contradictions" too glaring to pass unnoticed. They are willing to work, but there are not enough jobs to go around. The bourgeois "coupon clippers" who do not work are nevertheless comfortable and affluent. Their children, well fed and warmly clothed, go to school; the workers' children—malnourished, hungry, and ill-clad—beg in the streets and dig through garbage for scraps of food. Seeing these contradictions leads workers to reflect critically on the causes of their misery. In this process, moreover, Marx's theory intervenes to make a contribution of its own; it supplies an explanation of how things came to be this way. It also proposes a solution: the overthrow of the ruling bourgeoisie. Because Marx believed that the workers would sooner or later arrive at this conclusion on their own, he saw himself as merely a "midwife" reducing the "birth pangs" by hastening the revolutionary process along the most direct and least painful course.

Seizure of State Power   Marx predicted that objective economic conditions (the economic crises resulting in the immiseration of the proletariat) and subjective conditions (revolutionary class consciousness) would combine to form a politically explosive mixture. Beginning with apparently unrelated, small, spontaneous strikes, boycotts, demonstrations, and riots, the revolutionary movement quickly coalesces into a more militant, organized, and unified force for the overthrow of the ruling class. Marx believed that this could come about in a number of ways. One possibility is that a nationwide general strike will cripple the economy and bankrupt the capitalists almost overnight. Another possibility is a bloody civil war pitting capitalists, soldiers, and police against armed proletarians. A third possibility, albeit an unlikely one (except perhaps in Holland and the United States, Marx said), is that the bourgeoisie will be overthrown not by bullets, but by ballots in a free and fair election. In any case, the workers have the advantage of solidarity and sheer force of numbers. The struggle will be protracted, difficult, and probably violent. But, by whatever means, the proletariat will at last take state power out of the hands of the bourgeoisie and into their own.

The Dictatorship of the Proletariat   Having seized state power, the proletariat proceeds to establish what Marx called the **revolutionary dictatorship of the proletariat**. By this inflammatory phrase, Marx meant merely this: the bourgeois state, being a system of class rule, amounted to the dictatorship of the bourgeoisie. When the workers take state power into their hands, they become the new ruling class. The workers, in other words, will rule in their own interest. Their most pressing interest is to preserve the gains of the revolution and prevent the defeated bourgeoisie from regrouping and mounting (possibly with outside assistance) a counterrevolution to regain power. The working class, accordingly, uses the apparatus of the state—the schools, courts, prisons, and police—in as dictatorial a manner as necessary to prevent this possibility.

Marx expects the victorious workers to be democratic and open in their deal-ings with each other. Theirs is to be a dictatorship of and by, not over, the proletariat.

The Withering Away of the State   In one of his later writings, the *Critique of the Gotha Programme*, Marx states that the proletariat's defeat of the bour-geoisie will inaugurate a period of socialism, which he describes as a form of society that makes the transition from capitalism to communism possible. Be-cause the old competitive ways of thinking typical of bourgeois society will not disappear immediately, the socialist phase of development will include not only the dictatorship of the proletariat, but also continued use of wage incentives to encourage people to work hard. Under socialism, according to Marx, the rule should be: "From each according to his ability, to each according to his labor." But the abiding interest of the proletariat, the "universal class," is in abolishing classes and class distinctions. This will begin to happen once the workers take control of the workplace and transform the conditions of labor, ending exploita-tion and alienation. The withering away of the state will then occur as the bourgeoisie die out, or see the error of their ways. The need for coercion will gradually fade, and Marx expects that the dictatorship of the proletariat will lose its reason for existing and simply "wither away."

Communism   Marx said remarkably little about the specific features of a fu-ture communist society. One reason for this is that he—unlike earlier utopian socialists, with their detailed blueprints—refused to write "recipes for the kitchens of the future."[30] The shape of any future society, Marx thought, could only be decided by the people who would inhabit it. Even so, Marx did hint at several features that he thought such a society will have. For one, it will be open and democratic, with all citizens taking an active part in governing it. For another, the major means of production—mills, mines, factories, and so on— will be publicly owned. Economic production will be planned and orderly. And distribution of goods and services will be based not on privilege or wealth, but on need. Under communism, then, the rule will be: "From each according to his ability, to each according to his need." People living in a communist society will at last be truly free. Having overcome the obstacles of exploitation, alien-ation, and ideological illusions, that is, they will be free to develop their many-sided personalities. Marx thus envisioned a future society in which every human being, not just a fortunate few, will be free to become well-rounded Renaissance figures.

> In communist society, where nobody has one exclusive sphere of activity but each can become accomplished in any branch he wishes, society regulates the general production and thus makes it possible for me to do one thing today and another tomorrow, to hunt in the morning, fish in the afternoon, rear cattle in the evening, criticize after dinner, just as I please, without ever becoming hunter, fisherman, shepherd or critic.[31]

Marx died in 1883—too early to witness attempts to put his ideas into political practice. Others, however, calling themselves Marxists and claiming to speak in his name, were soon busy interpreting, reinterpreting, and adapting his ideas in ways that would almost certainly have astonished, and in some cases appalled, Karl Marx. Whether Marx would have liked it or not, he gave rise to Marxism. And Marxism after Marx, as we explain in the next chapter, has had an interesting career of its own.

NOTES

1. For one history of socialism among many, see George Lichtheim, *A Short History of Socialism* (New York: Praeger, 1970).
2. Plato, *The Republic* (books 3 and 4, 412B–421C).
3. Thomas More, *Utopia*, ed. J. Churlton Collins (Oxford: Clarendon Press, 1904), pp. 43–44. More wrote *Utopia* in Latin, and Collins reprints Ralph Robynson's translation of 1551. We have altered this translation, especially the spelling, to bring it up to date, as we do in the selection from *Utopia* in Terence Ball and Richard Dagger, eds., *Ideals and Ideologies: A Reader* (New York: HarperCollins, 1991), selection 29.
4. Ibid., p. 68.
5. Gerrard Winstanley, *A New Yeers Gift for the Parliament and Armie* (1650); reprinted in David Wooton, ed., *Divine Right and Democracy* (Harmondsworth: Penguin Books, 1986), pp. 317–333, at p. 318. See also Winstanley, *The Law of Freedom* (1652; New York: Schocken Books, 1973).
6. Claude-Henri de Saint-Simon, *Social Organization, The Sciences of Man, and Other Writings*, ed. Felix Markham (New York: Harper Torchbooks, 1964).
7. Auguste Comte, *August Comte and Positivism: Selections from His Writings*, ed. Gertrude Lenzer (New York: Harper & Row, 1975), p. 88.
8. See Frank E. Manuel, *The Prophets of Paris* (Cambridge, Mass.: Harvard University Press, 1962).
9. See the selection from Fourier in Ball and Dagger, eds., *Ideals and Ideologies*, selection 30.
10. Robert Owen, *A New View of Society and Other Writings*, ed. G. D. H. Cole (London: E. P. Dent, 1927); Keith Taylor, *The Political Ideas of the Utopian Socialists* (London: Cass, 1982); and Lichtheim, *A Short History of Socialism*, pp. 37—42.
11. David McLellan, *Marx: His Life and Thought* (London: Macmillan, 1973).
12. G. W. F. Hegel, *Phenomenology of Mind*, trans. J. B. Baillie (New York: Harper & Row, 1967), pp. 228–240.
13. Karl Marx, *Capital* (New York: International Publishers, 1967), vol. 1, "Afterword to the Second German Edition," p. 20.
14. Karl Marx and Friedrich Engels, *The Manifesto of the Communist Party*, in Lewis S. Feuer, ed., *Marx and Engels: Basic Writings on Politics and Philosophy* (Garden City, N.Y.: Doubleday Anchor, 1959), p. 7; also in Ball and Dagger, eds., *Ideals and Ideologies*, selection 31.
15. All quotations in this paragraph are from Marx and Engels, *The German Ideology* (New York: International Publishers, 1947), part 1.
16. *Manifesto*, p. 9; *Ideals and Ideologies*, selection 31.
17. *German Ideology*, p. 39; *Manifesto*, p. 26.
18. *Manifesto*, p. 9; *Ideals and Ideologies*, selection 31.
19. Ibid., pp. 9–10; *Ideals and Ideologies*, selection 31.

20. Ibid., p. 12; *Ideals and Ideologies*, selection 31.
21. Ibid., p. 10; *Ideals and Ideologies*, selection 31.
22. Ibid., p. 14; *Ideals and Ideologies*, selection 31.
23. Ibid., p. 22; *Ideals and Ideologies*, selection 31.
24. *German Ideology*, p. 14.
25. *Manifesto*, p. 22; *Ideals and Ideologies*, selection 31.
26. Ibid., pp. 12–13; *Ideals and Ideologies*, selection 31.
27. *Critique of Hegel's Philosophy of Right*, in Feuer, ed., *Marx and Engels: Basic Writings on Politics and Philosophy*, pp. 141–142.
28. *Manifesto*, p. 29; *Ideals and Ideologies*, selection 31.
29. Ibid., p. 32; *Ideals and Idealogies*, selection 31.
30. Marx, *Capital*, vol. 1, p. 17.
31. *German Ideology*, p. 22.

FOR FURTHER READING

Avineri, Shlomo. *The Social and Political Thought of Karl Marx* (Cambridge and New York: Cambridge University Press, 1968).

Ball, Terence, and James Farr, eds. *After Marx* (Cambridge and New York: Cambridge University Press, 1984).

Berlin, Isaiah. *Karl Marx: His Life and Environment*, 4th ed. (Oxford and New York: Oxford University Press, 1978).

Carver, Terrell. *Marx's Social Theory* (Oxford: Oxford University Press, 1982).

Kolakowski, Leszek. *Main Currents of Marxism*, trans. P. S. Falla, 3 vols. (Oxford: Clarendon Press, 1978).

Manuel, Frank E. *The Prophets of Paris* (Cambridge, Mass.: Harvard University Press, 1962).

McLellan, David. *Karl Marx: His Life and Thought* (London: Macmillan, 1973).

Singer, Peter. *Marx* (Oxford and New York: Oxford University Press, 1980).

Taylor, Keith. *The Political Ideas of the Utopian Socialists* (London: Cass, 1982).

Wilson, Edmund. *To the Finland Station* (New York: Doubleday Anchor, 1953).

Chapter
6

Socialism and Communism After Marx

[A]ll of us really owe the comparative decency of our lives to poor drudges underground, blackened to the eyes, with their throats full of coal dust, driving their shovels forward with arm and belly muscles of steel.

George Orwell

*A*t the end of the twentieth century, socialism—especially of the authoritarian, central planning variety—seems to be an idea whose time has passed. Toward the end of the nineteenth century, by contrast, socialism seemed to many in Europe and North America to be an idea whose time had come. The period from Karl Marx's death in 1883 until the outbreak of World War I in 1914 was a time of political and theoretical ferment—and growing popular support—for socialism and socialist parties. One observer has called this the golden age of socialism, and of Marxism in particular.[1]

It was an age of Marxian socialism, to be sure, but it was also an age of Christian socialism, Fabian socialism, anarcho-communism, and other non-Marxian variants. Even those who called themselves Marxists often subscribed to different interpretations of what Marx meant and what Marxism was. Friedrich Engels advanced his own distinctive interpretation of Marxism, as, later, did Lenin and the Bolsheviks, who thought of themselves as "scientific socialists" remaking the world in the fiery forge of revolution. Others were skeptical or critical, or both. The "revisionists," for example, criticized the revolutionary thrust of Marx's theory. They thought that socialism, and later communism, would come about peacefully, by "evolutionary" means. Other critics, such as the anarcho-communist Mikhail Bakunin, suspected that Marxism harbored authoritarian or even totalitarian tendencies and should therefore be rejected as a guide to political practice.

Such faction and ferment has characterized socialism in the twentieth century. As we shall see, there have been many voices in the socialist chorus, not all singing in the same key, and some marching to different drummers and singing altogether different songs. Even so, Marx's voice has until recently boomed louder than anyone else's. Virtually every socialist since his time has thought it necessary to come to terms with Marx's theory, either to accept it, to reject it outright, or to modify it almost beyond recognition.

MARXISM AFTER MARX

Several years before his death, Marx learned that a group of admiring French workingmen were calling themselves Marxists. The idea that anyone would reduce his complex and supposedly scientific theory to a sectarian ideology or simplistic "ism" appalled the old man. As Marx told his son-in-law, "what is certain is that I am not a Marxist."[2] But if Marx did not regard himself as a Marxist, many others were happy to claim the title. Chief among these was Marx's old friend and coauthor, Friedrich Engels.

Engels's Marxism

Although a fierce critic of capitalism, Engels was himself a capitalist. His father, co-owner of the German textile firm of Ermen and Engels, had sent the young Engels to England in 1842 to manage the firm's factory in Manchester. Always a reluctant capitalist, Engels nevertheless enjoyed the good life. He was a connoisseur of fine wines and good cigars, and he kept a mistress, an Irish woman named Mary Burns who worked in his factory. She showed Engels the appalling conditions in which workers lived in Manchester. These he then described memorably and in grisly detail in *The Condition of the English Working Class* (1844), a work that greatly impressed Marx and has since become a minor sociological classic.

In the mid-1840s Marx, the radical philosopher, teamed with Engels, the capitalist. Their partnership was in many ways unique. Each was strong where the other was weak. Marx quickly came to depend on Engels, not least for financial assistance during the early years of his exile in England, where the Marx family had moved in 1849, living for years in dire poverty. For his part, Engels depended on Marx for political inspiration and intellectual stimulation. Marx, as Engels readily acknowledged, was the deeper and more original thinker. But Engels was the better writer, with a knack for turning memorable phrases and writing with ease and speed in several languages. In the works they wrote together—including the *Communist Manifesto* (1848)—the ideas were mainly Marx's, but much of the prose was Engels's. During Marx's lifetime, then, Engels did much to simplify and popularize his friend's ideas.

In the years immediately following Marx's death, however, Engels added his own ideas to Marx's. Engels adapted and interpreted—one might even say, radically reinterpreted—Marx's theory. Indeed, some scholars have suggested that it was Engels, not Marx, who invented Marxism, so that later Soviet Marxism (Marxism-Leninism) owes more to Engels than to Marx.[3] We will examine the latter claim shortly. But first we must look more closely at Engels's political situation and his contribution to Marxism.

The political situation in which Engels found himself in the 1880s was pe-

Friedrich Engels (1820–1895).

culiar. After Marx's death in 1883 he claimed to speak for Marx on a wide variety of subjects, including the direction in which the German Social Democratic party (SDP) should be heading. The SDP had been formed in 1875 by an alliance of two rival German socialist parties—the United German Labor party, founded in 1863 and led by Ferdinand Lassalle (1825–1864), and the Social Democratic Workers' party, established in 1869 by Marx's disciples August Bebel and Wilhelm Liebknecht. Lassalle had been Marx's main rival for the theoretical and intellectual leadership of the German socialist movement, and each devoted considerable energy to criticizing the other. Their contrasting visions of socialism were matched only by differences in their respective appearances and personalities. Marx—short, stout, and every inch the thorough and studious scholar—distrusted the tall, handsome, popular, and flamboyant Lassalle. A dashing and romantic figure, Lassalle was a spellbinding orator and a gifted writer of plays, poems, and political tracts of which Marx heartily disapproved.

Unlike Marx, an internationalist who held that the working class has no homeland, Lassalle was an ardent nationalist who believed that workers of every nation should seek their own path to socialism. The political tactics that would work for German socialists, for example, would not necessarily work for the French. Moreover, Lassalle believed, working people tend to be deeply patriotic and protective of their respective countries. To try to weld them into a unified international movement would therefore be ill-conceived and bound to fail. Also unlike Marx, Lassalle was a statist who believed that the state could not, should not, and would not "wither away." It must instead be captured electorally and controlled democratically by workers and their elected representatives. Socialism was to be imposed from above by a beneficent and all-powerful state.

Even after Lassalle's premature death in 1864—he was killed in a duel over a love affair with a seventeen-year-old girl—the Lassallean wing of the SDP continued to be a thorn in Marx's side. Its reformist tendencies, its eclecticism and romanticism, its German nationalism—all ran counter to Marx's vision of a broad, unified, and international workers' movement.

From the time of Marx's death in 1883 until his own in 1895, Engels was the guardian of Marxian orthodoxy to whom Marxists in Germany and elsewhere looked not only for theoretical inspiration and clarification, but for practical advice as well. In addition to offering advice about political tactics, Engels supplied a simplified version of Marx's theory that is in several respects difficult to square with Marx's own views. In particular, Engels made two very important moves. First, he claimed for Marxism the honorific title of "scientific socialism." And second, Engels reinterpreted what Marx meant by **materialism.**

Scientific Socialism   In his speech at Marx's graveside, Engels called Marx "the man of science," comparing his achievement to that of Charles Darwin. "Just as Darwin discovered the law of development of organic nature, so Marx discovered the law of development of human history."[4] There is at first sight an air of plausibility about the comparison. After all, Marx did believe that his inquiries were "scientific." By "science" (the German word is *Wissenschaft*) Marx meant a body of organized knowledge that can be tested and found to be true or false. Scientific knowledge, he held, is not static and closed, but open to criticism and refutation. Marx was highly critical of earlier thinkers—including Adam Smith and many others—for being insufficiently scientific in this sense. But he could also be quite critical of himself, and he repeatedly revised and amended his theory in the light of new evidence.

Marx's open and self-critical conception of science contrasts sharply with Engels's closed and uncritical view. Consider, for example, their respective views of the nature and function of scientific generalizations or "laws." Some nineteenth century thinkers maintained that just as there are immutable laws of gravity, thermodynamics, and other natural phenomena, so too are there unchangeable laws governing history and human society. Marx agreed that there are social and historical laws, but he believed that these were historically changeable artifacts—mutable features characteristic of particular social formations rather than fixed features of all past, present, or possible societies. The so-called law of supply and demand, for example, is not a timelessly true law, but merely an artifact of capitalist market society. When capitalist society is superseded, that so-called *law* will no longer be valid. In this respect, the laws social scientists seek are quite unlike the laws discovered by physicists, chemists, and other natural scientists.[5]

Engels, by contrast, believed that the new "science" of **dialectics** showed that the laws governing nature and society were one and the same. According to dialectics, everything—nature, history, even human thought—is nothing more than matter moving in accordance with the timeless "laws" of dialectics. And "dialectics," he wrote, is "the science of the most general laws of all motion. Therein is included that their laws must be equally valid for motion in nature and human history and for the motion of thought." Just as "all true knowledge of nature is knowledge of the eternal, the infinite, and hence essentially absolute," so too, Engels claimed, is all true knowledge of human beings and their history absolute and unchanging.[6]

On this dogmatic and rigidified "science" of "dialectics" Engels erected his claims for scientific socialism. Engels maintained that scientific socialism—that is, his (and, he claimed, Marx's) version of socialism—was not simply one political ideology among many competitors, but an unchallengeable scientific account of how things were and must always be. Any socialist who argued otherwise was merely a "utopian" whose views rested more on sentiment or opinion than on science.[7] Such dogmatic self-certitude represented a dramatic departure from the young Marx's call for a "relentless critique of all that exists"—including existing conceptions of science.

Materialism   As we saw in the preceding chapter, Marx called himself a materialist, largely in order to distinguish his views from those of Hegel and other philosophical idealists of whom he was highly critical. But he was no less critical of earlier "crude" materialists like Thomas Hobbes, who believed that the world and everything (and everyone) in it consisted of nothing but physical matter in motion. According to this view, human thoughts and actions are merely the effects of physical forces beyond human control. In the "Theses on Feuerbach," Marx heaped ridicule upon this kind of crude **materialism:**

> The materialist doctrine that men are products of circumstances and upbringing, and that, therefore, changed men are products of other circumstances and changed upbringing, forgets that it is men that change circumstances and that the educator himself needs educating. . . .[8]

Marx was a materialist in another and altogether different sense. He was not concerned with "matter" per se, but with the ways in which human beings organize themselves in order to survive and flourish by transforming raw materials into humanly useful objects, artifacts, and commodities. These ways, in their turn, "influence" or "condition" (*bedingen*) the way in which people think about themselves and their world.

Engels's version of materialism has more in common with the materialism of Hobbes than with that of Marx. Everything, Engels asserts, is reducible to matter and its transformations. However extensive the changes, matter remains eternally the same, its "motions" governed by timeless "iron laws":

> [W]e have the certainty that matter remains eternally the same in all its transformations, that none of its attributes can ever be lost, and therefore, also, that with the same iron necessity that it will exterminate on the earth its highest creation, the thinking mind, it must somewhere else and at another time again produce it.[9]

Thus Engels's emphasis on matter in motion stands in curious contrast to Marx's emphasis on human beings in motion, making and remaking their world into a more humanly habitable place.

The Revisionists

At the turn of the century some Marxists favored revising Marxian theory in the light of economic and political developments that had occurred since Marx's death. The leading theorist among this group, which came to be known as the **revisionists**, was Eduard Bernstein (1850–1932). A prominent figure in the German Social Democratic party, Bernstein believed that some aspects of Marx's theory were either false or out of date and should, accordingly, be rejected or revised. Hence the name *revisionist*.

An early and active member of the SDP, Bernstein had to flee Germany to avoid imprisonment under the antisocialist laws in effect from 1878 to 1890. Bernstein's "temporary" exile in England was to last 20 years. He met Marx and Engels there, and found both old men to be a good deal less dogmatic than many self-styled Marxists were. While in England, Bernstein also came under the influence of **Fabian socialism** (discussed later in this chapter), which favored a strategy of gradual reform as the best way of creating a socialist society in Britain. Bernstein, too, came to believe that an evolutionary path to socialism was morally and politically preferable to a violent revolutionary one—as the title of his *Evolutionary Socialism* (1899) implies.

Bernstein regarded himself as a Marxist, in spirit if not always in letter. To reject those aspects of Marx's theory that were false and to revise those that were outmoded was, he thought, in the best critical scientific spirit of Marx himself, for the mark of a genuinely scientific theory is that its truth is open to question and criticism. Just as Marx had criticized his predecessors, so Bernstein did not flinch from criticizing Marx. His criticisms fall into three categories: moral, political, and economic.

Moral Criticism Bernstein believed, first of all, that Marx and later Marxists had been too little concerned with ethics or morality. This omission had two aspects. For one thing, Marx had maintained that ethical values and beliefs belong to the **ideological superstructure** of society and therefore depend upon the economic **base**. From this it follows that ethical views and values are dependent upon nonethical factors; they can be effects, but never causes, of social actions and institutions. On this point, however, Bernstein followed the German philosopher Immanuel Kant (1724–1804), who held that one's will is free of outside influences or causes. A person is free, then, to choose (or will) as one pleases; but one also has a duty to make morally responsible choices.

A second and even more worrying aspect is that Marxian socialists had focused on the *end*—the coming of a communist society—without worrying about the morality or immorality of the *means* used to arrive at that end. "To me," Bernstein wrote, "that which is generally called the ultimate aim of socialism is nothing, but the movement is everything."[10] By this Bernstein meant that socialists should think about the morality of the means by which they propose to bring about a socialist society. A society born in blood is unlikely to be as peaceful and democratic as one that evolves by nonviolent means. Since ends and means are inextricably bound together, a just society cannot be created by unjust means. Nor can a democratic society come about by undemocratic means. And socialism without democracy is not worth having—indeed, without democracy socialism cannot exist.[11] Moreover, Bernstein believed that Marxists who focus upon distant aims rather than on shorter-term goals were themselves naively and dangerously utopian. To the extent that Marxists—including Marx himself—fix their gaze exclusively on the final victory of socialism, there "remains a real residue of Utopianism in the Marxist system."[12] His own brand of "practical political socialism," by contrast, "places near aims in front of distant ones."[13] In these respects, then, Bernstein was echoing what Lassalle had said earlier about the relation between ends and means:

> Show us not the aim without the way.
> For ends and means on earth are so entangled
> That changing one, you change the other too;
> Each different path brings different ends in view.[14]

Political Criticism   Besides his ethical reservations, Bernstein expressed doubts about some of Marx's political pronouncements. He pointed to a number of remarkable developments since Marx's death—developments that ran counter to Marx's expectations. For one, the labor movement in Germany and elsewhere had grown larger and stronger, partly because working-class males in most industrial countries could now vote. The socialist parties that maintained close ties with trade unions and other working-class organizations had also gained size and strength. The antisocialist laws passed by Bismarck in 1878 had been repealed in 1890, making it possible for socialist parties to organize, to recruit members openly, and to send representatives to the *Reichstag* (the German parliament), where they could propose legislation favoring working-class interests, including the graduated income tax and a shorter workweek. For the first time it appeared that the state, instead of suppressing the workers, could—as Lassalle had insisted—be their ally and guardian. These, in Bernstein's view, were hopeful developments pointing toward the possibility of a peaceful transition to socialism.

Economic Criticism   No less important, Bernstein claimed, were certain newly emergent economic facts and trends that tended to undermine Marx's theory. Indeed, he charged, "certain statements in *Capital* . . . are falsified by facts."[15] For example, Marx had predicted that wealth would be concentrated in fewer and fewer hands, until the few were very rich and the many were very poor. But, Bernstein noted, this has not happened in the advanced capitalist countries. Far from growing poorer and more miserable, the workers had, on the whole, become better off. Citing statistics, Bernstein showed that the real income of workers had risen in the latter part of the nineteenth century. Consequently, more workers were able to afford decent housing, better food and clothing, and other of life's amenities. These developments were not due to the generosity of the bourgeoisie, but to the success of trade unions in raising wages and improving working conditions.

To critics who complained that comfortable workers suffer from **false consciousness** and are apt to lose sight of socialist goals and aspirations, Bernstein replied:

> One has not overcome Utopianism if one assumes that there is in the present, or ascribes to the present, what is to be in the future. We [socialists] have to take working men as they are. And they are neither so universally pauperised as [Marx and Engels had predicted] in the *Communist Manifesto*, nor so free from prejudices and weaknesses as their courtiers wish to make us believe. They have the virtues and failings of the economic and social conditions under which they live.[16]

For his part, Bernstein had no doubt that these conditions were gradually improving and would continue to improve as long as workers continued to organize themselves into trade unions and political parties that would promote their interests.

When Bernstein brought these ideas back to Germany in the late 1890s, they proved to be both influential and controversial. The German Social Democratic party did, in the end, come to favor a peaceful parliamentary path to socialism, but not without a good deal of fighting and feuding within party ranks. Former friends and allies, including Karl Kautsky (1854–1938), broke with Bernstein over the issue. Some years later, Kautsky, who initially maintained that revolution remained a viable possibility for socialists, finally came to share Bernstein's view.[17] Other breakaway socialist factions, such as the Spartacists, led by Rosa Luxemburg and Karl Liebknecht, remained revolutionists who were adamantly opposed to Bernstein's revised version of Marxism. And Russian Marxists branded Bernstein a traitor to Marxism.[18] While revisionist Marxism was carrying the day in Germany and other advanced capitalist countries, a very different variant was taking shape to the east.

Soviet Marxism-Leninism

The Russian Context   Compared with North America and most of the countries of western Europe, Russia in the late nineteenth century was economically and politically backward. Its economy was mainly agricultural, its industrial base relatively small, and its factories few and inefficient. The vast majority of its people were not proletarian wage laborers working in factories, but peasants who tilled the land in exchange for a portion of the produce. And Russia was as politically primitive as it was economically backward. Its institutions were undemocratic, its tsar an autocratic ruler, and its hereditary nobility oppressive and largely indifferent to the suffering of the common people.

Such a semifeudal society seemed singularly unlikely to spawn the kind of revolution that Marx had expected. Proletarian revolution, after all, required a large proletarian class, not a class of peasants afflicted with what Marx in the *Manifesto* called "the idiocy of rural life." Largely illiterate and often strongly superstitious, such people seemed unlikely to make a revolution. Yet there was discontent—not only among peasants in the countryside, but also among workers and intellectuals in the cities. Many Russian intellectuals, particularly the more radical among them, saw themselves as the conscience and voice of a vast and still-sleeping majority who would one day wake up, feel their power, and remake Russian society from the ground up. Until then, the task of intellectuals was to try to rouse that sleeping giant and to prepare it for its destiny.

Different groups of intellectuals had different visions of what that destiny was to be. Some saw the Russian people, particularly the Slavs, as the most spiritual of the world's people, destined to live—and to show others how to live—spiritually rich and meaningful lives. Others saw Russians as future Europeans, destined to be united with other western European peoples. Still others saw Russia as a land ripe for a revolution that would shake the world and usher in a new era of equality, freedom, and communal harmony.

Tsarist Russia permitted virtually no freedom of debate or discussion. Opposition parties were outlawed. Police spies and informers were everywhere, and the jails and prisons were full of dissidents and political prisoners. Political discussions were generally confined to small groups of people who met in secret and at considerable risk to themselves, their friends, and their families. Their views reached a wider audience through illicit pamphlets and newspapers that were published secretly and passed from hand to hand. This atmosphere of secrecy and intrigue produced plots and conspiracies aplenty. Some became terrorists who tried to strike at the heart of the tsarist system itself by killing the Tsar. One of these, a young student named Alexander Ulyanov, paid with his life for his part in an unsuccessful attempt to assassinate Tsar Alexander II.

Alexander Ulyanov had an adoring younger brother, Vladimir, who wanted to be a lawyer and live a quiet and respectable life. But Alexander's execution changed all that. Vladimir Ilyich Ulyanov (1870–1924) became a revolutionary opponent of the tsarist regime, going underground, and taking a new identity and a new name—Lenin.

Lenin's Contributions   With the help of the Russian Marxist philosopher Georgi Plekhanov (1856–1918), Lenin plunged into an intensive study of the few works of Marx and Engels then available. These included *Capital* and the *Communist Manifesto*, but not *The German Ideology*, the *Economic and Philosophical Manuscripts* of 1844, or several other important works. The main lesson Lenin learned from his studies, and subsequently sought to apply in practice, is that class struggle is the chief driving force of historical development. For the revolutionary, rational political action consists of following strategies for intensifying and taking advantage of class divisions and differences. Anything that helps to accomplish that end is justifiable. For the sake of the political struggle one may lie, cheat, steal, embrace enemies, betray friends—all is acceptable if it serves the purpose of the class struggle.

The revolutionary, for Lenin, must be hardened against "softness" and "sentimentality," ready to reject the most elementary imperatives of "bourgeois" ethics if they interfere with the political struggle. Lenin heaped scorn on Bernstein and others who tried to supplement Marx's theory of history with Kant's theory of ethics. For Kantian moral imperatives—to keep one's promises and to treat others as ends, never as means—Lenin had nothing but contempt. "Promises," he wrote, "are like pie crusts—made to be broken." To the objection that Lenin's revolutionary morality permitted people to be treated as mere means to some supposedly greater end, Lenin replied, "You cannot make an omelette without breaking eggs"—the implication being that you cannot make a revolution without breaking heads. Revolution is a tough, dirty, mean, and bloody undertaking, and revolutionaries must face that fact. They must be hardened not only against the influence of bourgeois morality, but against anything that might sap their revolutionary will—even art and music. Lenin loved music but, as his friend Maxim Gorky recalled,

> One evening in Moscow, when Lenin was listening to Beethoven sonatas, . . . he said: "I know nothing greater than the Appassionata; I'd like to listen to it every day. It's beautiful, superhuman music. I always think proudly—it may be naive— what marvelous things people can do. . . . But I can't listen to music too often, it . . . makes you want to say kind, silly things, to stroke the heads of the people who, living in a terrible hell, can create such beauty. Nowadays you mustn't stroke anyone's head, you'd get your hand bitten off, you've got to hit them over their heads, without mercy, although, ideally, we're against the use of force. H'm, H'm, our duty is infernally hard."[19]

Lenin's view of the hardened revolutionary personality carried over to his vision of the communist party. Marx had viewed the communist movement as a large, inclusive, and broadly based organization of working people from many countries. But Lenin believed that the communist party should be small, exclusive, highly organized, tightly disciplined, and conspiratorial. No other party, he argued, could succeed in overthrowing the Russian police-state. Lenin's view was put to the test in 1903. A rival wing of the Russian Communist party wanted a less exclusive and more open party. Through some adroit maneuvering in this internal party struggle, Lenin's wing of the party gained control and began to call themselves Bolsheviks (meaning "majority"—i.e., the majority within the Russian Communist party).

In Lenin's view, the party's role is to agitate, organize, and educate the workers, teaching them where their "true" interests lie. The "function of the proletarian vanguard," Lenin wrote, "consists in training, educating, enlightening and drawing into the new life the most backward strata and masses of

V. I. (Ulyanov) Lenin (1870–1924).

the working class and the peasantry."[20] This was necessary, Lenin believed, because most working people suffer from false consciousness, the most pernicious form of which is "trade-union consciousness":

> the working class, exclusively by its own effort, is able to develop only trade-union consciousness, i.e. the conviction that it is necessary to combine in unions, fight the employers, and strive to compel the government to pass necessary labor legislation, etc.[21]

Revolutionary class consciousness cannot, or at all events should not be allowed to, come about spontaneously and by itself. It must instead be imported into the working class from outside, by a **vanguard party** whose leadership was to consist primarily of revolutionary intellectuals. Without such a vanguard to show the way, Lenin feared, the working class would not only fail to become a revolutionary force; it would become downright reactionary.

Yet this vanguard party was to be democratic in two rather restricted respects. The first was that it claimed to represent the real or true interests of the modern *demos*, the proletariat and the peasantry. Secondly, the party was to be, in itself, a microcosm of the democratic society that was to come. Inside the party, free discussion was to be permitted. But once a vote was taken and an issue decided, discussion was to cease and everyone was to follow the orders of the central leadership. This notion of internal party democracy Lenin called **democratic centralism**. Democracy throughout society was not yet feasible, he believed, because the masses still could not be trusted to know their own real interests. Left to their own devices, without a vanguard party to tutor and guide them, the workers would make wrong or even reactionary decisions.

Lenin's low opinion of the working-class mentality was even further confirmed in 1914, with the outbreak of World War I. Marx had argued that the proletariat was an international class, without a fatherland. Nevertheless, in 1914, workers—many of whom called themselves socialists—volunteered in droves to fight workers from other countries. What had happened? Was Marx wrong? Or were other factors at work that Marx had not taken into sufficient account?

What had happened, Lenin argued in *Imperialism, the Highest Stage of Capitalism* (1916), was that the workers in the advanced capitalist countries— England, Germany, Italy, France, Belgium, and eventually the United States as well—were willing to go to war against their fellow proletarians because they had come to have a stake in their respective countries' **imperialism**, or policies of colonization and exploitation of peoples in Africa, Asia, and South America. Each capitalist country had carved out "spheres of influence"—a polite phrase they used to mask brutal exploitation that exceeded even that of early capitalism in the West. World War I was a war for cheap labor, cheap raw materials, and foreign markets, Lenin said. The scene of the most brutal capitalist oppression had shifted from Europe and North America to the countries on the capitalist periphery—the Third World, as we say nowadays. Diamond miners in South Africa, tin miners in Bolivia, copper miners in Chile—these and scores of other Third World laborers were being worked to death for subsistence wages. Any attempt to organize unions or to strike for higher wages and improved working conditions was harshly suppressed by the armed forces of the occupying imperial power. That was why the U.S. Marines were in Latin America and the Caribbean, the British army in India, and the French Foreign Legion in north Africa.

Meanwhile, according to Lenin, European and American workers were being allowed to organize into trade unions to demand a larger share of an ever-expanding economic pie—an expansion made possible by the "super-profits" that their countries' capitalists were extracting from the land, labor, and resources of these poorer nations. The capitalists were thus able to "bribe" their "own" workers and trade unionists with higher wages, shorter hours, better working conditions, health insurance plans, and other benefits. This, said Lenin, is the real source of the rising wages and standard of living touted by Bernstein and the Revisionists.[22]

Four important and far-reaching conclusions followed from Lenin's analysis of *imperialism*. First, it reconfirmed Lenin's suspicion of the revisionists and his hostility toward them. He saw the revisionists as the allies of, and apologists for, the capitalist class that they claimed to oppose. Second, members of the working class in the advanced capitalist countries have been infected with trade-union consciousness. They have, in effect, become "bourgeois" and cannot be counted on to make the revolution that Marx had predicted—at least not without the help of a vanguard party to lead the way. Which brings us to the third conclusion: the party plays the important, indeed indispensable, role of raising the consciousness of the working class. A fourth and especially significant conclusion is that the revolution will come first to those areas in which the proletariat is both "immiserated" and led by an active vanguard party. Instead of occurring first in the most advanced capitalist countries, as Marx expected, proletarian revolutions will begin in the more "backward" nations of the world—in Russia and China, for example.

In 1917 revolution came to Russia. Afraid he would miss it altogether, Lenin returned from exile barely in time to take an active and leading part. The Russian Revolution of 1917 did not correspond to anyone's predictions—certainly not Marx's and not even Lenin's. The Tsar had committed the Russian army to join the English and French in fighting against Germany in World War I. Ill-trained, ill-equipped, and badly led, the Russian army suffered one defeat after another. Morale in the army was low and the casualty rate high. Meanwhile, back in Russia, the people—the peasants in particular—were suffering from shortages of food and fuel, high taxes, and the loss of their sons and brothers in an apparently endless and pointless war. They wanted an end to it. In March 1917 riots broke out in Petrograd (St. Petersburg) and other Russian cities. Tsar Nicholas ordered his soldiers to stop the revolt, but they refused. Less than two weeks later, the Tsar stepped down, to be replaced by a provisional government soon to be headed by Alexander Kerensky, a non-Bolshevik socialist committed to continuing the war against Germany. In October 1917 the Bolsheviks stormed the Winter Palace, seat of Kerensky's government, and seized state power. Lenin was named premier, and a government based on *soviets* (workers' councils) was declared.

The Bolshevik government attempted to restructure Russian society from the ground up. It seized mines, mills, factories, and other large manufacturing facilities and put them in the hands of the soviets. The new government also confiscated large tracts of land and gave them to the peasants. Although such measures were popular among peasants and workers, they were viewed with alarm by wealthy landowners and other privileged groups, who soon started a civil war or counterrevolution to regain state power. From 1918 to 1920, the Red or revolutionary forces fought the White or reactionary forces, the latter with the help of troops and supplies from England, the United States, and other capitalist countries. By 1920 the Whites were defeated, but there was dissension within the ranks of peasants and workers. There were revolts and strikes and even a sailors' mutiny at the Kronstadt naval base. Lenin realized that the new government could not consolidate its power without rebuilding an economy wrecked by war, revolution, and counterrevolution. His solution was the New Economic Policy (NEP) of 1921, which replaced the more radical socialist measures (known as "war communism," because of the shortages brought about by World War I) instituted earlier. Under the NEP (1921–1928) the government retained control of the major manufacturing concerns but permitted peasants to farm their own land and sell their produce for a profit. The NEP gave the Bolshevik government a breathing space and bought it time to consolidate state power. It was during this period that the secret police—the forerunner of today's KGB—was established to keep an eye on potential counterrevolutionaries. During this period also, Lenin's health began to decline. In 1924 he died.

Stalin's Contribution   Before his death, Lenin warned his fellow Bolsheviks to beware of Joseph Stalin. The warning proved prophetic. From 1929 until his death in 1953, Stalin ruled the Soviet Union and its Communist party with a ruthlessness virtually unmatched in history, leaving a legacy of political repression that lingers to this day. He also left his mark on Marxism-Leninism, the ideology by which he justified his actions and policies for nearly a quarter of a century.

Joseph Stalin (1879–1953) was born Iosif Djugashvili in Russian Georgia. The son of pious parents, he was sent in 1894 to the Tbilisi seminary to be educated for the priesthood in the Russian Orthodox Church. Before he was expelled from the seminary, he apparently learned several valuable lessons that he never forgot. One was to put the best face on a convoluted or even logically invalid argument so as to make it appear straightforward and logically valid. Another was that, if logical argument does not convince, simplification and ritualistic repetition will. All "lessons" must be hammered home with an air of infallibility and a certain repetitive intensity. And, not least, young Djugashvili took away the lesson that texts—even sacred texts—are open to interpretation and sometimes, even, to radical reinterpretation. To have one's own interpretation of a sacred text accepted as authoritative can itself be a source of considerable power.

After leaving the seminary in 1899, Djugashvili drifted into politics, joining the Russian Social Democratic Labor party in 1901. When that party split into two factions in 1903, he sided with Lenin and the Bolsheviks. Like many of his fellow party members he, too, took on a new name—Stalin (meaning "man of steel"). The name was well chosen. Stalin had an appetite for danger and intrigue. He participated in several bank robberies to fatten the coffers of the fledgling party, for instance, and soon developed a reputation for undertaking dirty and difficult tasks for the party. His stature within the party grew apace. Partly because Stalin was so ruthless and cunning, Lenin came to distrust his Georgian comrade. But with Lenin's death in 1924, the main obstacle to Stalin's advancement was removed.

Joseph (Djugashvili) Stalin (1879–1953).

In the late 1920s Stalin began consolidating his own power within the Party and the country by discrediting and eventually eliminating all remaining opposition, whether personal, political or theoretical. Although he was no match for theorists like Lenin or Leon Trotsky (1879–1940), Stalin nevertheless felt it necessary to portray himself as the Party's preeminent theorist. What he lacked in subtlety he more than made up for in simplicity. As the Soviet historian Roy Medvedev observes:

> In philosophy Stalin was at best a dilettante. He lacked both systematic training and genuine self-education. He never made a real study of Hegel, Kant, . . . or, judging by his pronouncements, the philosophical works of Marx, Engels, and Lenin. All his philosophical writings are marked by primitivism, oversimplification, superficiality, and a penchant for dogmatic schematization.[23]

In Stalin's writings, Medvedev adds, "originality is notable by its absence. Propositions that were hailed as great discoveries by propagandists of the

[Stalin] cult were actually trivial platitudes. But it must be granted that Stalin was a master at making these platitudes seem important."[24]

To ensure that his interpretation of Marxism-Leninism was beyond question and above criticism, Stalin proceeded to eliminate questioners and critics—particularly those who had some knowledge of Marxian theory. This serves to explain why Stalin's emergence as the preeminent Marxist-Leninist theoretician coincided with the political purges and show trials of the 1930s. Leading Bolsheviks—many of them heroes of the October Revolution that brought the Communists to power—were purged from the party, put on public trial to "confess" to crimes they had not committed, and shot or sent to Siberia to starve or freeze to death. Trotsky, living in exile in Mexico, was murdered on Stalin's orders. By these brutal means Stalin sought to eliminate not only potential political opponents, but theoretical or ideological critics as well. Ironically, the purge extended even to the writings of Marx and Engels themselves. Stalin suppressed publication of the authoritative edition of Marx and Engels's works, the *MEGA* (*Marx-Engels Gesamteausgabe*), and ordered its editor, David Riazanov, shot. He also saw to it that several of Lenin's writings were excluded from his *Collected Works*.[25] At the same time he directed the rewriting of Russian history, falsely portraying himself as Lenin's closest confidant, advisor, ally, and natural heir.

What, then, are the distinguishing features of Stalinism as a variant of (some would say a departure from) Marxism-Leninism? Three features are especially noteworthy. One concerns the role of the party and party leadership. Lenin had held that the working class suffers from false consciousness and needs a vanguard party to guide it. Stalin held that the party itself is afflicted with false consciousness and needs a vanguard—a single, all-wise, all-knowing genius—to guide it. That all-knowing guide was, of course, Stalin himself. This is the "theoretical" foundation for the "cult of personality" that Stalin built around himself.

A second feature of Stalinism is its notion of "socialism in one country." Socialism, said Stalin, must be created and consolidated in one country—the Soviet Union—before it can be constructed anywhere else. This is at odds with what Marx and Engels had to say about the international character of the socialist movement. Proceeding from this premise, Stalin's rival Leon Trotsky not only denied that it was possible to build socialism in a single country; he also advocated "permanent revolution"—by which he meant that the revolution, even in the Soviet Union, can realize its aims only if the party remains vigorous, vital, and alert to the dangers of despotism within its own ranks. Trotsky ceased saying such things after one of Stalin's secret agents buried an ice-axe in the back of his head.

A third feature of Stalinism is to be found in Stalin's strategy of justification and legitimation. Stalin employed "dialectics" to justify virtually every plan, policy, and result. According to Stalin's version of **dialectical materialism** (or **DiaMat**)—a phrase, incidentally, that Marx never used—there are no accidents or coincidences; all is determined by the movement of matter and everything that happens had to happen as it did.[26] That this doctrine of "historical inevitability" commits the elementary logical fallacy of *post hoc, ergo propter hoc*—roughly, if one event occurred before another, the first must have caused the second—did not trouble Stalin.[27] His brand of logic was itself "dialectical." With it even the most brazen contradiction could be reconciled "dialectically." Consider the following example:

> We stand for the withering away of the state. At the same time we stand for the strengthening of the dictatorship of the proletariat, which is the mightiest and strongest state power that has ever existed. . . . Is this "contradictory"? Yes, it is contradictory. But this contradiction is bound up with life, and it fully reflects Marx's dialectics.[28]

What Stalin omits to note, of course, is that Marx believed that the purpose of criticism was to expose contradictions as a prelude to overcoming them, and not—as Stalin would have it—to accepting or acquiescing in them. By means of such casuistry Stalin offered "dialectical" justifications for any position or action, however heinous.

Stalin's reign of terror came to an end with his death in 1953. Three years later the new leader of the Soviet Union, Nikita Khrushchev (1894–1971), denounced Stalin's crimes before the Twentieth Party Congress. His anti-Stalinist successors, including Mikhail Gorbachev, have continued to do so, despite opposition from a small but vocal pro-Stalinist faction within the Party. Today, as the Soviet Union enters the last decade of the twentieth century, it is still haunted by Stalin's ghost. Whether or to what extent that ghost can or will be exorcised by means of **glasnost** (openness) and **perestroika** (restructuring) remains to be seen.

Chinese Communism

The other global power whose ruling party calls itself communist is the People's Republic of China. With its increasing industrial might and a population of more than a billion—one out of five people alive today is Chinese—China plays an increasingly important role on the world's stage. If we are to understand current Chinese thinking and actions, we must know something about China's past and its revolutionary path to the present.

The Chinese Context   The ideological thread of Chinese history over the last century consists of many complex strands. The oldest is Confucianism, a body of doctrine drawn from the teachings of Confucius (551–479 B.C.). As a political perspective, Confucianism stresses order, hierarchy, respect for the monarchy and one's parents, and a bureaucracy managed by a learned elite, the Mandarins. A second strand, Chinese nationalism, was born of a reaction against nineteenth century European, American, and Japanese colonialism and foreign occupation. For a proud and ancient people to be economically dominated by "barbarians" was especially galling. Repeated attempts by the Chinese to drive the foreigners out—as in the Boxer Rebellion of 1899, for example—were suppressed by better armed foreign forces. In 1905 the Nationalists under Sun Yat-sen established a nominally independent Chinese Republic. After a series of setbacks China was unified under the Nationalist leader, Generalissimo Chiang Kai-shek, in 1928.

But Chiang's Nationalist party was not without rivals. The still-new Chinese Communist party (CCP), founded in 1921, represents a third strand in China's ideological configuration. While a young library assistant at Beijing University, Mao Ze-dong (1893–1976) was among the first to join the newly formed CCP. Mao had been electrified by the news of the 1917 Russian Revolution and had set about studying the works of Marx, Engels, and Lenin to see what lessons they might contain for China. Unable to read any language other than Chinese, however, Mao's choice of readings was severely restricted. Most of the works of Marx and Engels—with the exception of the *Communist Manifesto* and several other short works—had not yet been translated into Chinese. But a number of Lenin's essays were beginning to appear in translation. One of these, Lenin's *Imperialism*, was to have a decisive influence on Mao's thinking.

Mao was drawn to Lenin's theory of imperialism for several reasons. First, it seemed especially well-suited to Chinese conditions. For one thing, China had no sizable industrial proletariat; the vast majority of its people were peasants who tilled the soil. For another, the imperialist powers found in China vast resources—abundant raw materials and cheap labor—and a large foreign market for their own manufactured goods. Little wonder, Mao reasoned, that the advanced capitalist countries sought "superprofits" in China. But Lenin's analysis not only served to explain several puzzling features of modern Chinese history; it also offered a prescription—revolution not as the internal class war that Marx had predicted, but as an anti-imperialist "war of national liberation" waged by the people of an economically backward nation against their foreign capitalist oppressors.

Certainly China in the 1920s was neither prosperous nor powerful. Most of its people were pitifully poor. Nearly three out of four were poor peasants who owned less than an acre of land, or none at all, and survived by working for the landlords of vast estates. There was little heavy industry. Only about one of every two hundred Chinese could be classified as proletarians in Marx's sense. The rest were mostly so-called rich peasants who, like Mao's parents, owned and farmed small plots. Mao's most original contribution to—or perhaps departure from—Marxism was his proposal to make a revolution that would downplay the importance of the urban proletariat and concentrate instead on harnessing the pent-up resentments of the peasants.

The Rural Proletariat   Mao's proposal to rely on the Chinese peasantry rested on several factors. First, poor peasants constituted an overwhelming majority of the Chinese population. Once organized and mobilized, they would be an almost irresistible force. Second, they were also the poorest and most oppressed sector of the populace. They therefore had everything to gain and little to lose by waging an all-out struggle against their oppressors. And finally, Mao believed that the peasants were endowed with a kind of practical wisdom or common sense that comes not from books or theories, but from experience.

Mao Ze-dong (1893–1976).

If a revolution was to be made in China, it must be made by peasants led by
a party whose leaders spoke their language and thought as they thought. Many
of Mao's speeches and writings were, accordingly, directed against abstract
theorizing and couched in a folksy style calculated to appeal to peasants:

> Marxism-Leninism has no decorative value, nor has it mystical value. It is only
> extremely useful. It seems that, right up to the present, quite a few have regarded
> Marxism-Leninism as a ready-made panacea: once you have it, you can cure all
> your ills with little effort. This is . . . childish. . . . Those who regard Marxism-
> Leninism as religious dogma show this type of blind ignorance. We must tell them
> openly, "Your dogma is of no use," or to use an impolite phrase, "Your dogma is
> less useful than excrement." We see that dog excrement can fertilize the fields,

and man's can feed the dog. And dogmas? They can't fertilize the fields, nor can they feed a dog. Of what use are they?[29]

Mao's Amendments   Although many of Mao's writings are concerned with "practice"—particularly with ways in which to mobilize the peasantry and the appropriate military strategy and tactics to use in different situations—he did amend Marxian theory in several significant ways. The first, as we have noted already, was to downplay the importance of the urban proletariat and to mold the peasantry into a revolutionary force. Revolution was to begin in the countryside. As the rural revolutionary forces gained strength, they could then encircle the cities and force them into submission. A second significant amendment was to downplay the importance of "objective" conditions, stressing instead the central role of "subjective" factors. In Mao's later life, especially, his revision of Marxian theory placed "consciousness" or political "will" above material or objective conditions. A third distinctive contribution was Mao's recasting of the concepts of class and class struggle. In Mao's hands the concept of class, which was of course central to classical Marxism, was largely replaced by the concept of nation. More specifically, Mao redescribed international relations in terms of class. China, he claimed, was a poor and oppressed "proletarian" nation that needed to throw off the yoke of the wealthy "bourgeois" oppressor nations. Far from being a purely internal struggle, then, the Chinese Revolution pitted proletarian nationalist forces against the representatives of international capitalism. The Nationalist party, some of whose leaders had encouraged and profited from foreign investment, was merely the Chinese agent or representative of the bourgeois nations. The struggle against Chiang and the Nationalists was therefore a struggle against the United States and other capitalist nations, which supported Chiang. The Chinese Revolution was, moreover, to be the model or prototype for revolutionary activity in Asia and Africa.[30] In a series of wars of national liberation, the proletarian nations of the Third World will surround and starve the wealthy capitalist nations into submission. In short, Mao advocated that national liberation movements in the Third World employ the tactics that had proved so successful in the CCP revolutionary victory of 1948–1949.

All these amendments are a far cry from anything that Marx had anticipated. But, on reflection, this is not entirely surprising. Mao had initially viewed Marx and Marxism through Leninist lenses. He adopted Lenin's notion that the Communist party must be the vanguard that leads the people to revolution, for instance, and must then serve as the dictator in the name of the proletariat. Even his Leninist views were later filtered through Stalin's supposedly authoritative interpretations of what Lenin said, or meant. Mao's was therefore Marxism seen as through a glass darkly, and even suspiciously. Yet even as Mao maintained that one should not be an uncritical worshipper at the shrine of Marx or any other Marxist, he nevertheless proclaimed the purity and sanctity of his own version of Marxism. As he and the Chinese Revolution grew older, Mao became more and more a cult figure and object of veneration. The hero of the Chinese Revolution was transformed into a larger-than-life figure, "The Great Helmsman," whose every thought and deed were magnified to mythic proportions.

Reds and Experts   By the mid-1960s Mao's cult of personality was building toward a disruptive and in many ways disastrous conclusion—the so-called Cultural Revolution. To understand the theoretical roots of the Cultural Revolution, we must take note of Mao's distinction between being "red" and being "expert." To be "red" was to be ideologically pure and correct; to be "expert" was to emphasize technical proficiency instead of ideological correctness. Mao, who favored the former over the latter, felt that by the mid-1960s the pendulum had swung too far in the direction of the expert. Ideological purity was in danger. So he called for a "cultural revolution" that would oust the experts and restore the reds to their rightful role. Workers were encouraged to humiliate managers and engineers, and students to humble their professors. Many experts were killed or imprisoned or removed from their posts and sent to work in the fields. What had been up was now down, and vice versa. In this topsy-turvy situation, industrial and agricultural production fell drastically, with widespread suffering the result. So disruptive was the Cultural Revolution that Mao finally agreed to call the army in to restore order in factories, in universities, and throughout society.

The Cultural Revolution left many of China's institutions and its economy in a shambles. It also damaged Mao's reputation among the Chinese. The radicals, including Mao's wife, were discredited, and pragmatists like Deng Xiaoping (1904–) gained the upper hand after Mao's death in 1976. Since then China has concentrated its energies on building its economic infrastructure. Under Deng's leadership, China began to reintroduce some features of a free market economy, including extensive commerce with capitalist countries. Some steps were also taken in the direction of freedom of speech, especially the freedom to criticize the Communist party leadership; but these were halted when the tanks and troops of the People's Liberation Army crushed the peaceful demonstration of Chinese students and their supporters in Beijing's Tiananmen Square in June 1989. In the wake of this incident and the wave of brutal repression that followed it, the fate of China and the future of Mao's uniquely Chinese brand of Marxism—"Mao Zedong thought"—remains unclear.

NON-MARXIST SOCIALISM

Marx and his followers have been the most influential of all socialists. For much of the twentieth century, in fact, about one-third of the world's population lived in countries governed by regimes that claimed to be Marxist. But Marx and the Marxists have by no means been the only founts of socialist or communist theory and practice. As we noted earlier, there have been, and continue to be, many non-Marxian voices in the socialist chorus. Indeed, there are so many varieties of non-Marxian socialism that we can scarcely list them, much less describe them in any detail. We conclude our history of socialism, then, with brief discussions of several of the more important and influential varieties of non-Marxist socialism.

Anarcho-communism

Marx's main rivals within the ranks of the European socialist movement were the *anarchists*.[31] We have already seen, in Chapter 1, that anarchists agree only on one key point: that the state is an evil that ought to be replaced by a system of voluntary cooperation. But there the agreement ends. Some anarchists are radical individualists; others are communalists. Some advocate the violent overthrow of the state; others are pacifists who advocate a more peaceful path to a cooperative society. With the exception of the libertarian or individualist anarchists discussed in Chapter 3, however, all have played a part in the socialist tradition.

One of the earliest attempts to articulate and defend anarchism was William Godwin's *Enquiry Concerning Political Justice* (1793). Godwin (1756–1836), an Englishman, maintained that the state was by its very nature oppressive, and likely to become more so unless it were somehow stopped. One way to do this, he thought, was by making communities small enough to be governed directly by their members, so as not to need the coercive control of the state. So far as property ownership was concerned, however, Godwin was not a consistent communist.[32] In this respect he differs from many later anarchists who held that the state is necessary as long as property is privately owned. For these socialist anarchists, or proponents of **anarcho-communism**, the abolition of the state and the abolition of private property are two sides of the same coin.

In contrast to the popular image of the bomb-throwing anarchist, many anarcho-communists have also made a strong moral case for pacifism and non-violence. One of these, Count Leo Tolstoy (1828–1910)—the author of *War and Peace* and other great novels—held fast to the pacifist principle that violence in any form is always wrong. A devout Christian, Tolstoy believed that this principle applies to the violence that the state does or is prepared to do to its citizens. Why else, he asked, does it maintain a system of police, courts, tax collectors, and prisons? Why else does it employ an executioner? Without these means whereby one human being does violence to another, the state would not exist. The state is, by its very nature, a violent institution. Violence being categorically wrong, the only moral thing to do is to get rid of the state, replacing it with a system of voluntary cooperation in which every person assists others and is in turn assisted by them.

How can such a society be brought into being? Peacefully, Tolstoy believed. The transition to anarchy can and should be accomplished by the power of persuasion—by persuading the rich to part with their wealth and by persuading everyone to withdraw support from the state and its institutions. But on this point there has been considerable disagreement among anarchists. Some, such as Tolstoy's countrymen Peter Kropotkin (1842–1921) and Mikhail Bakunin (1814–1876), have held that violent means may be required to eliminate the main source of violence, the state. For Bakunin, destruction can even be creative, as it is when people rise up to destroy the state—the master that enslaves them—and liberate themselves.

It is easy to see why Marx regarded the anarchists with contempt, and why they viewed him with suspicion. Marx, as we noted in Chapter 5, believed that the transition from capitalism to communism required that the victorious revolutionaries seize state power in order to prevent the defeated bourgeoisie from mounting a counterrevolution. When it was no longer needed, this transitional state, the dictatorship of the proletariat, would finally wither away. In *Statism and Anarchy* (1874), Bakunin mounted a prophetic and withering criticism of Marx's claim that the state would, or could, spontaneously self-destruct. The state, said Bakunin, is not like that; its natural tendency is not to disappear, but to acquire more and more power, to grow ever more oppressive and violent, and to subject its citizens to increasingly stringent scrutiny and control. This is as true of a so-called workers' state as of the state that existed under the bourgeoisie. In fact, said Bakunin, the workers' state is likely to be even more oppressive, for it—unlike the bourgeois state—has no militant and organized working class to oppose it and to check its growth.[33]

A rather different defense of anarchism was advanced by Peter Kropotkin, particularly in *Mutual Aid* (1902). A prince who had renounced his title in order to express a sense of solidarity with the common people, Kropotkin was closely watched by the Russian police. In 1874 he was arrested for illegal political activities and sent to Siberia. After serving two years of his sentence he made a daring escape and, like many political refugees, made his way to England— and to an exile that was to last 42 years. Much influenced by the writings of Charles Darwin and other prominent nineteenth century scientists, Kropotkin accepted the view that all species evolve according to inexorable laws of development. This meant that the human species was steadily evolving and that society would eventually become more peaceful and cooperative. By means of concerted political action, he thought, these processes of change could be speeded up, and the state abolished and replaced by a noncoercive anarchist society. Indeed, he argued that the political lesson of Darwin's theory—contrary to the **Social Darwinists'** emphasis on competition between individuals— is that survival is likely to be the reward of those who learn to cooperate or engage in mutual aid.[34]

Fabian Socialism

The Fabian Society, founded in London in 1884, took its name from the Roman general Fabius (died 203 B.C.), who refused to fight pitched battles, favoring instead a strategy of retreating and wearing down the enemy, finally getting them to surrender without shedding blood. It was in this spirit and by peaceful parliamentary means that the *Fabian Socialists* sought to nudge England in an ever more markedly socialist direction.[35] Its leading members—including George Bernard Shaw, H. G. Wells, Graham Wallas, Sidney and Beatrice Webb, and Bertrand Russell—were mostly (with the exception of the aristocratic Russell) middle-class writers and social reformers. They put their considerable talents to political use in the socialist cause, mainly by writing popular essays, plays, and books. Shaw's play *Pygmalion* (which later became the Broadway musical and movie *My Fair Lady*) poked fun at the English class system, and his *The Intelligent Woman's Guide to Socialism and Capitalism* (1928) explains socialist economic and political principles in a clear and witty way.

The Fabian philosophy of a peaceful parliamentary path to a socialist society was incorporated into the British Labour party, founded in 1900. The Labour party first won control of the British government in the election of 1924, when Ramsay MacDonald became Britain's first socialist Prime Minister. Since then, the Labour party has been in and out of office many times and has succeeded in implementing such policies as the *nationalization* (i.e., government ownership and operation) of certain services and industries, such as coal and steel, railroads and airlines, telecommunications, and others. The Labour party also instituted a comprehensive social-welfare system that includes a national health program providing free medical and dental care. In the 1980s the Conservative party, under the leadership of Prime Minister Margaret Thatcher, curtailed many social services and *privatized* (i.e., sold to private investors) a number of industries that had been nationalized by the Labour party. Unable to agree about the best way of opposing the conservatives, the opposition Labour party has since split into feuding factions and a small splinter group calling itself the Social Democratic party.

American Socialism

The United States has a long, but not very strong, socialist tradition. Exactly why socialism has not proved appealing to most Americans is a question we will address in a moment. First, though, let us look briefly at the thought of one of the few original socialist thinkers that the United States has produced.

Edward Bellamy (1850–1898) was the author of a best-selling utopian novel, *Looking Backward*, published in 1888. The novel's hero, Julian West, falls into a deep coma-like sleep and awakens in the year 2000 to find an America vastly different from the one he knew at the end of the nineteenth century. The United States, he discovers, has ceased to be a competitive capitalist society and has become a cooperative socialist society. When he tries to tell his new-found friends about life in the old society, they can hardly believe their ears. Why, they want to know, would anyone willingly live in a dog-eat-dog society? Julian West replies by

> compar[ing] society as it then was to a prodigious [stage-] coach which the masses of humanity were harnessed to and dragged toilsomely along a very hilly and sandy road. The driver was hunger, and permitted no lagging. . . . Despite the difficulty of drawing the coach at all along so hard a road, the top was covered with passengers who never got down, even at the steepest ascents. These seats on top were very breezy and comfortable. Well up out of the dust, their occupants could enjoy the scenery at their leisure, or critically discuss the merits of the straining team. Naturally such places were in great demand and the competition for them was keen,

every one seeking . . . to secure a seat on the coach for himself and to leave it to his child after him. . . . [Yet the seats at the top] were very insecure, and at every sudden jolt . . . persons were slipping out of them and falling to the ground, where they were instantly compelled to take hold of the rope and help to drag the coach. . . . It was naturally regarded as a terrible misfortune to lose one's seat, and the apprehension that this might happen to them . . . was a constant cloud upon the happiness of those who rode.[36]

The people on top, Bellamy continues, would express sympathy for and shout words of encouragement to those dragging the coach, and would sometimes send down salves and bandages for their bleeding hands and feet; but none of them ever got down to help. Such, says Bellamy, is the nature of competitive capitalist society.

Against this bleak picture Bellamy counterposes a socialist vision of mutual assistance and cooperation. The United States in the year 2000 has no poverty and no unemployment. All able-bodied people work willingly, and all are compensated equally for their labors. Those who work at unpleasant jobs, such as garbage collecting, work fewer hours per week than those with easier or more pleasant jobs. There are no wages, for there is no money. Instead, everyone has a credit card (remarkably prophetic, that!) with which one buys from state-owned stores what is required to satisfy one's basic needs. Through these and other ingenious arrangements, people live in equality, harmony, and freedom.

This vision apparently appealed to many Americans, who formed Bellamy Clubs by the thousands to discuss how best to put these ideas into practice. Bellamy's popularity proved to be short-lived, but his influence is evident in subsequent socialist theorizing. His version of socialism became one of several, and its main themes were incorporated into the thinking of various populists and progressives at the turn of the century. Much has happened in the interim. But what clearly has not happened is the coming of a socialist society. Indeed, today in the United States, unlike many other countries, many people consider "socialism" a dirty word, even though (as several public opinion surveys suggest) most are unable to define it. One of the first questions that many foreigners ask is, "Why do so many Americans find socialism so unappealing?"

Several explanations are possible. One is that the United States is essentially a two-party system in which third parties have little chance of significant electoral success. (Even so, Socialist party presidential candidate Eugene V. Debs received nearly a million votes in the 1920 presidential election.) Another explanation is that socialism is a working-class movement and ideology, and surveys show that most Americans—whether blue- or white-collar—think of themselves as belonging to the middle class. A third and closely related explanation is that the fluidity of class distinctions, and a corresponding possibility of "moving up" socially and economically, renders socialism unappealing to people who think of themselves as upwardly mobile. A fourth explanation is that the long and still strong tradition of liberal-individualism in the United States makes "collectivist" ideologies unappealing. The idea of "rugged individualists" who "pull themselves up by their bootstraps" retains a powerful appeal among many Americans.

Some recent American socialists, such as the late Michael Harrington (1928–1989), maintain that the picture of the rugged and self-reliant individual is an ideological fantasy that is out of touch with contemporary American realities. To be sure, America has great wealth and abundant opportunities, but these are unjustly distributed. A genuinely just society would not permit any of its citizens to go hungry, to be homeless, or to remain unemployed for long periods. The root of the problem lies not with these poor people, but with the system of profit and privilege that rewards "winners" and punishes "losers" and—worse yet—their children, who are themselves caught up in a cycle of poverty and despair. The only truly *free* society would be one in which opportunities to develop one's talents and abilities to their fullest would be equally distributed. And such a society, say the socialists, would necessarily be socialist.[37]

SOCIALISM TODAY

If the 1880s and '90s were the Golden Age of Marxism, as Leszek Kowlakowski has claimed, how should we regard the 1980s and '90s, a time of dramatic and astonishingly swift change in the socialist world? From one point of view, these decades seem to signal the end of socialism as a compelling political ideology; from another, the turbulence of these years may mark a revival of socialism. As old institutions and dogmas are discredited and overturned, socialists confront new opportunities and challenges—especially the challenge of deciding what forms and directions socialism should take. This challenge is likely to inspire a debate among socialists that may well lead to a burst of creativity.

At this point it seems that the Marxist-Leninist version of communism is dying, if not already dead. In 1989, a year that future historians may consider as significant as 1789, the Soviet Union and Poland began to allow non-Communists to compete for political office, which resulted in an overwhelming electoral defeat for the Communists in Poland; the ruling Communist party in Hungary, the Hungarian Socialist Workers' party, dissolved itself; the Communist government of East Germany, under the pressure of massive demonstrations and emigration, opened the Berlin Wall and promised its people free elections; the Communist regime in Czechoslovakia collapsed and a dissident playwright, Václav Havel, was elected President; and Communist party rule was openly challenged in Rumania, which overthrew and executed its dictatorial leader. Not all signs pointed in the same direction in 1989, of course, for this was also the year in which the Communist government of China violently suppressed the reform movement led by students. Yet even in China Marxism-Leninism was under challenge—a challenge that began with the economic reforms initiated when Deng Xiaoping became head of the Chinese Communist party in 1978. In some respects, the Chinese who gathered in Tiananmen Square to call for an end to corruption in government and respect for human rights were only seeking to extend Deng's economic reforms to the political arena as well.

But what does it mean to say that communism is dead or dying? Although this question could be answered in many ways, two points are especially worth noting. The first is that the Communist party has lost its claim to speak for and in the name of the proletariat. Instead of leading the way through socialism to the new world of communist society, the Party became a stodgy, rigid, bureaucratic institution, more interested in maintaining the power and privileges of its leaders than in bringing an end to exploitation and alienation. Whether this was inevitable or avoidable is open to debate. But it is clear that, wherever the Communist party has held power, democratic centralism has been far more centralist than democratic.

The second point follows from the first. Communists typically have taken democratic centralism to mean that political power *and* economic planning are to be under the control of the Communist party. Thus communists have adopted the view that the economy must be centrally controlled and planned. In particular, communists have instituted a **command economy,** a top-down, authoritarian system in which wages, prices, production, and distribution are determined not by the competitive market's law of supply and demand, but by the decisions and commands of the government. By the 1980s, however, many communists had concluded that centralized control of property and resources was too cumbersome and inefficient. The most prominent spokesman for this disaffection is Mikhail Gorbachev, head of the Communist party of the Soviet Union, who announced his policy of *perestroika* shortly after he assumed office in 1985. Like Deng Xiaoping in China, Gorbachev has sought to decentralize control of the economy and introduce elements of a competitive, market economy into the Soviet Union. Although his efforts have yet to overcome the serious economic difficulties facing the USSR, there is no sign of a retreat to the old-style communist command economy. So if communism is dead or dying, it is largely because the communist notion of a centrally controlled economy has lost its appeal, even for communists.

For both these reasons, communism seems no longer to have the ability to inspire heroic sacrifices and a dedicated and loyal following. In this sense, it is dying. Nevertheless, not all elements of Marxism-Leninism, much less socialism in general, are breathing their last. To many people in Asia, Africa, and Latin America, Lenin's account of imperialism still supplies the most powerful explanation of the plight of the countries of the Third World, which they see as dominated economically and politically by the capitalist powers of Europe, North America, and Japan. If communism is not the solution to their problems it once seemed, these people are still not likely to concede that capitalism is, either.

Indeed, it would be a great mistake to conclude that the death of communism will automatically mark the triumph of capitalism. In many cases, the people who are abandoning communism are not necessarily abandoning socialism. They continue to believe that, in some way or other, the major means of production in a society ought to be in the hands not of private persons, but of the public at large. They may have given up on the ideas of the one-party state and the command economy, but not on socialism in some form or other.

As we noted at the beginning of our discussion of socialism in Chapter 5, socialists have long been divided over two questions: how much and what kind of property is to be in public hands? and how is society to exercise control over this property? From Saint-Simon to the Soviet communists, some socialists have responded by calling for centralized control and ownership of most forms of property—factories and farms, mills and mines, and other means of production. But from the beginning, other socialists have responded to one or both of these questions in a more modest fashion. Owen and Fourier, with their visions of societies divided into small, self-sufficient, self-governing communities, called for highly decentralized forms of socialism. And in the twentieth century, a growing number of socialists have advocated **market socialism.**[38] As the name indicates, market socialism attempts to blend elements of a free market economy with social ownership and control of property. Although different socialists propose to blend these elements in different ways, the basic idea is that the major resources—large factories, mines, power plants, forests, mineral reserves, and others—will be owned and operated directly for the public good, while private individuals will be free to own small businesses, farms, houses, cars, and so on. Even the publicly owned firms will compete in the marketplace for profits. If there are four or five steel factories in a country, in other words, the workers in each factory will choose their supervisors, control their working conditions, and set the price of the finished steel, which they will then try to sell in competition with the other factories—and perhaps foreign competitors, too. Any profits will then be shared among the factory's workers as they see fit. If the factory loses money, it will be up to the workers to decide how to cope with the losses and become more competitive.

Some form of market socialism, then, seems to be the future of socialism. It promises neither the utopia of the early socialists, nor the brave new world that Marx and his followers envisioned as the ultimate product of historical development. But it does promise to promote cooperation and solidarity rather than competition and individualism, even as it aims at reducing, if not completely eliminating, the class divisions that spawn exploitation and alienation. In these respects, the modest, decentralized version of socialism that seems to be emerging continues to draw on themes that have long inspired people to seize the socialist banner. If communism is dying, then, it need not take socialism to the grave with it. On the contrary, communism's death could conceivably breathe new life into other forms of socialism.

CONCLUSION

Socialism as an Ideology

Like liberalism and conservatism, socialism comes in so many varieties that it sometimes seems not one, but many different ideologies. Socialists do share certain core assumptions or beliefs, however, just as liberals and conservatives do. We can best explain them in terms of the four functions that all political ideologies perform.

Explanation   To begin with, how do socialists try to explain social conditions? In general, they explain them in terms of economic and class relations. Rather than appeal to the choices of individuals, as liberals typically do, socialists are inclined to say that individuals are always caught up in social relations that shape and structure the choices available to them. Individuals may make choices, but they cannot choose to do just anything they wish. As Marx put it, "men make their own history, but they do not make it just as they please. . . ."[39] Some will have more to choose from than others. In particular, capitalists will have more options than workers, and the choices the capitalists make will sharply limit the choices available to the workers. A capitalist faced with declining profits can decide to expand or reinvest in his or her business, for instance, or move it to a different region or country, or simply sell or close it. Within the limits of his or her resources, the capitalist can do as he or she sees fit. But the worker can usually do nothing more than react to the choice the capitalist makes. And when the capitalist decides to close the business, the worker has little choice but to look elsewhere for work.

For these reasons, socialists maintain that social conditions must be explained by referring to economic or class relations. Since so much of what happens in society depends upon the way people organize themselves to work and produce goods and services—beginning with the food they need to live—then conditions in society can only be accounted for in terms of the division of society into classes. To explain the problem of crime, for example, socialists are not likely to point to the weakness of human nature, as conservatives do. Instead, they are inclined to say that much criminal activity is the result of the exploitation and alienation of working-class people who lack the power to improve their condition in a class-divided society.

Evaluation   The class-division factor carries over to the second function of ideologies, that of evaluating social conditions. In this case, the key factor is the sharpness of class divisions in a society. If one class has firm control of the wealth, so that it is able to limit sharply the choices open to the working class, then conditions are, from a socialist point of view, exploitative and unjust. If class divisions are slight, or if there are no apparent classes at all, conditions will be good. But this can only happen, socialists say, if control of the means of production is somehow shared by all members of the society.

Orientation   With regard to orientation, then, socialists tell people that they should think of themselves mainly in terms of their position in the class structure. Some socialists have taken this notion to the extreme, saying that class differences are the only differences that matter. When Marx said that the workers have no homeland, for instance, he seemed to say that nationality or citizenship should play no real role in one's identity. Not race or religion or nationality, but only class position really makes a difference in the world. Although most socialists do not go this far, all believe that our position in the class structure is an important factor in shaping our identities. We see things as we do and we are who we are largely because of class position.

If the preceding notion is true, then what is the point of telling people that they should see themselves as members of this or that class? The point, according to socialists, is that class consciousness is a necessary step on the path to a classless society. Before a capitalist can see the error of his or her ways, the capitalist must first understand that he or she is a member of the class that exploits and oppresses the workers. Only then is there any chance that the capitalist will surrender control of wealth and resources to their rightful owner—society at large. More importantly, it is only when the workers see that they form a large and oppressed class that they will be able to take action to free themselves. If they fail to develop this awareness of their social position, they will have no more chance of liberating themselves than the slave who thinks that his or her slavery is altogether natural and proper.

Program For most socialists, then, orientation is necessary to the programmatic function of their ideology. The socialist goal is simple: to bring about a society that is as nearly classless as possible. Exactly how they propose to do this will vary from one time and place to another, of course. Some look for an almost spontaneous revolution, while others believe a single highly disciplined party must lead the way; some rely on persuasion and the force of example, while others favor violent revolution and the force of arms. But in all cases they maintain that steps must be taken to promote equality and cooperation among all members of society in order to give everyone greater control over his or her own life.

Socialism and the Democratic Ideal

In its pursuit of equality, socialism is an ideology committed to democracy, in one or another sense of that contested term. As many socialists will quickly admit, leaders like Stalin have been more interested in acquiring personal power than in promoting democracy; but these leaders, they say, were not true socialists. True socialism requires government of, by, and for the people. It aims to give everyone an equal voice in the decisions that affect his or her life in direct and important ways. But this can only happen, socialists say, if no one person or class controls most of the wealth and resources—and thus most of the power—within a society. Wealth and resources must be shared evenly, owned and controlled for the benefit of the whole society, if true democracy is ever to take shape. Otherwise, they insist, we shall have nothing but government of the wealthy, by the wealthy, and for the wealthy.

NOTES

1. Leszek Kolakowski, *Main Currents of Marxism*, vol. 2; *The Golden Age* (Oxford: Clarendon Press, 1978).
2. Quoted in David McLellan, *Karl Marx: His Life and Work* (London: Macmillan, 1973), p. 443.

3. See Terrell Carver, *Engels* (Oxford: Oxford University Press, 1981), and *Marx and Engels: The Intellectual Relationship* (Brighton, U.K.: Harvester Press, 1983); Terence Ball, "Marxian Science and Positivist Politics," in Terence Ball and James Farr, eds., *After Marx* (Cambridge and New York: Cambridge University Press, 1984), chap. 11.

4. Friedrich Engels, "Speech at Marx's Graveside," in Karl Marx and Friedrich Engels, *Selected Works*, 1 vol. (New York: International Publishers, 1968), p. 435. For an inquiry into the Marx-Darwin myth, see Terence Ball, "Marx and Darwin: A Reconsideration," *Political Theory*, 7 (1979):469–483.

5. See James Farr, "Marx's Laws," *Political Studies*, 34 (1986):202–222; and "Marx and Positivism," in Ball and Farr, eds., *After Marx*, chap. 10.

6. Friedrich Engels, *Dialectics of Nature* (New York: International Publishers, 1963), p. 314.

7. Engels, *Socialism, Utopian and Scientific*, in Marx and Engels, *Selected Works*. See the excerpt in Terence Ball and Richard Dagger, eds., *Ideals and Ideologies: A Reader* (New York: HarperCollins, 1991), selection 32.

8. Marx, "Theses on Feuerbach," in Marx and Engels, *Selected Works*, p. 28.

9. Engels, *Dialectics of Nature*, p. 25.

10. Eduard Bernstein, *Evolutionary Socialism* (New York: Schocken Books, 1961), p. 202. See, also, Kolakowski, *Main Currents of Marxism*, vol. 2, chap. 4; and Peter Gay, *The Dilemma of Democratic Socialism*, 2nd ed. (New York: Collier Books, 1962).

11. Bernstein, *Evolutionary Socialism*, p. 106.

12. Ibid., p. 210; also in Ball and Dagger, eds., *Ideals and Ideologies*, selection 33.

13. Ibid., p. 202.

14. Ferdinand Lassalle, *Franz von Sickingen* (1859), act 2, sc. 5, lines 93–97.

15. Bernstein, *Evolutionary Socialism*, p. 211; also in Ball and Dagger, eds., *Ideals and Ideologies*, selection 33.

16. Ibid., p. 219; also in Ball and Dagger, eds., *Ideals and Ideologies*, selection 33.

17. See Gary P. Steenson, *Karl Kautsky, 1854–1938: Marxism in the Classical Years* (Pittsburgh: University of Pittsburgh Press, 1978), esp. pp. 116–131 and 186.

18. See V. I. Lenin, "Marxism and Revisionism," in Lenin, *Selected Works*, 1 vol. (Moscow: Progress Publishers, 1968), pp. 25–32; also in Ball and Dagger, eds., *Ideals and Ideologies*, selection 34.

19. Quoted in Bruce Mazlish, *The Revolutionary Ascetic* (New York: Basic Books, 1976), p. 140.

20. Lenin, " 'Left Wing' Communism—An Infantile Disorder," in *Selected Works*, p. 535.

21. Quoted in Kolakowski, *Main Currents of Marxism*, vol. 2, p. 386.

22. Lenin, *Imperialism, the Highest Stage of Capitalism*, in Lenin, *Selected Works*, pp. 171–175, 240–247.

23. Roy A. Medvedev, *Let History Judge: The Origins and Consequences of Stalinism*, trans. Colleen Taylor (New York: Alfred A. Knopf, 1972), p. 519. See also Robert C. Tucker, ed., *Stalinism* (New York: Norton, 1977); and Adam B. Ulam, *Stalin: The Man and His Era* (New York: Viking Press, 1973).

24. Medvedev, *Let History Judge*, p. 510.

25. Ibid., chap. 14.

26. Here, as elsewhere, Stalin's views stand in sharp contrast with those of Marx. On the role of chance and accident in history, see Marx's letter to Ludwig Kugelmann (17 April 1871) in Karl Marx and Friedrich Engels, *Selected Correspondence* (Mos-

cow: Progress Publishers, 1975), p. 248: "World history . . . would . . . be of a very mystical nature, if 'accidents' played no part."

27. For an examination and critique of claims about "historical inevitability," see Isaiah Berlin, "Historical Inevitability," in his *Four Essays on Liberty* (New York: Oxford University Press, 1970), essay 2.

28. Joseph Stalin, "Political Report of the Central Committee to the Sixteenth Congress," in Stalin, *Selected Works* (Moscow: Foreign Languages Publishing House, 1952–1955), vol. 12, p. 381.

29. Mao Ze-dong, "The Chen-Feng Movement," in Conrad Brandt, Benjamin Schwartz, and John King Fairbank, eds., *A Documentary History of Chinese Communism* (New York: Atheneum, 1966), pp. 384–385.

30. See Bruce D. Larkin, *China and Africa, 1949–1970: The Foreign Policy of the People's Republic of China* (Berkeley and Los Angeles: University of California Press, 1971).

31. See Paul Thomas, *Karl Marx and the Anarchists* (London: Routledge & Kegan Paul, 1980).

32. William Godwin, *An Enquiry Concerning Political Justice*, ed. Isaac Kramnick (Harmondsworth: Penguin, 1976). Also see Mark Philp, *Godwin's Political Justice* (London: Duckworth, 1984).

33. See Mikhail Bakunin, "On Marx and Marxism," in Ball and Dagger, eds., *Ideals and Ideologies*, selection 36.

34. Peter Kropotkin, *Mutual Aid* (London: Heinemann, 1902); and "Anarchist Communism," in Ball and Dagger, eds., *Ideals and Ideologies*, selection 37.

35. See Norman MacKenzie and Jean MacKenzie, *The First Fabians* (London: Weidenfeld & Nicholson, 1977); and A. M. McBriar, *Fabian Socialism and English Politics, 1884–1914* (Cambridge: Cambridge University Press, 1966); Margaret Cole, *The Story of Fabian Socialism* (Stanford, Calif.: Stanford University Press, 1961).

36. Edward Bellamy, *Looking Backward* (New York: New American Library, 1960), pp. 26–27; also Ball and Dagger, eds., *Ideals and Ideologies*, selection 38.

37. See Michael Harrington, "Why America Needs Socialism," *Dissent* (May–June, 1970); also in Ball and Dagger, eds., *Ideals and Ideologies*, selection 39.

38. See Alec Nove, *The Economics of Feasible Socialism* (London: Allen & Unwin, 1983).

39. Karl Marx, "The Eighteenth Brumaire of Louis Bonaparte," in Marx and Engels, *Selected Works*, p. 97.

FOR FURTHER READING

Ball, Terence, and James Farr, eds. *After Marx* (Cambridge and New York: Cambridge University Press, 1984).

Carr, E. H. *Michael Bakunin* (London: Macmillan, 1937).

Carver, Terrell. *Engels* (Oxford and New York: Oxford University Press, 1981).

Cole, Margaret *The Story of Fabian Socialism* (Stanford, Calif.: Stanford University Press, 1961).

Crick, Bernard. *Socialism* (Minneapolis: University of Minnesota Press, 1987).

Gay, Peter. *The Dilemma of Democratic Socialism: Eduard Bernstein's Challenge to Marx* (New York: Collier Books, 1962).

Kolakowski, Leszek. *Main Currents of Marxism*, 3 vols., trans. P. S. Falla (Oxford: Clarendon Press, 1978).

Lichtheim, George. *A Short History of Socialism* (New York: Praeger, 1970).

Lukes, Steven. *Marxism and Morality* (Oxford and New York: Oxford University Press, 1985).

Medvedev, Roy A. *Let History Judge: The Origins and Consequences of Stalinism*, trans. Colleen Taylor (New York: Knopf, 1972).

Miller, David. *Anarchism* (London: Dent, 1984).

Starr, John B. *Continuing the Revolution: The Political Thought of Mao* (Princeton, N.J.: Princeton University Press, 1979).

Tucker, Robert C., ed. *Stalinism* (New York: Norton, 1977).

Wolfe, Bertram D. *Three Who Made a Revolution* (New York: Dell, 1964).

Woodcock, George. *Anarchism* (Harmondsworth: Penguin, 1963).

Chapter
7

Fascism

The sleep of reason brings forth monsters.

Goya

Future historians may well remember the twentieth century as the age of world wars, nuclear weapons, and a new kind of political regime—**totalitarianism.** All these developments are connected to political ideologies in one way or another, but none more closely than totalitarianism. For totalitarianism is the attempt to take complete control of a society—not just its government, but all its social, cultural, and economic institutions—in order to fulfill an ideological vision of how society ought to be organized and life ought to be lived. This is what happened in the Soviet Union when Stalin imposed his version of Marxist socialism on that country. This also happened in Italy and Germany when Benito Mussolini and Adolf Hitler introduced varieties of a new and openly totalitarian ideology called fascism.

In fact, Mussolini and the Italian Fascists coined the word "totalitarian." They did this to define their revolutionary aims and to distinguish their ideology from liberalism and socialism, each of which advocates its own form of democracy. Democracy requires equality, whether it be the liberal ideal of equal opportunity for individuals or the socialist vision of equal power for all in a classless society. Mussolini and his followers regarded these ideals with contempt, as did Hitler and the Nazis. They did appeal to the masses for support, to be sure, but in their view the masses were to exercise power not by thinking, speaking, or voting for themselves, but by blindly following their leaders to glory. As one of Mussolini's many slogans put it, *credere, obbedire, combattere* (believe, obey, fight). Nothing more was asked, nothing more was desired of the people. By embracing totalitarianism, then, fascists also rejected democracy.

In this respect, fascism is a **reactionary** ideology. It took shape in the years following World War I as a reaction against the two leading ideologies of the time, liberalism and socialism. Unhappy with the liberal focus on the individual and the socialist emphasis on contending social classes, the fascists provided a view of the world in which individuals and classes were to be absorbed into an all-embracing whole—a mighty empire under the control of a single party and a supreme leader. Like the Reactionaries of the early 1800s, they also rejected the faith in reason that they thought formed the foundation for liberalism and socialism alike. Reason is less reliable, both Mussolini and Hitler declared, than intuitions and emotions—what we sometimes call "gut instincts." This is why Mussolini exhorted his followers to "think with your blood."

To say that fascism is in some ways a reactionary ideology does not mean, however, that fascists are simply reactionaries or extreme conservatives. In many ways they are quite different. Unlike Joseph de Maistre and the other Reactionaries we discussed in Chapter 4, fascists do not reject democracy, liberalism, and socialism in order to turn the clock back to a time when society was rooted in ascribed status, with church, king, and aristocracy firmly in power. On the contrary, many fascists have been openly hostile to religion, and few of them have had any respect for hereditary monarchs and aristocrats. Nor have they sought to return to the old, established ways of life. On the contrary, fascism in its most distinctive forms has been openly revolutionary, eager not only to change society, but to change it radically. This by itself sets fascists apart from conservatives, who cannot abide rapid and radical change. So, too, does the fascist plan to concentrate power in the hands of a totalitarian state led by a single party and a supreme leader. Nothing could be further from the conservative's desire to disperse power among various levels of government and the other "little platoons" that make up what they take to be a healthy society than the fascist vision of a unified state bending to the will of a single, all-powerful leader.

Fascism, then, is neither conservative nor simply reactionary. It is, as the original fascists boasted, a new and distinctive ideology. To appreciate how distinctive it is, we must explore its background in the *Counter-Enlightenment*, in *nationalism*, and in other intellectual currents of the nineteenth century. We shall then examine fascism in its purest form in Mussolini's Italy, following that with a look at other varieties of fascism in Nazi Germany and elsewhere.

FASCISM: THE BACKGROUND

Although fascism did not emerge as a political ideology until the 1920s, its roots reach back over a century to the reaction against the intellectual and cultural movement that dominated European thought in the eighteenth century—the **Enlightenment.** In various ways the thinkers of the Enlightenment dreamed a dream of reason. Taking the scientific discoveries of the seventeenth and eighteenth centuries as their model and inspiration, the Enlightenment philosophers claimed that the application of reason could remove all the social and political evils that stood in the way of happiness and progress. Reason can light the minds of men and women, they proclaimed, freeing them from ignorance and error and superstition.[1] The two great political currents that flow from the Enlightenment are liberalism and socialism. Different as they are in other respects, these two ideologies are alike in sharing the premises of the Enlightenment. These premises include:

1. *Humanism*—the idea that human beings are the source and measure of value, with human life valuable in and of itself. As Immanuel Kant (1724–1804) put it, human beings belong to the "kingdom of ends." Each person is an end in himself, in Kant's words, not something that others may use, like a tool, as a means of accomplishing their own selfish ends.

2. *Rationalism*—the idea that human beings are rational creatures and that human reason, epitomized in scientific inquiry, can solve all mysteries and reveal solutions to all the problems that men and women face.

3. *Secularism*—the idea that religion may be a source of comfort and insight, but not of absolute and unquestionable truths for guiding public life. The Enlightenment thinkers differed from one another in their religious views. Some, like John Locke and Kant, remained Christians; others, like Voltaire (1694–1778), rejected Christianity but believed in a God who had created a world as well-ordered as a watch, which the "divine watchmaker" had wound and left to run; still others were skeptics, agnostics, or atheists. But even those who took their Christianity seriously regarded religion as something to be confined largely to private life, and therefore out of place in politics. The irreligious among the Enlightenment philosophers simply dismissed religion as an outmoded superstition that must give way to rational and scientific ideas.

4. *Progressivism*—the idea that human history is the story of progress, or improvement—perhaps even inevitable improvement—in the human condition. Once the shackles of ignorance and superstition have been broken, human reason will be free to order society in a rational way, and life will steadily and rapidly become better for all.

5. *Universalism*—the idea that there is a single universal human nature that binds all human beings together, despite differences of race, culture, or religious creed. Human beings are all equal members of Kant's kingdom of ends who share the same essential nature, including preeminently the capacity for reason.

These Enlightenment views are often linked to liberalism, but they provided much of the inspiration for socialism as well. Indeed, modern socialism arose in part from the complaint that liberalism was not going far enough in its attempt to remake society in the image of Enlightenment ideals. Fascism, however, grows out of the very different conviction that the ideals of the Enlightenment are not worth pursuing—a claim first put forward in the late eighteenth and early nineteenth centuries.

The Counter-Enlightenment

A diverse group of thinkers some call the **Counter-Enlightenment** mounted a counterattack on the Enlightenment.[2] Among them were the linguist Johan

Gottfried von Herder (1744–1803); the royalists and reactionaries Joseph de Maistre (1753–1821) and Louis Gabriel de Bonald (1754–1840); the Marquis de Sade (1740–1814), now notorious as a libertine and pornographer; and racial theorists like Joseph-Arthur de Gobineau (1816–1882). None of them rejected every premise of the Enlightenment, and each had particular concerns and complaints that the others did not share. But they were alike in dismissing the major premises of the Enlightenment as fanciful, false, and politically dangerous.

They were united, for instance, in denouncing "universalism" as a myth. Human beings are not all alike, they said; the differences that distinguish groups of people from one another run very deep. Indeed, these differences— of sex, race, language, culture, creed, and nationality—actually *define* who and what people are, shaping how they think of themselves and other people. For Herder, linguistic and cultural differences mattered most; for Gobineau, it was race; and for de Sade, it was gender. Men, de Sade observed, do not admit women to the kingdom of ends. They treat them as means, as objects to be used, abused, and humiliated—and this is as it should be. Not surprisingly, our words *sadism* and *sadistic* come from the name de Sade.

The Counter-Enlightenment critics brought similar complaints against the Enlightenment's faith in reason. The problem with rationalism, they said, is that it flies in the face of all human experience. The prevalence of *un*reason, of superstition and prejudice, shows that reason itself is too weak to be relied on. Most people, most of the time, use reason not to examine matters critically and dispassionately, but to rationalize and excuse their desires and deepen their prejudices. With this in mind, the Counter-Enlightenment writers often deplored the Enlightenment assault on religion. Some of them wrote from sincere religious conviction, but others simply held that religious beliefs are socially necessary fictions. The belief in heaven and hell, they maintained, may be all that keeps most people behaving as well as they do; to lose that belief may be to lose all hope of a civilized and orderly society. If that means that government must support an established church and forsake religious tolerance, so be it.

Each in his own way, these critics challenged the fundamental premises of the Enlightenment. Out of their challenge a different picture of human beings emerged. According to this picture, humans are fundamentally nonrational, even irrational, beings; they are defined by their differences—of race, sex, religion, language, and nationality; and they are usually locked in conflict with one another, a conflict sparked by their deep-seated and probably permanent differences. Taken one by one, there is nothing necessarily "fascist" about any element of this picture. Combining the elements, however, gives us a picture of human capacities and characteristics that prepared the way for the emergence of fascism. This should become clearer as we look at another feature of fascism—**nationalism.**

Nationalism

Nationalism, as we noted in Chapter 1, is the belief that the people of the world fall into distinct groups, or nations, with each nation forming the natural basis for a separate political unit, or **nation-state.** This sovereign, self-governing political unit is supposed to draw together and express the needs and desires of a single nation. Without such a state, a nation or people will be frustrated, unable either to govern or express itself.

Although nationalistic sentiments are quite old, nationalism itself emerged as a political force in the wake of the Napoleonic Wars of the early 1800s. As they swept across Europe, Napoleon's armies—the armies of the French *nation*—created a backlash, inspiring people in Germany, Italy, and elsewhere to recognize their respective nationalities and to struggle for unified nation-states of their own.

This first stage of nationalism is apparent in the works of the linguist Herder and the philosopher Johann Gottlieb Fichte (1762–1814). Both appealed to the sense of German nationality, with Fichte laying particular stress on the distinctiveness of the German language—the only truly original European language, he said, for Latin had smothered the originality in the others.[3] In the winter of 1807–1808, still smarting from Napoleon's defeat of the Prussian army in 1806, Fichte delivered his *Addresses to the German Nation* in Berlin. In the *Addresses* he maintained that the individual finds much of the meaning and value of life in being connected to the nation into which he or she was born. Rather than think of ourselves merely as individuals, in other words, we must think of ourselves as members of the larger and lasting community of the nation. Hence, Fichte said,

> the noble-minded man will be active and effective, and will sacrifice himself for his people. Life merely as such, the mere continuance of changing existence, has in any case never had any value for him; he has wished for it only as the source of what is permanent. But this permanence is promised to him only by the continuous and independent existence of his nation. In order to save his nation he must be ready even to die that it may live, and that he may live in it the only life for which he has ever wished.[4]

Longing for membership and meaning, the individual lives, according to Fichte, in and through the nation. And though Fichte thought the German nation was especially worth defending, neither he nor Herder was simply a *German* nationalist. All nations have value, they said, for all nations give shape and significance to the lives of their people. Against the universalism of the Enlightenment, then, Herder and Fichte argued that every nation brings something distinctive or unique to the world—something for which it deserves recognition and respect.

Yet neither Herder nor Fichte called for every nation to be embodied politically in its own distinct state. That development came later, most notably in the words and deeds of an Italian nationalist, Giuseppe Mazzini (1805–1872), and a German nationalist, the "Iron Chancellor" Otto von Bismarck (1815–1878).

In the early 1800s Italy was as fragmented as Germany. Since the fall of the Roman Empire around 500 A.D., the word Italy named a geographical and cultural region, but never a politically united country. Divided into kingdoms, duchies, and warring city-states, and often overrun by French and Spanish armies, Italy became the center of commerce and culture during the Renaissance, but it was far from the center of European political power. Niccolò Machiavelli called attention to this in the sixteenth century when he concluded his famous book, *The Prince*, with "An Exhortation to Liberate Italy from the Barbarians"—but to no avail. Italy remained divided until the 1800s, when Mazzini and others made it their mission to unify the country. Other nations had found statehood—England, for instance, and France and Spain—and now, Mazzini said, it was time for Italy to join their ranks as a nation-state. Italy must be united not only geographically and culturally, but politically as well. A nation cannot truly be a nation unless it can take its place among the powers of the earth. So Italians must be brought together, Mazzini argued, as citizens under a common government. Only in this way could they achieve freedom and fulfill their destiny as a people.

But Mazzini did not confine his nationalism to his native country. Like Herder and Fichte, he supported nationalism as an ideal for all nations, not just his own. Mazzini sometimes suggested that geography testified to God's intention of creating a world of distinct nations. Why else, he asked, did rivers, mountains, and seas separate groups of people from one another and foster the development of separate languages, cultures, and customs? Mazzini even envisioned a world in which each nation had its own state, and every nation-state lived in harmony with all the others—all following the example of a politically united Italy.

The nineteenth century nationalists used the press, diplomacy, and occasionally the force of arms to achieve their goal, and by 1871 both Italy and Germany had finally become nation-states. The nationalistic impulse has persisted and grown and today continues to figure in the politics not only of Europe, but of Africa, Asia, and the American continents. It contributed to Zionism—the movement to establish a homeland, or nation-state, for Jews in Israel—and has taken a liberal direction in some cases, communist or socialist directions in others. That is a story for another chapter, however. In this chapter we concentrate on the nationalistic elements in fascism. But first we must examine two more intellectual currents of the late 1800s that contributed to the rise of fascism—*elitism* and *irrationalism*.

Elitism

As we pointed out in earlier chapters, many nineteenth century social thinkers regarded theirs as the age of democracy and "the common man." Although many applauded this development, others abhorred it, and some, like Alexis de Tocqueville and John Stuart Mill, regarded it with mixed emotions. Democracy did expand opportunities and possibilities for the common person, they said, and to that extent it was good; but it also posed a threat to individuality—the threat of the "tyranny of the majority." Marx and the socialists largely dismissed or ignored this threat. For them, democracy—or socialist democracy, at any rate—would afford everyone an equal chance to live a creative, fruitful, and self-directed life. But this could only happen, they said, in a classless society, which socialists assumed could be created with sufficient effort. This assumption came under sharp attack in the late nineteenth and early twentieth centuries by thinkers who emphasized the importance of *elites* in society.

These so-called elite theorists included Gaetano Mosca (1858–1941), Vilfredo Pareto (1848–1923), and Roberto Michels (1876–1936). In one way or another, each contributed to the idea of **elitism** by concluding that a classless society was impossible. On the basis of historical studies, for instance, Mosca concluded that societies always have been, and always will be, ruled by a small group of leaders, even when it appears that the majority is ruling. Pareto, an Italian economist and sociologist, reached a similar conclusion. Perhaps most strikingly, so did Michels, a Swiss sociologist who undertook a study of the socialist parties of Europe, which professed to be working to achieve a classless society. Yet Michels's study revealed that even these parties, despite their proclaimed faith in democracy and equality, were controlled not by the majority of members, but by a relatively small group of leaders.

This discovery led Michels to formulate his *iron law of oligarchy*. In all large organizations, he said, and certainly in whole societies, power cannot be shared equally among all the people. For the organization or society to be effective, real power must be concentrated in the hands of a small group—an elite, or oligarchy. This is simply the nature of large organizations, and there is nothing that can change it. According to Michels, then, this "iron law" is destined to defeat the well-meaning designs of democrats and egalitarians. Like Mosca and Pareto, he concluded that elites rule the world; they always have, and they always will.

The views of these elite theorists reinforced arguments advanced earlier by the German philosopher Friedrich Nietzsche and others. According to Nietzsche (1844–1900), outstanding accomplishments were the work of a few great men—the kind of person he called the *übermensch* ("overman" or "superman"). Yet, he complained, all the tendencies of the age are toward a mass society in which these outstanding individuals will find it ever harder to act in bold and creative ways. Elitism *should* be the rule, Nietzsche suggested; Mosca, Pareto, and Michels concluded that it *was*. Their notion of the elite may have been different from Nietzsche's, but the two views in combination helped to prepare the way for the explicitly elitist ideology of fascism.

Irrationalism

The final element in the cultural and intellectual background of fascism was *irrationalism*. This term captures the conclusions of a variety of very different thinkers who all came to agree with the thinkers of the Counter-Enlightenment that emotion and desire play a larger part in the actions of people than reason. Among these thinkers was Sigmund Freud (1856–1939), the founder of psychoanalysis, whose observations of his patients—and even of himself—led him to detect the power of instinctive drives and "the unconscious" in human conduct. In a similar vein, the American philosopher and psychologist William James (1842–1910) wrote that most people have a "will to believe." Exactly what they believe is less important to them, James said, than that they believe in *something*. Psychologically speaking, people need something—almost anything, in fact—in which to believe, to give their small lives a larger and more enduring meaning.

Another social theorist who contributed to the development of irrationalism—and one who seems to have had a special influence on Mussolini—was the French social psychologist, Gustav Le Bon (1841–1931). In his classic work, *The Crowd*, Le Bon argued that human behavior in crowds is different from the behavior of individuals. Acting collectively and therefore anonymously, people will participate in acts of barbarism that they would never engage in as lone individuals. The psychology of lynch mobs, for example, is quite different from the psychology of the individuals who compose that mob. People acting *en masse* and in mobs are not restrained by individual conscience or moral scruple. A mob psychology or "herd instinct" takes over, shutting down individual judgments regarding right and wrong.

In a similar spirit, Pareto examined the social factors influencing individual judgment and behavior, concluding that emotions, symbols, and what he called "sentiments" are more important than material or economic factors. And Mosca suggested that people are moved more by slogans and symbols, flags and anthems—by "political formulae," as he called them—than by reasoned argument and rational debate.

All these thinkers—Freud, James, Le Bon, Pareto, and Mosca—were more immediately concerned with explaining how people acted than in leading people to action. Not so Georges Sorel (1847–1922), a French engineer who became a social theorist and political activist. Sorel insisted that people are more often moved to action by political "myths" than by appeals to reason. To bring about major social changes, then, it is necessary to find a powerful myth that can inspire people to act. For Sorel, the idea of a nationwide "general strike" could prove to be such a myth. The general strike was a myth, in other words, in that there was no guarantee that it would really lead to the revolutionary overthrow of the bourgeoisie and capitalism. If enough people could be brought to believe in the myth of the general strike, however their efforts, fueled by this belief, would indeed lead to a successful revolution. What matters most, Sorel concluded, is not the reasonableness of a myth, but its emotional power, for it is not reason but emotion that leads most people to act. And when the people act *en masse*, they can smash almost any obstacle in their path.

This was advice that Mussolini, Hitler, and other fascist leaders quite obviously took to heart. The slogans, the massive demonstrations, the torchlight parades—all were designed to stir the people at their most basic emotional and instinctive levels. But stir them to do what? To create powerful nation-states, then mighty empires, all under the leadership of the fascist elite. So it was not only irrationalism, but elitism and nationalism and the attitudes of the Counter-Enlightenment, too, that came together in the early twentieth century in the totalitarian ideology of fascism. To see how fascism combined these elements, we turn next to the clearest case of fascism—Italy under Mussolini's regime.

FASCISM IN ITALY

Because the rise and fall of Italian Fascism is so closely associated with one man, Benito Mussolini, we can conveniently chart its course through an account of Mussolini's life. Some historians even suggest that Italian Fascism was little more than a vehicle for Mussolini's ambitions—a loose and incoherent set of ideas that he cobbled together to help him achieve and keep power. There is surely some truth to that view; Mussolini was an opportunist who trimmed and shifted his ideological position to suit his changing political needs. Yet even his shifts and inconsistencies reveal a certain coherence to his views, for they emphasize his faith in his own intuition and his conviction that the most important form of power is willpower.

Mussolini and Italian Fascism

Benito Mussolini was born in a village in rural Italy in 1883, the year that Karl Marx died. Mussolini's father was a blacksmith and an atheist, his mother a schoolteacher and a Catholic. As a young man, Mussolini also taught school for a short while, but he soon left the classroom to take up political journalism. Calling himself a Marxist, Mussolini wrote articles for socialist newspapers. In 1912 he became editor of *Avanti!* (*Forward!*), the largest of Italy's socialist journals. As editor he remained a revolutionary socialist, proclaiming that capitalism would fall only after a violent proletarian uprising. Even at this early stage, however, Mussolini already placed more emphasis on the *will* to engage in revolutionary struggle, than on economic factors and the contradictions of capitalism.

Mussolini's break with socialism came during World War I. Before the war, socialists across Europe had agreed that they would take no part in any "capitalist" war. If the bourgeoisie of France, England, and Germany wanted to slaughter one another, so be it; the socialists would urge the working classes of all countries to stay out of the war and wait for the opportunity to create socialist societies once the capitalist powers had destroyed one another. But when World War I erupted in August 1914 almost all the socialist representatives in the legislatures of the warring countries voted to support their own countries' war efforts. This, said some observers, was a sign that nationalism was a far stronger force in human life than loyalty to one's social class.

Mussolini agreed and began to urge Italy to join the war—a stance that cost him his position as editor, since the official socialist policy in Italy was to stay out of the war. Italy did enter the war on the side of England and France, though, and Mussolini was eventually drafted into the army, where he served until a mortar he was loading exploded and wounded him seriously.

For Mussolini, World War I proved once and for all that Marx was wrong: workers *do* have a fatherland—at least they want to *believe* that they do. Any political party or movement that denies this is doomed to failure. Socialists, he said, "have never examined the problems of *nations* [but only of classes. Contrary to Marx], the nation represents a stage in human [history] that has not yet been transcended. . . . The 'sentiment' of nationality exists; it cannot be denied."[5] And so Mussolini set out to affirm and take political advantage of the widely shared sentiment of nationalism.

He did this by forming first the *fasci di combattimento*, or combat groups, that consisted largely of World War I veterans, and soon the Fascist party itself. The party program sometimes seemed revolutionary, sometimes conservative, but always nationalistic. When World War I ended, Italy had been united for less than fifty years, and many Italians felt that their country, unlike France and England, had not received its fair share of the spoils when Germany and Austria surrendered. Playing upon this resentment, the Fascists promised action to end the "bickering" between the various Italian political factions. There has been too much talk, too much debate, they declared; the time has come for forceful action, even violence, if Italy is to take her rightful place among the major powers of Europe.

This emphasis on national unity was apparent in the word *fascism*, which derives from the Italian *fasciare*, to fasten or bind. The aim of the Fascist party, then, was to bind the Italian people together, to overcome the divisions that weakened their country. Fascism also appealed to the glories of the ancient Roman Empire by invoking one of the old Roman symbols of authority, the *fasces*—an axe in the center of a bundle of rods, all fastened together as a symbol of the strength that comes from unity. To achieve this unity, the Fascists said, it was necessary to overcome certain obstacles. One of these was liberalism, with its emphasis on individual rights and interests. No nation can be strong, according to the Fascists, if its members think of themselves first and foremost as individuals who are concerned to protect their own rights and interests. Another obstacle was socialism, with its emphasis on conflicting social classes. Mussolini, the former Marxist, particularly attacked Marxian beliefs about class divisions and class struggle, which he regarded as enemies of national unity. Italians must not think of themselves either as individuals or as members of social classes, he said; they must think of themselves as Italians first, foremost, and forever.

So Mussolini and his followers, who adopted black shirts as their uniform, set out to seize power. They ran candidates for office, they used the press, and they sometimes simply beat up or intimidated their liberal and socialist opponents. In October 1922, Mussolini—now known to the Fascists as *Il Duce*, the leader—announced that the Fascists would march on Rome, the seat of the Italian government, and seize state power if it were not given to them. The March began on October 27. It seems clear that the Italian army could have sent Mussolini's Blackshirts scurrying, but the Italian king overestimated the strength of the Fascists and overruled the prime minister's declaration of martial law. On October 29 he invited Mussolini to form a government as the new prime minister of Italy.

Once in office, Mussolini moved to entrench himself and his Fascist party in power. He ignored the Italian Parliament; outlawed all parties except the Fascist; struck a compromise with the Catholic church; gained control of the mass media; and stifled freedom of speech and assembly. He also set out to

Benito Mussolini (1883–1945).

make Italy a military and industrial power so that it would again be the center of a great empire. Indeed, Mussolini made no secret of his ambitions for Italy—ambitions that included war and conquest. In his speeches and writings, Mussolini often spoke of war as the true test of manhood, and he had warlike slogans stencilled on the walls of buildings throughout Italy. "War," one of them proclaimed, "is to the male what childbearing is to the female!" "A minute on the battlefield," according to another, "is worth a lifetime of peace!"[6]

Mussolini made good his threats by launching several military adventures, most notably the conquest of Ethiopia in 1935–1936. His imperial ambitions soon led him into an alliance with Adolf Hitler and Nazi Germany, and from there into World War II, which Italy was woefully unprepared to fight. In July 1943 the king, with the support of the Grand Council of Fascists, stripped Mussolini of his dictatorial powers and placed him under house arrest. That September German troops rescued Mussolini and established him as head of a puppet government in northern Italy. But in April 1945, as the war was coming to an end, Mussolini and his mistress were captured and shot by antifascist Italian partisans. Their bodies were taken to Milan and strung upside down over one of the city's squares. Thus ended the career of *Il Duce*.

Fascism in Theory and Practice

While in power, Mussolini encouraged the belief that Italian Fascism rested on a philosophical or ideological basis. The Fascists had a plan, he said, for transforming Italy, and this plan grew out of a coherent view of the world. Included in that view were distinctively fascist conceptions of human nature and freedom.

For the fascist, the individual human life had meaning only insofar as it was rooted in and realized through the life of the society or the nation as a whole. Fascists rejected atomism and individualism, in other words, and insisted on the truth of the organic view of society. The individual, on his or her own, can accomplish nothing of great significance, they said. It is only when the individual dedicates his or her life to the nation-state, sacrificing everything to its glory, that the individual finds true fulfillment.

The Italian Fascists also stressed the value of the state, which they saw as the legal and institutional embodiment of the power, the unity, and the majesty of the nation. To be dedicated to the service of the nation was thus to be dedicated to the state—and to its great and glorious leader, *Il Duce*. The state was to control everything, and everyone was to serve the state. As the Italian people were reminded over and over, "everything in the state, nothing outside the state, nothing against the state."

This meant that *freedom* for the fascists was not, and is not, individual liberty, but the freedom of the *nation*, the integrated, organic whole that unites all individuals, groups, and classes behind the iron shield of the all-powerful state. Individual liberty, in fact, is an obstacle to freedom because it distracts people from their true mission to "believe, obey, fight." Freedom of speech, freedom of assembly, freedom to live as one chooses—these are all "useless liberties," according to the fascists. The only freedom that truly matters is the freedom to serve the state. In terms of our triadic definition of freedom, then, the Italian Fascists conceived of liberty as shown in Figure 7.1.

True freedom, in the fascist view, is found in serving the state, and there is nothing more fulfilling than doing one's part, however small, to promote its glory. But how was the glory of the state to be achieved? Through military conquest, Mussolini said, and conquest required the discipline and loyalty of the Italian people. This Mussolini and the Fascists attempted to win through massive propaganda efforts, always designed to appeal to the emotions and instincts of the people. The people were a mass, a herd incapable of ruling

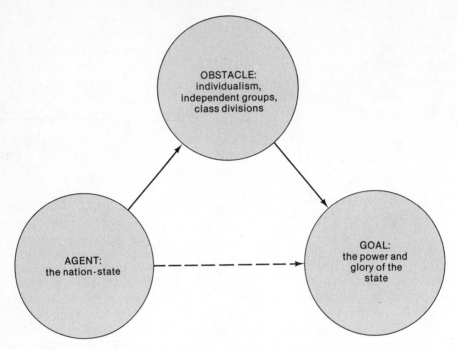

Figure 7.1 The Fascist conception of freedom.

themselves. They needed an elite to guide them, and they especially needed a dictator with an almost mystical ability to know where their "real" or "true" interests lay. Hence the people were told, in schools and in speeches and in slogans emblazoned on walls, that "Mussolini is always right!" Everything—newspapers, radio, schools—was to be used to instill this conviction in the people. In 1936, for instance, the compulsory reader for eight-year-olds in Italian schools contained the following:

> The eyes of the Duce are on every one of you. No one can say what is the meaning of that look on his face. It is an eagle opening its wings and rising into space. It is a flame that searches out your heart to light there a vermillion fire. Who can resist that burning eye, darting out its arrows? But do not be afraid; for you those arrows will change into rays of joy.
>
> A child, who, even while not refusing to obey, asks "Why?," is like a bayonet made of milk. . . . "You must obey because you must," said Mussolini, when explaining the reasons for obedience.[7]

But indoctrination and propaganda are not enough to convert a people into a modern military machine; they also need weapons and fuel and food. To this end, Mussolini tried to encourage industrial production in Italy. He did this through the policy of **corporativism,** according to which property was to remain in private hands even as it was put to public use. To prevent disputes between owners and workers from disrupting business and production, however, the Ministry of Corporations was supposed to supervise economic affairs. The economy was divided into 22 sectors, or corporations, each of which was administered by representatives of capital, labor, and the Ministry of Corporations. The representatives of the ministry were supposed to look after the interests of the public as a whole, and the three groups were supposed to work together in harmony for the good of all Italians. In practice, however, the Fascist representatives of the ministry could do much as they pleased. They were often pleased to accept bribes and to do the bidding of those who paid the bribes—usually the business owners.

The two decades of Fascist rule in Italy proved to be a time of remarkable corruption. Partly for this reason, Mussolini was unable to realize his military ambitions. Nor was Mussolini, despite all his talk about totalitarianism, able to convert Italy into a society in which the Fascist party and state truly controlled all aspects of life. That was his aim, however, and that is surely the important point. To the north of Italy, another variety of fascism appeared in the 1920s with the same totalitarian aim—and came much closer to succeeding.

FASCISM IN GERMANY: NAZISM

Hitler and Nazism

Just as Italian fascism was closely associated with Benito Mussolini, so its German counterpart, nazism, was inextricably linked with Adolf Hitler. Hitler was born in Austria, near the German border, in 1889. Moving to Vienna when he was 18, Hitler tried, unsuccessfully, to establish himself as an artist. He remained there for several years, living practically as a vagrant, until World War I began. Hitler then joined the German army and served with distinction, twice winning the Iron Cross for bravery. He was in the hospital when the war ended in 1918, and shortly thereafter his political career began.

When Germany surrendered to end World War I, German troops were still on French soil, and many Germans believed that surrender was unnecessary. Germany had not been defeated on the battlefield, they charged, but betrayed by traitorous politicians. Hitler shared these sentiments. After his release from the hospital, Hitler remained with the army as a spy. In this role he attended the meetings in Munich of a tiny group that called itself the German Workers' party. Hitler somehow saw an opportunity in this group, which he joined in 1920. He soon became the leader of the party under its new name, the National Socialist German Workers' party—or Nazis, as they were called from the abbreviation of the first two words.

The party grew quickly under Hitler's direction. To give an impression of discipline and strength, the Nazis established a paramilitary organization, the brown-shirted Storm Troopers, which they used to break up meetings of the Socialist and Communist parties. In 1923, perhaps hoping for the same luck Mussolini had enjoyed with his March on Rome the year before, Hitler launched the Beer Hall *Putsch*. This was an attempt to overthrow the government of the German province of Bavaria in the hope that this would topple the whole German government and bring the Nazis to power. The *putsch* (or *coup*

Adolf Hitler (1889–1945).

d'état) failed, however, and Hitler was arrested and tried for treason. Yet for his part in this armed uprising against the government, Hitler received only a five-year prison sentence and served only nine months of it. During his imprisonment, he wrote the first part of his autobiography, *Mein Kampf*, or *My Battle*.

In that book Hitler made clear the basic outlines of his ideology. Germany has a great destiny, he wrote, if only the German *volk* (folk or people) can join forces and throw off those enemies who divide and betray them—particularly the communists and Jews. But the German people will not be able to do this without a single party and supreme leader to forge them into a united and invincible force. As he wrote in *Mein Kampf*:

> The psyche of the great masses is not receptive to anything that is half-hearted and weak.
>
> Like the woman, whose psychic state is determined less by abstract reason than by an indefinable emotional longing for a force which will complement her nature, and who, consequently, would rather bow to a strong man than dominate

a weakling, [so] likewise the masses love a commander more than a petitioner and
feel inwardly more satisfied by a doctrine tolerating no other beside itself, than by
the granting of liberalistic freedom . . . .[8]

This was Hitler's notion of the *Führerprinzip*—the leadership principle—
according to which the masses and the *Führer*, or leader, were bound together.
The relationship, as Hitler's words indicate, is erotic and even sadistic in the
original Sadean sense.

Once out of prison, Hitler returned to his political agitation, relying on a
combination of ordinary political campaigning and strong-arm tactics. By 1933
the Nazis were the largest of several parties in the German *Reichstag*, or Parliament, although they did not control a majority of the seats. When Hitler was
appointed Chancellor, he quickly proved even more adept than Mussolini at
converting his position as head of government into an outright dictatorship. He
then moved to create a Third *Reich* (empire) in Germany, one that would sur-
pass the first two—the Holy Roman Empire and the German Empire that Bismarck had consolidated by 1871. This would be a Thousand Year *Reich*, and
throughout this millenium Germany would be the political and cultural leader
of Europe.

To accomplish this goal, Hitler planned to do two things. First, provide
Germany with *lebensraum*, the "living room" or breathing space it needed to
become a great empire. Hence Hitler looked to the east—to Poland and the
Soviet Ukraine in particular—as the future "bread basket" of Germany. The
lands to the east were to be conquered and their "inferior" people were to be
enslaved. Hitler set this part of his plan in motion when he invaded Poland on
September 1, 1939, thus beginning World War II.

The second of Hitler's plans was to eliminate all enemies standing in the
way of the Thousand Year *Reich*. These included the communists, both in Germany and elsewhere, and the Jews. In attempting to fulfill this plan, Hitler in
1941 invaded the Soviet Union, with which he had signed a nonaggression
pact, and undertook the "Final Solution" to the "Jewish Problem." This led,
during World War II, to the systematic murder of some six million Jews and
other supposedly "inferior" peoples.

World War II ended for Germany in the spring of 1945 with English and
American armies moving toward Berlin from the west and the Soviet army
entering it from the east. In the last days of April, while confined to his bunker
in Berlin, Hitler married his mistress, bid farewell to his staff, and, with his
new bride, committed suicide. To avoid meeting the same humiliating fate as
Mussolini and his mistress, Hitler left orders that their bodies be burned. Thus
ended the career of *Der Führer*, whose thousand-year *Reich* had lasted scarcely
a dozen years.

Nazism in Theory and Practice

In most respects nazism in Germany closely resembled fascism in Italy. There
was the same hatred of liberalism and communism, for instance; the same atti-

tude toward the masses, which were to be molded to the will of the great leader through propaganda and indoctrination; the same reliance on an organic conception of society; the same appeal to military might and the need for discipline and sacrifice; the same emphasis on nationalism; and the same totalitarian spirit. Neither Hitler nor Mussolini had much interest in economic matters, moreover, at least not as long as they thought that their countries were producing enough weapons and other war materiel. The inclusion of the word "socialist" in the name of the Nazi party has led to some confusion on this point, but Hitler certainly was no socialist. As he explained in a speech,

> Every truly national idea is in the last resort social, i.e., he who is prepared so completely to adopt the cause of his people that he really knows no higher ideal than the prosperity of this—his own—people, he who has so taken to heart the meaning of our great song *"Deutschland, Deutschland über alles,"* that nothing in this world stands for him higher than this Germany, people and land, land and people, he is a socialist. . . . [He] is not merely a socialist but he is also national in the highest sense of that word.[9]

For Hitler, then, socialism was merely another name for nationalism. The "nation," moreover, did not include everyone born within the borders of Germany, but only those born into the racial group to which the German *volk* belonged.

From the beginning nazism relied, and continues to rely, on the idea that race is the fundamental characteristic of human beings. Race was never an important matter for the Italian Fascists—not, that is, until pressure from Hitler led Mussolini to take some steps against Jews in Italy. Fascism was not, and need not be, a racist ideology, in other words; nazism was and is. Indeed, the belief that one race is innately superior to others is at the core of nazism—so much so that we can define nazism in terms of the simple formula, fascism + racism = nazism. This is especially clear in the nazi views of human nature and freedom.

For Hitler and his followers, the fundamental fact of human life is that human beings belong to different races. There is no such thing as a universal human nature, in their view, because the differences that distinguish one race from another mark each race for a different role or destiny in the world. There was nothing really new in this, for racist theories had been around for a long time and had become particularly influential in the nineteenth century through the work of Joseph-Arthur de Gobineau and other Counter-Enlightenment thinkers.

According to Gobineau, race was the key to the rise and fall of great civilizations. Like many other people over the centuries, Gobineau wondered why once mighty empires such as Rome lost their power and collapsed. The answer he hit upon was *miscegenation*, the mixture of races. A people rose to power, Gobineau concluded, when its racial composition was pure and vigorous. But as it expanded its control over conquered peoples—as it became an empire— the original racial stock was weakened by interbreeding with other races. The result was an inferior people, incapable of maintaining its identity and power.

And the result of that was the loss of the empire. Furthermore, the world's races were not created equal. The white race is superior to the yellow, Gobineau said, and the yellow is superior to the black. This is the pattern of nature, as he saw it, and it ought to be observed in society as well.

Ideas like Gobineau's were much in the air in the late nineteenth century, as were those of the **Social Darwinists.** As advanced by Herbert Spencer and William Graham Sumner, Social Darwinism was not a racist doctrine. Its emphasis on the struggle for survival, however, lent itself to a racist interpretation. All one had to do was say that the struggle for survival was not a struggle between *species*, as Darwin's theory said, nor a struggle between *individuals*, as Spencer and Sumner said, but a broader struggle between entire *races* of people. This was, and continues to be, the essence of the nazi position. One race is superior to all others, Hitler proclaimed. It is the "master race," and nature intends it to rule the other, "inferior" races.

Which was the master race? Hitler's answer was usually the **Aryans,** though he sometimes referred to the Nordic race. By referring to the Aryan race, he drew, probably unconsciously, on the studies of several nineteenth century scholars, especially linguists. In studying various languages, they found evidence that not only the European languages, but also those of the Middle East and some of India shared a common source. Some scholars concluded that these languages, and all the civilizations of India, Europe, and the Middle East, must have emerged from a single group of people, which they referred to as the Aryans. Gradually the notion grew that the Aryans were an extraordinary race, the fountain of most of what was civilized and worthwhile in the world. On the basis of this speculation, the Nazis decided that it was the destiny of Aryans to rule others, to subjugate the inferior races so that culture could advance and reach new and glorious heights.

To realize their destiny, however, the Aryans would have to become aware that the inferior races hated them and plotted their destruction. The Aryans would have to respond ruthlessly, destroying their most dangerous racial enemies and enslaving others. And this is precisely what Hitler proposed to do.

As far as Hitler was concerned, the Aryan race was the source—the "culture creating" source—of European civilization. And the Germanic people were the highest or purest remnant of the Aryan race. Thus the destiny of the German *volk* was clear: to dominate or even exterminate so-called lesser peoples—particularly Jews, Gypsies, Slavs, and other "inferior" races and nationalities. Out of this domination would come the glorious Thousand Year *Reich*.

The Nazis also drew upon this racial view of human nature in developing their conception of freedom. Like the Italian Fascists, they opposed the liberal view that freedom is a matter of individual liberty, favoring instead the idea that freedom properly understood is the freedom of the nation or *volk*. But the Nazis gave this idea their characteristic racial twist. The only freedom that counts, they said, is the freedom of the *volk* who belong to the master race. Freedom should be the freedom of Aryans because that is nature's plan. But there are obstacles in the way of the Aryan race's freedom to realize its destiny. Besides inferior races who are doing all they can to drag the Aryans down

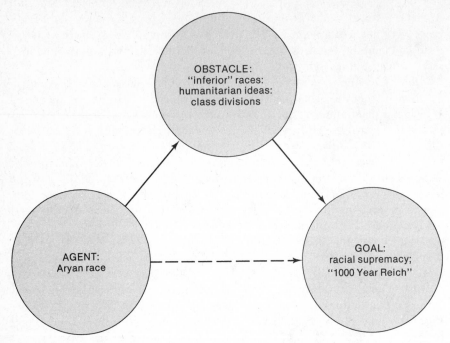

Figure 7.2 The Nazi conception of freedom.

to their own level, there is also the obstacle presented by certain ideas and ideals—specifically, the humanist ideas of the Enlightenment. These, according to Hitler, were "Jewish ideas," ideas that made even Aryans soft and squeamish. Because these ideas of universal brotherhood and equality are at the core of liberalism and Marxism, it followed for Hitler that these ideologies are not merely obstacles, but enemies to be rooted out and destroyed. This was the rationale for censorship, for book burnings, for toughening the minds of the young to make them into willing servants of *Führer* and *volk*.

Every individual, in the Nazi view, is merely a cell in the larger *volkish* organism. The destiny of the organism is also the individual's destiny. Outside the *Volksgemeinschaft*—the racially pure "folk community"—nothing worthwhile exists. In seeking to create and sustain such a community, therefore, one must not be distracted by softness or compassion or pity. "Inferior" peoples must be regarded as subhuman animals or "vermin" to be destroyed without a moment's thought or hesitation. Only in that way can the Aryan people be free to achieve their great destiny. For nazis, then, freedom takes the form shown in Figure 7.2.

FASCISM ELSEWHERE

Although fascism has been most closely identified with Italy and Germany in the period from World War I to World War II, it was not confined to those two countries. Fascist parties and movements spread throughout Europe in the 1920s and 1930s, from Romania to France and England, and made a brief appearance in the United States in the 1930s. Aside from Italy and Germany, however, the only European country in which fascism came to power was Spain under the regime of General Francisco Franco. Franco's forces won the Spanish Civil War (1936–1939) with the aid of both Italy and Germany. Once the Civil War was over, though, and especially when World War II began to go against the fascist powers, Franco ousted the more ardent fascists from his government and moved in the direction of a conservative, even reactionary, dictatorship. Franco was more concerned, that is, with maintaining firm authority in a quiet Spain than in mobilizing mass support in order to win glory and a new empire for his country.

Fascism also enjoyed some success outside Europe, notably in Argentina in the 1940s and 1950s under the leadership of Juan Perón, an army officer who won a large following among the Argentine working class. There have been—and continue to be—strong elements of fascism in South Africa, too. Although they try to distance themselves from Hitler and nazism, the official South African policy of **apartheid,** or racial separation, is justified by invoking ideas about the organic unity of a racially superior Afrikaner *volk*.

Apartheid literally means "apartness," and there are two senses in which the South African government has pursued a policy of apartness. The first is segregation of the races. Since 1948, when the Afrikaner Nationalist party first won control of the government, the people of South Africa have been officially divided into four racial groups: African, Asian, Coloured (i.e., of mixed descent), and White. Although the Africans are easily the largest part of the population—more than 72 percent of the total, according to the 1980 census—the ruling Nationalist party has denied them voting rights and virtually shut them out of the country's regular political process. Since 1984, Asians and Coloureds have been able to vote, but only for representatives to the Asian and Coloured houses of the legislature—with a third house, reserved for Whites, holding the ultimate power. There have also been laws prohibiting marriage between whites and nonwhites, *pass laws* (recently repealed) that require Africans to obtain permission before they enter white urban areas, and attempts to confine the Africans to ten territorial "homelands" located in some of the poorest and most barren areas of South Africa.

White South Africans, especially descendants of Dutch and German colonists known as Afrikaners, have typically justified this policy by appealing to the belief that racial differences are fixed and unchanging features of life. Each race has its own distinct characteristics, in this view, and no good can come from attempts to bring the races together. Each race can best develop along the lines nature intends only if it remains separate from the others—hence the notion that the different races of South Africa are pursuing "separate development." Separate, but not equal. For one race, the White, is supposedly superior to the others. Not only must Whites keep apart from other races, they must also exercise the leadership necessary to make separate development possible for all.

This brings us to the second sense in which *apartheid* means apartness in South Africa. Many Afrikaners believe that they are a special people, chosen by God to carry out His plan in their country. One Afrikaner leader stated this view in 1944:

> In every People in the world is embodied a Divine Idea and the task of each People is to build upon that Idea and to perfect it. So God created the Afrikaner People with a unique language, a unique philosophy of life, and their own history and tradition in order that they might fulfill a particular calling and destiny here in the southern corner of Africa. We must stand guard on all that is peculiar to us and build upon it. We must believe that God has called us to be servants of his righteousness in this place.[10]

So the Afrikaner *volk*, who compose the majority of the White population, are a special people with a special calling. They are a breed apart from others, and if they are to accomplish their mission they must remain apart.

To their sense of the racial superiority of Whites in general, then, white Afrikaners added a belief in their national destiny as a distinctive people or *volk*. These elements, as we have seen, were among the key ingredients of nazism in Germany, and, except for the racism, of fascism in Italy. To be sure, there has also been some loosening of restrictions on the African, Asian, and Coloured citizens of the country in recent years. Still, the policy of *apartheid* remains in place; and resting as it does on the two pillars of racism and nationalism, it bears more than a passing resemblance to fascist and nazi doctrine.

As the example of South Africa indicates, fascism is not altogether dead and gone, not even in the two countries in which it seemed so thoroughly defeated. The Fascist party is outlawed in Italy, as is the Nazi party in Germany, but neofascists and neonazis still run for office, and organize marches and rallies, under different names. There has, in fact, been a small revival of fascism throughout Europe in recent years. This seems to be the result of a renewed nationalism that has been brought to the fore by resentment of foreign workers and immigrants. In the United States, too, the Nazi party and other groups with fascist leanings—the Ku Klux Klan, the Aryan Nation, and assorted "skinheads"—sometimes make their presence felt.

So fascism as an ideology is not dead. It lives on, at least as a possibility, wherever the sense of national or racial difference leads to a longing for national unity.

CONCLUSION

Fascism as an Ideology

One feature of fascism is clear. No matter what the form, fascists have always tried to win mass support by appealing to people in the simplest, most emotional terms. This becomes evident as we look at how fascism and nazism perform the four functions of political ideologies.

Explanation   Why are social conditions the way they are? Fascists typically answer this question with some account of heroes and villains. Usually they concentrate on the scoundrels or traitors who conspire to keep the nation or *volk* weak in order to serve their own partisan interests. They look for scapegoats on whom to blame their problems. This is what the Nazis did to the Jews, for instance, and what neonazis and other white supremacists do to blacks, or hispanics, or other "inferior" and "foreign" groups.

Evaluation   Whether a situation is good or bad, according to fascists, will usually depend on some evaluation of a nation's or *volk's* unity and strength. If the people are fragmented, at odds with one another, then it is time to look for the scoundrels who are tearing the *volk* or nation apart. If the people are united behind their party and their leader, on the other hand, then all is well.

Orientation   What is one's place in the world, one's primary source of belonging or identification? According to the Italian Fascists it is the nation-state; to the nazis, the nation defined in racial terms. In either case, the individual should recognize that he or she is of no significance as an individual, but only as a member of the organic whole—the nation-state or the race—that gives meaning and purpose to his or her life.

Program   What is to be done? Again, the answer is simple—believe, obey, fight! Follow one's leaders in the struggle against the enemies of the nation or race, and do whatever is necessary to bring glory to one's people by helping to establish it as a leading power in the world. Give everything to the state, keep nothing from the state, and do nothing against the state.

Fascism and the Democratic Ideal

In its strongest forms, then, whether it be Italian fascism or German nazism, fascism is a totalitarian ideology. Of all the political ideologies, it is the only one to reject democracy altogether. Although it responds to the democratic ideal, it responds with contempt. For the fascist, democracy is merely another name for division and weakness in a world where unity and strength are what truly matter.

NOTES

1. For a clear statement of this view, see Immanuel Kant, "What Is Enlightenment?," in Terence Ball and Richard Dagger, eds., *Ideals and Ideologies: A Reader* (New York: HarperCollins, 1991), selection 17.
2. We take the term *Counter-Enlightenment* from Isaiah Berlin's essay, "The Counter-Enlightenment," in Berlin, *Against the Current: Essays in the History of Ideas* (Harmondsworth: Penguin, 1982), pp. 1–24.
3. Hans Kohn, *Nationalism: Its Meaning and History* (Princeton, N.J.: D. Van Nostrand, 1955), p. 36.

4. William Y. Elliot and Neil McDonald, eds., *Western Political Heritage* (New York: Prentice-Hall, 1949), p. 797.
5. Quoted in A. James Gregor, *Contemporary Radical Ideologies* (New York: Random House, 1968), p. 131.
6. Quoted in William S. Halperin, *Mussolini and Italian Fascism* (Princeton, N.J.: D. Van Nostrand, 1964), p. 47.
7. Both passages quoted in Denis Mack Smith, "The Theory and Practice of Fascism," in Nathanael Greene, ed., *Fascism: An Anthology* (New York: Thomas Y. Crowell, 1968), pp. 109–110.
8. Adolf Hitler, *Mein Kampf*, trans. Ralph Manheim (Boston: Houghton Mifflin, 1943), p. 42; also in Ball and Dagger, eds., *Ideals and Ideologies*, selection 42.
9. Quoted in Gregor, *Contemporary Radical Ideologies*, p. 197.
10. Quoted in Leonard Thompson, *The Political Mythology of Apartheid* (New Haven, Conn.: Yale University Press, 1985), p. 29.

FOR FURTHER READING

Arendt, Hannah. *The Origins of Totalitarianism* (Cleveland and New York: Meridian Books, 1958).

Bullock, Alan. *Hitler: A Study in Tyranny*, rev. ed. (New York: Harper & Row, 1964).

Kohn, Hans. *The Idea of Nationalism: A Study in Its Origin and Background* (New York: Collier, 1967).

Mosse, George. *The Crisis of German Ideology: Intellectual Origins of the Third Reich* (New York: Grosset & Dunlap, 1964).

Nolte, Ernst. *Three Faces of Fascism: Action Française, Italian Fascism, National Socialism*, trans. Leila Vennewitz (New York: Holt, Rinehart & Winston, 1965).

Smith, Denis Mack. *Mussolini* (New York: Alfred A. Knopf, 1982).

Thompson, Leonard. *The Political Mythology of Apartheid* (New Haven, Conn.: Yale University Press, 1985).

PART
Three

POLITICAL IDEOLOGIES TODAY AND TOMORROW

Chapter
8

Liberation Ideologies

Man is born free, yet everywhere he is in chains. . . . The one who thinks himself the master of others is as much a slave as they.

Jean-Jacques Rousseau

*I*n the past quarter-century or so, several ideologies have affixed the word *liberation* to their name. The call for *black liberation* came out of the ferment of the 1960s, as did the *women's liberation movement*. These were followed by the *gay liberation* movement in Europe and North America, *liberation theology* in Latin America, and even an increasingly militant *animal liberation* movement in Europe and the United States. In many respects, of course, these are very different movements with vastly different ideologies. Each has its distinctive arguments and each addresses a particular audience. Yet, despite their differences, all share common features that mark their respective ideologies as members of an extended family.

This family resemblance should become clear in this chapter as we examine the extent to which these liberation ideologies have a common core. Do they share a similar conception of freedom or liberty? How does each fulfill the four functions of an ideology? And how does each define the democratic ideal?

LIBERATION IDEOLOGIES: COMMON CHARACTERISTICS

An interest in liberation is, of course, nothing new. All political ideologies have stressed the importance of liberty, although, as we have seen, each conceives of liberty in very different ways. In some respects, then, contemporary liberation ideologies simply extend or amend the views of earlier ideologies, especially liberalism and socialism. But these new ideologies seek liberation from forms of oppression and domination that, in the liberationists' view, earlier ideologies have wrongly neglected or overlooked. They also recommend new and distinctive strategies for overcoming or ending oppression.

Liberation ideologies share several core, or common, features. The first is that each addresses a particular audience—blacks, or women, or homosexuals, or poor peasants, or even people distressed by the mistreatment of animals. (As we note later, the ideology of animal liberation runs into theoretical difficulties faced by no other liberation ideology.) A second common feature is that each of the groups addressed is supposedly mistreated or oppressed by some dominant group. The term "oppression" refers to the many means—institutional, intellectual, legal, even linguistic—that some people use to "press down," "crush," or otherwise "deform" others.[1] It is in this sense that blacks have been and still are oppressed by whites, women by men, homosexuals by heterosexuals, poor peasants by wealthy landowners, and animals by humans.

A third feature common to all liberation ideologies is that they aim to liberate an oppressed group not only from "external" restraints or restrictions, such as unjust or discriminatory laws, barriers to entry in education, housing, employment, and others, but from "internal" restrictions as well. Internal restrictions are those beliefs and attitudes that oppressed people have come to accept—uncritically and unconsciously—as true, and which then serve to inhibit their quest for freedom or liberation. Liberation ideologies are addressed, then, to people who have in some sense participated in their own oppression or victimization. In this view, for example, some blacks have internalized "white" values and racist attitudes toward blacks; some women have accepted men's diagnoses and explanations of their discontent; many homosexuals have felt guilty because they are not "straight" or heterosexual; many Latin American peasants have accepted their "lot" in life as fate or as the will of God; and if not animals, then at least those humans who eat their flesh and wear their fur have accepted the claim that humans are a "higher" species with the right to eat or skin members of "lower" species. The dominance of the ruling race, gender, sexual orientation, class, or species depends on the oppressed group's continuing acceptance of their condition as natural, normal, or inevitable. To break the grip and the legitimacy of the dominant group requires a change of outlook and attitude on the part of the oppressed.

From this there follows a fourth feature common to all liberation ideologies: all aim to "raise the consciousness" and change the outlooks of people who have somehow participated—however unwillingly, unwittingly, or unconsciously—in their own oppression or victimization. Such participation may take many forms. For example, a black person might feel socially or intellectually inferior to whites; women might think themselves to be helpless, or at least less powerful than men; homosexuals might feel guilty for being "gay" or homosexual, rather than "straight"; and so on. The aim of the various liberation ideologies is to confront and criticize the sources of these feelings of inadequacy, inferiority, or guilt—and in so doing to liberate or emancipate members of oppressed groups by helping them to help themselves.

Fifth and finally, liberation ideologies also aim to liberate the oppressors—to free them from the illusion of their own superiority and to help them recognize their former victims as fellow human beings. The aim of all liberation ideologies, in short, is to break those "mind-forged manacles" about which William Blake wrote a century and a half ago.[2]

Since each of these liberation ideologies addresses a specific audience or group, we can best understand their structure, arguments, and appeal by looking at the groups to which each is addressed.

BLACK LIBERATION

The ideology of black liberation has two main variants. These are not entirely distinct from one another, since they share the same goal—an end to the **racism** that oppresses black people—and sometimes adopt similar tactics. But there is a significant difference of emphasis in the two approaches to black liberation. The first, the *civil rights* variant, is essentially liberal in outlook. That is, it is concerned with protecting and extending rights to people previously denied them. Thus the civil rights movement of the 1960s, led by Dr. Martin Luther King, Jr., and others, addressed itself mainly to overt discrimination in such matters as voting rights, education, transportation, housing, and jobs. Many gains were made, and many battles won; but the struggle continues against widely and persistently held racist beliefs and attitudes among white people—and, perhaps surprisingly, among some blacks as well. From the sec-

Martin Luther King, Jr. (1929–1968).

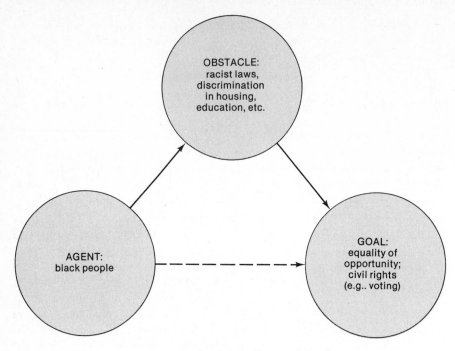

Figure 8.1 The "civil rights" view of freedom.

ond, or *black liberationist* perspective, the most pernicious form of racism may well be that which lodges itself inside, and damages, the psyche of blacks. This is the particularly subtle and insidious kind of racism that the ideology of black liberation addresses and seeks to overcome. (See Figure 8.1.)

People of color, and perhaps black people in particular, have long felt the sting of prejudice and racial discrimination. Whether in the form of racial slurs, stereotypes, or jokes, such prejudice wounds the pride and undermines or even destroys the dignity and self-respect of racial minorities. However hard a black person may work to earn the respect of others, he or she is still likely to be viewed and assessed in racially stereotypical terms. To shed the burdens of the racist stereotype he or she may try to "pass"—if not actually to pass as white, then at least to be accepted by whites by, for example, straightening one's hair, adopting "white" tastes in music, food, clothes, and friends, and taking care not to use "black" expressions or turns of phrase. Since such attempts are almost always unsuccessful, one might then turn one's anger inward, toward oneself, hating one's own blackness more than one hates white racists.

This double rage—hatred not only of one's oppressors, but of oneself and one's race—has often been noted by black writers. It has been voiced eloquently by the novelists Richard Wright and James Baldwin, the black poet Langston Hughes, and Malcolm X, the assassinated Black Muslim leader, in *The Autobiography of Malcolm X*. Having been suppressed and turned inward by blacks, this anger sometimes comes to the surface in self-destructive ways. Psychoanalysts call this process "sublimation" or "the return of the repressed." It may take a skilled psychoanalyst to help someone delve deep inside his or her psyche to bring such long-suppressed anger to light. So perhaps it is not surprising that some of the most far-reaching analyses of black self-loathing have been made by psychoanalysts. Two of them, Drs. William Grier and Price Cobbs, call the syndrome "Black Rage"—an anger against whites that blacks vent on themselves and each other.[3] This, in conjunction with poverty, despair, lack of educational opportunities, and other social and economic inequalities, may help to explain the disturbingly high homicide and drug addiction rates among inner-city blacks in the United States.

Nor are these pathologies confined to North America. In *Black Skins, White Masks*, the Algerian psychoanalyst Frantz Fanon described the despair of black Africans who tried to adopt white European attitudes and values, and in the attempt lost their identity and sense of self-worth. Their French may be exquisite and more eloquent than that of their colonial masters, their European suits of impeccable cut and quality, and their manners charming; but, try as they might, they are not and never will be white Europeans. The result, as Fanon recounts it, is an unrequited love for white Europeans and all things European, on the one hand, and an abiding hatred of all things black and African, on the other. Such self-loathing gives rise to self-destructive behavior.[4] The only way out of this impasse, says Fanon, is for black people to break out of their mental prisons; not to be freed by others, but to free themselves from the false beliefs and illusions in which they have for too long been ensnared. The process of healing, of recovering from the massive psychic injury that whites have visited upon blacks (and blacks upon themselves), begins by calling white culture into question, by showing that the standards of white culture are not necessarily the true or the only standards of intelligence, beauty, and achievement. Black people need to recognize that their so-called ugliness and inferiority is a "mind-forged manacle"—or, to change the metaphor, an illusory bubble that bursts as soon as it is seen for what it is.

The ideology of black liberation tries to burst this bubble by several means. One is to recover black history—the story of how blacks, in the long history of their bondage, have triumphed time and again against their white masters; how they have retained their dignity despite the indignities heaped upon them by slave-owners and other oppressors; and how they have developed an affirmative culture—art, music, poetry, and literature—that has infused and influenced the dominant culture of today. (It is in fact almost impossible to think of modern mainstream "American" music—blues, jazz, and rock-and-roll—without acknowledging its black roots.) Another is to repudiate "white" views of blacks (and some blacks' internalized views of themselves) by reclaiming and proclaiming "black" values and standards. This can be done, for example, by affirming that "black is beautiful," that curly or "knappy" hair is attractive, and that "black" English and dress should be proudly displayed as badges of black identity and solidarity. In these and other ways, the ideology of black liberation has attempted to instill a sense of racial pride and identity.

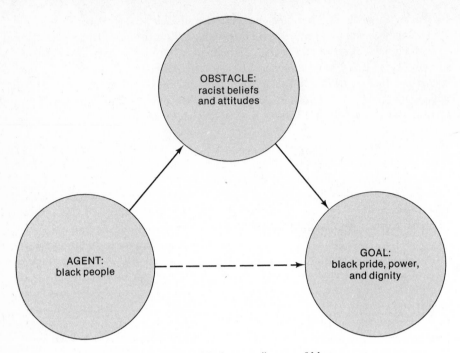

Figure 8.2 The "black power" view of liberty.

Pride and identity are necessary steps on the road to liberation, according to this view. This will be liberation not only for oppressed black people, furthermore, but liberation for their oppressors as well. On this point the civil rights and liberationist variants of black liberation agree. Like the master in Hegel's parable of the master and slave (see Chapter 5, pp. 128–129), whites cannot be free as long as they refuse to acknowledge that blacks are equally worthy as human beings. Martin Luther King, Jr., who had studied Hegel's philosophy in divinity school, gave eloquent statement to this view in a speech in 1962.

> Many Southern leaders are pathetically trapped by their own devices. They know that the perpetuation of this archaic, dying order [of racial segregation] is hindering the rapid growth of the South. Yet they cannot speak this truth—they are imprisoned by their own lies. It is history's wry paradox that when Negroes win their struggle to be free, those who have held them down will themselves be freed for the first time.[5]

The black power and black pride movements of the late 1960s and 1970s— as found, for example, in the Black Muslim religion and the Black Panther party—may have lost their militancy and perhaps much of their appeal, but their legacy remains. If blacks are no longer so militant, that may be because they have made their point—to white people and, more importantly, to themselves. In South Africa, however, the ideology of black liberation—as found, for example, in the African National Congress (ANC) led by Nelson Mandela and the Black Power movement led by the late Steve Biko—remains very much alive and vital in the face of continuing repression.

The conception of freedom (or liberty) at the core of the ideology of black liberation is schematically summarized in Figure 8.2.

WOMEN'S LIBERATION

It might be thought that the women's liberation movement and its ideology began only in the 1960s. In fact, the ideology of women's liberation has a long history. Yet this history has until recently remained half-hidden, and women's voices have been submerged or ignored. Some of these voices have come down to us, however. Writing to her husband, John Adams, who was attending the 1776 Continental Congress, Abigail Adams asked him to "remember the ladies and be more generous and favorable to them than your ancestors. Do not put such unlimited power into the hands of the husbands. Remember, all men would be tyrants if they could. If particular care and attention is not paid to the ladies, we are determined to foment a rebellion, and will not hold ourselves bound by any laws in which we have no voice or representation."[6] In a similar spirit, Mary Wollstonecraft chided Thomas Paine for writing *The Rights of Man* and neglecting the rights of women, which she then defended in *A Vindication of the Rights of Woman* (1792). The nineteenth century saw an increasing militancy on the part of women. Suffragettes in England and the United States demanded that women be allowed to vote, while others lobbied for changes in the laws regulating marriage and divorce. Many in the early nineteenth-century American women's movement—Margaret Fuller, Lucy Stone, Sojourner Truth, Elizabeth Cady Stanton, and others—were also active in the antislavery movement. As they pointed out, the condition of women and slaves were similar in many ways: both were denied the right to vote, to run for public office, to own property in their own name, or to leave an abusive master or husband. Others, such as Susan B. Anthony, were active in the temperance movement because many wives and children were sexually abused, beaten, neglected, and abandoned by alcoholic husbands and fathers. The women's movement began, then, not only as an attempt to further the cause of women, but of other oppressed people as well.

The response of many, perhaps most, men was either to ignore or to ridicule women who dared to make such outlandish and radical demands. John Adams, for example, replying to Abigail's letter, wrote, "I cannot but laugh." As it gained strength in the nineteenth century, the women's movement became the butt of jokes and cartoons; newspaper editorials predicted that if these women had their way, husbands would look after the children while their wives worked and went to the saloon to drink whisky and smoke cigars. Not all men laughed, however; some risked ridicule by siding with the women. In England, William Thompson issued *An Appeal of One-Half of the Human Race* (1822) and John Stuart Mill decried *The Subjection of Women* (1869), as did Friedrich Engels in *Origins of the Family, Private Property and the State* (1884). In the United States the former slave Frederick Douglass spoke and wrote on behalf

Mary Wollstonecraft, later Mary Wollstonecraft Godwin (1759–1797).

of the fledgling women's movement and the antislavery advocate William Lloyd Garrison editorialized in defense of women's rights.[7]

In the twentieth century there have been a number of different variations or variants of a feminist perspective, often in combination with other ideologies such as socialism and anarchism. Socialist feminists, for example, argue that women cannot be free until capitalism has been replaced by socialism.[8] Anarchist feminists claim that women will be oppressed as long as the state exists.[9] Lesbian separatist feminists claim that women will be oppressed as long as they associate with and are dependent upon men.[10] But perhaps the two most influential contemporary variants are the *liberal feminist* and the *women's liberationist* perspectives.

The early women's movement represents largely the first or liberal feminist view. Like the Civil Rights variant of the movement for black liberation, it has been motivated mainly by a desire to overcome overt forms of discrimination—in marriage, educational opportunities, legal rights and, above all, the right to vote. The last was won in the United States in 1920, with the ratification of the Nineteenth Amendment to the Constitution. The removal of these and other legal and institutional barriers has been the aim of liberal feminists. Their goal has been to give women the same rights and opportunities that men enjoy. Their conception of freedom is schematically summarized in Figure 8.3.

The second and more militant Women's Liberation movement and its ideology first appeared in the late 1960s. It has been concerned not only with overt sexual discrimination, but also with exposing and overcoming more subtle forms of discrimination that go under the heading of **sexism.** Sexism is a set of beliefs and attitudes about women's supposedly innate inferiority and various inadequacies—intellectual, physical, emotional, spiritual, and otherwise—that prevent them from being men's equals. The ideology of women's liberation attempts to expose, criticize, and overcome these sexist attitudes and beliefs.

Such sexist attitudes and beliefs include, but are not limited to, the following: it is "unfeminine" to be successful in scholarly, athletic, or other endeavors, particularly in competition with males; girls are no good at math (or science, or sports); the same actions that are "bold" and "assertive" when a man

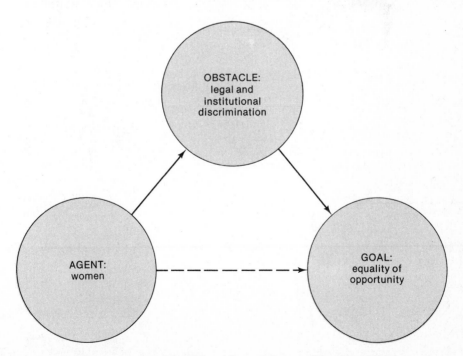

Figure 8.3 The "liberal feminist" view of freedom.

performs them are "bossy" and "aggressive" when undertaken by a woman; a man who makes a concession or a compromise is being "diplomatic," whereas a woman is showing "weakness"; men get "angry," women become "bitchy"; a woman who is raped probably provoked or invited the attack; and so on. These and many other sexist beliefs, attitudes, and stereotypes are widely held by men. But, say women's liberationists, women must not only address and attempt to overcome men's sexism, but their own as well. To the degree that women share these sexist views, they are afflicted with self-loathing and a lack of respect for themselves and for other women. Until women recognize that their chains are in part "mind-forged manacles," they cannot hope to break them. Women, in other words, need to recognize and overcome their own internalized sexist attitudes and beliefs about their sex's supposed limitations and liabilities.

The Women's Liberation movement has pursued several strategies for fighting sexism. In the 1960s and early 1970s especially, "consciousness raising groups"—small groups of women who met to talk about their experiences with and feelings about men, women, sex, love, marriage, children, parents, husbands, lovers, and friends—were formed for this purpose. So-called "Take Back the Night" marches and demonstrations were held to publicize the crime of rape. Women's counseling centers were opened and women invited to talk and to do something about their troubles. Women's studies programs were started in colleges and universities across the country to enable women to study women's history (or "herstory") and other subjects from a feminist or women's liberationist perspective. Through these and other means women's liberationists have confronted and resisted the sexist stereotypes, beliefs, and attitudes held by men and women alike.[11]

Unlike liberal feminists, who tend to stress the essential equality and sameness of the two sexes—especially equal rights, equal opportunities, and equal pay for comparable work—women's liberationists tend to emphasize *differences*. Men and women not only have different biological makeups; they also have different attitudes, outlooks, and values. Women should be free to be different, they argue, and these differences should be respected and protected. Nowhere are these differences more pronounced than in attitudes toward sex. Unlike most women, men tend to separate sex from love, trust, and respect. The sex act is therefore seen not as an integral feature of love and mutual respect, but as something that has no necessary relation to other emotions or activities. This attitude, in turn, carries over to men's attitudes in other areas as well. This is especially evident, for example, in the attitude toward women that is displayed in pornographic pictures and literature. There, women are depicted as mere bodies or body parts—as "sex objects"—rather than as whole people; they are shown to enjoy pain, degradation, and humiliation; and always they are subservient to men, who are depicted as proud, cruel, and uncaring. Not surprisingly, then, women's liberationists—unlike liberal feminists—often wage legal and political war against pornography and pornographers.

The view of liberty and liberation at the core of the ideology of the women's liberation movement may be summarized in Figure 8.4.

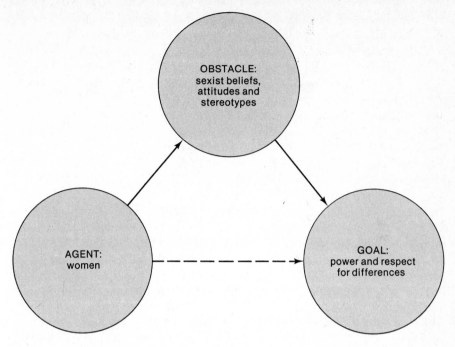

Figure 8.4 The "women's liberationist" view of freedom.

GAY LIBERATION

The **Gay** Liberation movement and its ideology are relatively recent arrivals on the political scene. This might at first seem surprising, since homosexuality is as old as heterosexuality. In the ancient Athens of Socrates, Plato, and Aristotle, for example, men acknowledged that heterosexual relations were necessary in order to produce children and continue the species; but they also pointed out that necessary activities, like eating and sleeping, are not necessarily noble or beautiful. As they saw it, homosexual love was superior to and more uplifting than heterosexual love because it represented an intimate relationship between equals (man to man or woman to woman) rather than between unequals (man to woman).[12] Similar attitudes often prevailed in ancient Rome.

If the classical world was hospitable to homosexuality, however, the religions that emerged from the Middle East took a decidedly different view of the matter. Jewish and Christian doctrine, as traditionally interpreted, have condemned homosexuality as perverted, unnatural, and sinful.[13] From these doctrines followed centuries of persecution of homosexuals. In Medieval Europe homosexuals were sometimes burned at the stake, and until very recently homosexuality was in most Western countries a crime punishable by imprisonment. In some countries of the Near and Middle East, it still is. Several American states still have sodomy laws prohibiting sexual relations between persons of the same sex. Even where legal penalties have been repealed or unenforced, other forms of discrimination persist. In many communities homosexuals face difficulties in securing employment, housing, and medical care—difficulties aggravated in recent years by the fear of AIDS. Lesbian mothers and homosexual fathers are often denied legal custody of their children. Teachers who admit to being gay sometimes lose their jobs, as do gays in the armed forces and other public service occupations.

The aim of the Gay Liberation movement has been twofold. Gay men and women have organized to repeal discriminatory laws and to gain access to opportunities previously denied them. And, in addition to opposing overt discrimination, gay liberationists have worked to overcome **homophobia**—fear of homosexuals and their influence—that stems from mistaken beliefs about, and attitudes toward, gay people. These **homophobic** beliefs include, but are not limited to, the following: all or most gays molest children; gay people generally seek to recruit children and young people into their ranks; all gays are sexually promiscuous; homosexuality is an abnormal or perverted sexual preference that can, and should, be corrected by psychiatric or other means; deep down, most gays really want to be straight; gays can be straight if they try hard enough; and so on. These and other homophobic beliefs are widely shared not only by heterosexuals, but even by some homosexuals who, by internalizing these attitudes, come to loathe themselves and other people like them. The newly emerging ideology of gay liberation aims to overcome both overt discrimination and homophobic attitudes and beliefs held by many heterosexuals and internalized by some homosexuals.[14] The movement has provided encouragement and support for gay men and women who wish to "come out of the closet" and publicly acknowledge their sexual preference. Their means of doing and affirming this include gay counseling centers, support groups, and "gay pride" marches and demonstrations.

The conception of freedom or liberty at the core of the gay liberation ideology is summarized in Figure 8.5.

LIBERATION THEOLOGY

A liberation movement of a different kind has emerged in the last quarter-century in the form of liberation theology. This movement aims to call attention to the plight of the poor, especially in Third World countries, and to inspire people, including the poor themselves, to help bring an end to their poverty. Although other Christian denominations are beginning to feel its influence, liberation theology has developed primarily within the Roman Catholic church. The center of its attention has been Latin America, where the population is overwhelmingly Catholic, and where many are desperately poor; but liberation theology also has advocates in Africa, Asia, Europe, and North America.

Liberation theology goes beyond the traditional Christian concern for saving souls for an afterlife. In addition, and perhaps more emphatically, it calls for political, even revolutionary action, on behalf of the poor in this earthly life. Not surprisingly, then, it is a subject of considerable controversy within the

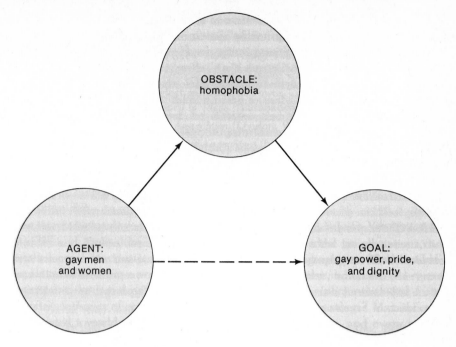

Figure 8.5 The "gay liberation" view of freedom.

Catholic church, particularly in Latin America. Some see liberation theology as an attempt to blend the teachings of Jesus with those of Marx, with critics complaining that there is more of Marx than Jesus in the mixture. As the liberation theologians see it, however, they are only following the example of Jesus in working for social justice. To do this work, they must draw on the insights of social theorists, such as Marx, who reveal the human sources of poverty and oppression. Thus they believe they act in the spirit of Jesus when they subject the church and the affluent parts of society to severe criticism. As a sympathetic writer describes it, liberation theology is

1. An interpretation of Christian faith out of the suffering, struggle, and hope of the poor.
2. A critique of society and the ideologies sustaining it.
3. A critique of the activity of the church and of Christians from the angle of the poor.[15]

To appreciate just how controversial liberation theology is, and to understand the purpose and point of the liberationists' arguments, we must look briefly at its historical background.

In earlier chapters we have noted how the Roman Catholic church has been a conservative force in European society. In prerevolutionary France, for instance, the church was the First Estate of the realm, a privileged part of the *ancien régime*. As a matter of policy, the church was usually hostile to liberalism, socialism, and any other movement that, in its view, paid too much attention to reason and progress and too little to faith and salvation. This remained the Catholic position until the late 1800s. Then, under the leadership of Pope Leo XIII, the position began to shift. Alarmed at the gap between social classes, and concerned that working-class men and women were leaving the church, Leo XIII issued *Rerum Novarum* in 1891. In this encyclical, or official statement of position, the Pope urged Christians to look upon themselves as equal members of God's family. Employers should not exploit workers, he said, and workers should give a full day's work for a full day's pay. But the main purpose of the encyclical was to praise the dignity of work and to demonstrate the church's concern for the just treatment of the working class. To a large extent, this new position meant that Catholicism was making its peace with democracy and reaching an accommodation with liberalism and socialism.

One result of this encouragement to take a greater interest in the earthly condition of the laboring class was the creation of Catholic trade unions. A later development was Christian Democracy—an attempt, as the name suggests, to combine Christian principles with democratic politics. From Christian Democracy came the Christian Democratic political parties that continue to play a major role in European politics today. These are generally moderate or center-right parties that support welfare programs and regulation of the economy, but not socialism as such.

Even more dramatic than *Rerum Novarum* was the change that Pope John XXIII initiated with the Second Vatican Council (Vatican II) of 1962–1965. Among other things, this council of Catholic bishops declared that church leaders can best keep and spread the faith by recognizing that they too are pilgrims who must make the journey of faith with the people. The church must become more directly involved in the lives and hopes of the people, in other words, and not simply administer the sacraments and teach the doctrines of Catholicism. In Latin America, a number of Catholic theologians took Vatican II as the sign of a new opportunity and a new challenge for the church. It was a step in the right direction, in their view, but only the first step on a long and arduous journey toward the liberation of the poor.

In 1968 a group of Catholic bishops from several Latin American countries met in Medellín, Colombia, to consider the implications of Vatican II. The general conclusion of the conference was that the church had devoted too many of its resources to the well-to-do in Central and South America and far too little to the poor. Catholic priests and nuns were often concentrated in the affluent areas of the cities, for example, where they taught and ministered to the middle class and wealthy. Intentionally or not, this led to the neglect of the great majority of the people, particularly the poor peasants of the countryside and the slum dwellers of the urban *barrios*. From Medellín, however, came a clear call for a change of direction as the bishops suggested that poverty was not simply the fate of the poor. Instead, poverty was largely the result of social conditions, or social structures, that were in turn the result of sinful conduct. To overcome poverty, the bishops said, "sweeping, bold, urgent, and profoundly renovating changes in society were necessary."[16]

Reflecting the work of several Latin American theologians, especially Gustavo Guttierez of Peru, the bold statement from Medellín brought liberation theology to public attention. Since then, Gutierez, Leonardo Boff of Brazil, and other Catholic theologians have urged the church to take a more active part in liberating the poor from poverty. The church, they say, should exercise its "option for the poor." To do this, however, it must move away from its traditional emphasis on rituals and sacraments. In helping people to reach and live in a "state of grace," in other words, the church has concentrated almost exclusively on orthodoxy—on teaching people the "correct beliefs." This is well and good, according to liberation theology, except that it has led to the neglect of the lives and needs of the poor, who find each day a struggle with misery and despair. In addition to orthodoxy, then, the church should promote **orthopraxis**—that is, "right" or "correct" action (*praxis*) in this world.

But what kind of action, according to liberation theologians, is right or correct? How should the church go about exercising the "option for the poor"? To answer these questions, liberation theologians rely heavily on the work of modern social thinkers. Thus they point out that the upper classes in Latin American countries have usually looked to economic development as a way of strengthening their countries' economies and raising the standard of living for their peoples. Such development means that countries try to promote industrial growth and productivity in the belief that this will create wealth that will eventually trickle down, through employment opportunities and other benefits, to the poor. But liberation theologians argue that development has been uneven and has led to "dependency." In order to develop their economies, that is, Latin American countries have had to rely upon investments and loans from the capitalist countries of Europe and North America, and this has made them dependent upon those foreign powers. Rather than developing their own economies, the result has been the continuous exploitation of the resources of Latin America, such as the destruction of the rain forests of Brazil, to meet the burden of foreign debt. Even worse, little of this so-called development ever provides any benefit for the poor. Instead, there is a great and growing gap between the wealthy and the middle class, on the one hand, and the poor and powerless, on the other.

What then is to be done? Liberation theology has produced no single or systematic program for change. A few seem willing to accept violent revolution as a necessary and acceptable means for winning justice for the poor. For the most part, however, liberation theologians see their mission, like other liberation ideologies, in terms of consciousness raising. We must follow the example of Jesus, they say, and go to live and teach among the poor. To this end, they have established "ecclesial base communities," where they instruct poor people not only in the Christian scriptures and faith, but also in reading, writing, health care, and social action. The core idea is to help the poor see that their poverty is *not* simply natural, part of the way life must be, but something that can and should be changed. Once they become aware of this, the poor will be able to take steps to free themselves from those sinful social structures that deny their human dignity and condemn them to poverty. In Gutierrez's words, we will have an authentic theology of liberation only when the oppressed themselves can freely raise their voice and express themselves directly and creatively in society and in the heart of the People of God, when they themselves "account for the hope," which they bear, when they are the protagonists of their own liberation.[17]

From the standpoint of liberation theology, in short, ending poverty is not simply a matter of growing more food and distributing it to more people. Poverty is the result of systematic oppression in Latin America and elsewhere. Some live in luxury and comfort while—and perhaps because—others barely survive. Poverty, then, is not just a matter of food and money, but a matter of liberation—of freeing people, and helping them to free themselves, from injustice and oppression. If this requires revolution, so be it. Some proponents of liberation theology actively supported the Sandinista regime in Nicaragua, and others have associated themselves in various ways with rebel or guerilla movements. Many have denounced what they regard as the injustice of the military and the rich; some have suffered the consequences. In El Salvador in 1989, for instance, six Jesuit priests, their housekeeper, and her daughter were murdered by an army death squad acting on orders to silence the priests' outspoken criticism of the Salvadoran regime. The best-known of these priests, all associated with the University of Central America, was Father Ignacio Ellacuria—rector of the university and an advocate of liberation theology.

Liberation theologians readily acknowledge that there are dangers involved in their struggle for liberation. But danger and suffering are the constant companions of poor people, they say, and those who exercise the option for the poor must be prepared to suffer as well. Nothing less than this is acceptable from Christians, whom liberation theologians remind of Jesus' promise to the righteous.

> "Then the King will say to those at his right hand, 'Come, O blessed of my Father, inherit the kingdom prepared for you from the foundation of the world; for I was hungry and you gave me food, I was thirsty and you gave me drink, I was a stranger and you welcomed me. I was naked and you clothed me, I was sick and you visited me, I was in prison and you came to me.'
>
> "Then the righteous will answer him, 'Lord, when did we see thee hungry and feed thee? or thirsty and give thee drink? And when did we see thee a stranger and welcome thee, or naked and clothe thee? And when did we see thee sick or in prison and visit thee?'
>
> "And the King will answer them, 'Truly, I say to you, as you did it to one of the least of these my brethren, you did it to me.' "[18]

Liberation theology combines religion with political action in a way that differs from the other liberation ideologies discussed in this chapter. Yet it clearly shares those five common features that, as we noted earlier, distinguish liberation ideologies from other ideologies. It is directed, first, to a particular audience—an audience composed of Christians. The poor are the principal subjects, of course, but liberation theology seeks to convert not only them, but all Christians to their interpretation of the Christian mission. Second, it also informs that audience about the ways in which the poor have been oppressed

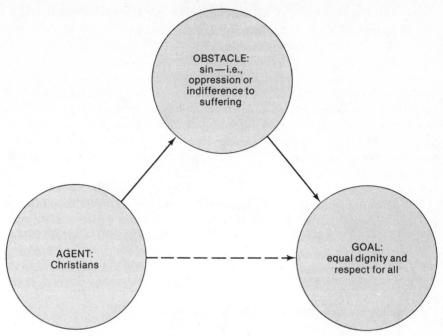

Figure 8.6 The liberation theology view of freedom.

by a dominant group—the affluent elite, both in Latin America and in those countries on which Latin America is dependent. Third, this oppression is not only external, but internalized in the form of a tendency among poor people to accept poverty as a normal part of life. Liberation theology says that the poor suffer from this internal oppression because they have been taught to see their poverty as their inevitable fate, as something that no one can control or change. This attitude, they say, must be overcome. In attempting to overcome this apathy, fourth, liberation theology tries to raise the consciousness of the poor so that they will be able to emancipate themselves. Again, however, it is not only the poor to whom liberation theology speaks. It also speaks, fifth and finally, to oppressors who sin directly against the poor and to bystanders who sin by their inaction. Those whose concern for themselves blinds them to the needs of the poor can be wealthy in worldly terms—houses, cars, cash—but suffer from a poverty of the spirit. Liberation theology thus addresses all Christians, rich and poor alike, for all need to be liberated from sin—including the sins of injustice, exploitation, and indifference to the sufferings of the poor.

The conception of freedom at the core of liberation theology may be understood as Figure 8.6 illustrates.

ANIMAL LIBERATION

We have left the ideology of animal liberation for last, not because it is unimportant or without influence—quite the contrary—but because it encounters a number of conceptual difficulties that other liberation ideologies do not face. Before examining these difficulties, however, we begin by looking briefly at the history of this ideology.

Human beings have long used animals for many purposes: as beasts of burden, as sources of food and fur, and more recently as pets. But human beings have also subjected animals to other less necessary and arguably more insidious uses. In the name of pleasure and entertainment, humans have used roosters in cock fights, bulls in bullfights, foxes in fox hunts, and dogs in dog fights. The proceedings and the results of such contests are too grisly to describe here. Suffice it to say that these contests are bloody, gruesome, and usually fatal to the animals forced to participate in them.

The forerunner of the ideology of animal liberation can be found in nineteenth century England, and more particularly in the increasingly widespread revulsion against the wanton use and abuse of animals for spectator sports.[19] Such suffering, said Jeremy Bentham (1748–1832), offends—or rather should offend—the moral sensibilities of any reasonably sensitive human being. At a time when growing numbers of people were actively attempting to free black slaves in America and elsewhere, Bentham wrote:

> The day may come when the rest of the animal creation may acquire those rights which never could have been with[held] from them but by the hand of tyranny. [Some] have already discovered that the blackness of the skin is no reason why a human being should be abandoned without redress to the caprice of a tormentor.[20]

But why, Bentham asked, are animals different? Is it because they have four legs? Or do animals deserve different treatment because they lack the use of reason? Or is it because animals cannot speak? To argue in this way, Bentham goes on to say, is self-defeating. Surely, he says,

> a full-grown horse or dog is beyond comparison a more rational, as well as a more conversable animal, than an infant of a day, or a week, or even a month, old. But suppose they were otherwise, what would it avail? The question is not, Can they reason? nor Can they talk? but, Can they *suffer*?[21]

This increasing awareness of and sensitivity to the suffering of animals led eventually to the formation of the Society for the Prevention of Cruelty to Animals in Britain, the United States, and elsewhere.

The animal liberation movement of the late twentieth century traces its origins to such nineteenth century figures as Bentham and Henry Salt (whose *Animal Rights*, first published in 1892, made the moral case for vegetarianism).[22] But to its moral argument it adds a certain militancy and a willingness to take personal and political risks to protect the rights of animals. Members of such groups as the Society for Animal Rights (SAR) and People for the Ethical Treatment of Animals (PETA) have not only lobbied their congressional representatives, but have picketed furriers' shops and animal laboratories. Some have freed caged animals, including mice, monkeys, and dolphins. The 1986 movie "Turtle Diary" is about three people who kidnap sea turtles from the London Zoo in order to release them into the ocean. In Britain, the Animal Liberation Front (ALF) has poured blood on expensive fur coats and set fire to furriers' warehouses. In 1988 animal liberationists in Sweden succeeded in their campaign to outlaw certain kinds of beef and poultry raising practices.

If the animals are unable to free themselves, say animal liberationists, then human beings acting on their behalf should be prepared to do so. Animal liberationists, in short, view their actions as emancipatory and their ideology as a fully formed liberation ideology. Let us look a little more closely at that claim.

As we noted at the beginning of this chapter, liberation ideologies share several features in common. The first of these is that each is addressed to a particular audience—to women, or black people, or homosexuals, or others. To whom is the ideology of animal liberation addressed? In one sense, of course, the audience—the group to be liberated—consists of animals; but, in another and more important sense, the ideology of animal liberation is addressed to human beings.

The second feature of any liberation ideology is that its audience must have been oppressed by some dominant group. In the case of animal liberation, however, human beings are both audience and oppressor. The ideology of animal liberation therefore directs its appeals to humans who (1) oppress or abuse animals, or (2) derive some benefit from such oppression, or (3) do not benefit but stand by and do nothing to prevent the further abuse and oppression of animals. An example of the first might be a hunter who clubs baby seals to death; of the second, a woman who wears a sealskin coat; of the third, those who take no action—for example, writing letters, making financial contributions, and so on—to protect baby seals.

The third feature of liberation ideologies is that they seek to liberate some group not only from external oppression but from psychological barriers or inhibitions that members of oppressed groups have internalized and made part of their own outlook. Obviously it is difficult, if not impossible, to talk about the psychological inhibitions of animals. But this difficulty is reduced considerably if we remember that the ideology of animal liberation is addressed primarily to human beings, who quite clearly do harbor certain beliefs and attitudes that have a bearing upon their treatment of animals. Many, perhaps most, of us subscribe to a set of ideas, beliefs, and attitudes that animal liberationists call **speciesism.** Simply put, speciesism is the belief—or rather, the unexamined prejudice—that human beings are superior to animals; that we have all the rights and they have none; that we may treat them in any way that we believe will benefit us, either as individuals (the steak on my plate) or as a species (the use of monkeys in medical experiments). The German Nazis, as animal liberationists remind us, also subscribed to their own version of speciesism: before murdering or performing medical experiments on Jews, they first took great pains to reclassify them as subhumans, as "animals" without rights and thus undeserving of humane treatment. This fact alone, say the animal liberationists, should give us pause. It should at least lead us to reflect on our beliefs about, and attitudes toward, the supposedly lower animals whose flesh we eat and on whom we perform experiments of various and often vicious kinds. These experiments range from the surgical removal of limbs and organs to testing the toxicity of detergents, bleaches, cosmetics and other products by injecting them into the eyes of rabbits and other laboratory animals.

In calling our attention to the abuse and mistreatment of animals, animal liberationism fulfills the fourth function of a liberation ideology. It aims to raise the consciousness of a particular audience, leading its members to examine critically what they had previously taken for granted. Many, maybe most, people simply assume that animals exist to serve our purposes and our pleasures. Their existence is justified only insofar as they provide meat, fur, or entertainment, or serve as experimental subjects in laboratories. The ideology of animal liberation poses a radical challenge to the set of unexamined assumptions and prejudices that it calls speciesism.

These arguments are brought together in Peter Singer's *Animal Liberation.*[23] Singer, an Australian philosopher, examines each of the arguments advanced in favor of speciesism and finds them either unwarranted, untenable, or incoherent. Consider, for example, the claim that humans are entitled to eat the flesh of "lower" animals, such as cows. On what, Singer asks, is this claim based? It rests on the belief that humans are a "higher" species. On what, then, is this claim to superiority based? It is based on the unique qualities of human beings—qualities that they do not share with lower and lesser creatures. These qualities include, preeminently, the facts that human beings have the use of speech and reason. But this claim, says Singer, is singularly self-subverting. By this logic we should be prepared to eat the flesh of severely retarded human beings, who lack the power of reason, and of humans who are unable to speak. That we are unwilling to do so only shows that the standard arguments in defense of human superiority are without rational and moral foundation. With the aid of these and other arguments, animal liberationists hope to raise the consciousness and critical self-awareness of human beings. Once they come to see their relationship with animals in a new and different light, they will no longer exploit or oppress them. Humans will at last be freed of their false and self-demeaning sense of their own innate superiority. The aim of animal liberation, then, is not only to deliver animals from human oppression but to deliver human beings from the confines of speciesism.[24]

We can conclude by noting that animal liberation, like other liberation ideologies, subscribes to its own distinctive conception of freedom or liberty, which is summarized in Figure 8.7.

CONCLUSION

Liberation and Ideology

Each of these ideologies takes a particular group, which it sees as oppressed, as the subject of its concern. But these groups can and do overlap, as in the case of black women, for example. They also share a family resemblance, as we have noted. For these reasons, we can treat them as a unit—as the family of liberation ideologies—as we examine the ways they perform the four functions of ideologies.

Explanation   Liberation ideologies do not try to explain all social conditions and circumstances. They begin, instead, with the condition of the specific

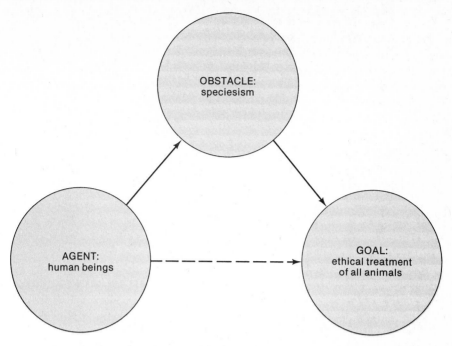

Figure 8.7 The animal liberationist conception of freedom.

group with which they are concerned—blacks, women, homosexuals, the poor, and nonhuman animals. This condition they then explain in terms of domination and oppression. They begin, that is, with the conviction that the plight of their group is not simply a natural fact of life that must be accepted, like the need to eat, sleep, and breathe. From this point they go on to explain how the suffering is the result of oppression—of blacks by whites, of women by men, and so on.

Evaluation   Just as "oppression" is the key word in the liberation ideologies' explanation of conditions, so too is it the key to their evaluations of these conditions. When oppression crushes or stifles people, and thus prevents them from living full and free lives, things are not as they should be. And every liberation ideology teaches that things are not yet as they should be, since each of the groups they address continues to suffer (or sometimes to cause) oppression. Rather than saying that conditions are good or bad, then, they tend to evaluate them in terms of better or worse. In societies and times in which women are relatively free to speak and think for themselves, for instance, conditions are better—less oppressive—for them than they are in societies and times in which women are treated simply as the property of men. To say that conditions are better, however, is not to say that they are already as good as they can and should be.

Orientation   One of the central features of liberation ideologies is the attempt to make members of oppressed groups aware of their oppression—to see themselves as the victims of some dominant or powerful group. This is a matter of orientation. People must understand their location in the world before they can do anything to change their circumstances. The victim of injustice must be brought to see that he or she is not responsible for the suffering he or she endures, nor is suffering simply his or her inevitable fate. So, too, must the oppressor be brought to see the injustice he or she is doing, wittingly or unwittingly, to other human beings or animals.

Program   Orientation or understanding by itself, of course, is not enough to overcome oppression. It must be joined to action. But action of what kind? Here the liberation ideologies take many different courses, depending upon the challenges they confront in different circumstances. Here the differences between liberal and liberationist variants of black liberation and womens' liberation become most pronounced. The liberal or Civil Rights variants typically try to bring about change by legal actions, such as the court cases brought by the National Association for the Advancement of Colored People (NAACP) and the attempt to add to the United States' Constitution an Equal Rights Amendment outlawing discrimination against women. The liberationist variants tend to favor activities that either challenge or circumvent the established social and legal powers, such as the formation of self-help and self-protection groups like the Black Panthers. Liberation groups of all sorts often resort to boycotts, demonstrations, and civil disobedience—public and peaceful acts of lawbreaking—to call attention to their views. Some advocates of liberation ideologies say that violence is justified, in some circumstances, as a form of self-defense against the oppressors who are doing violence to them.[25] But whatever their tactics, they all share the same general program: to bring an end to the oppression of a group of people (or of nonhuman animals) so that they may live full and free lives.

Liberation and the Democratic Ideal

One final question remains to be asked. How do liberation ideologies construe, or construct, the democratic ideal? They typically think of it as self-rule, which is consistent with the conception of democracy found in other ideologies. But liberation ideologies point out that self-rule is impossible unless people have a more or less well-developed sense of self-worth and self-respect. And so the various liberation ideologies aim to implant and reinforce that sense of dignity in their various audiences in the five ways that we listed earlier. Each addresses a particular audience—black people, women, homosexuals, the poor—whose experiences are historically unique, although all have experienced oppression of some sort. Each liberation ideology recognizes these experiences as real and valid, and leads those whom it addresses to examine the origins, memory, and effects of such oppression. Typically these include internalized inhibitions and barriers—for example, feelings of inferiority or inadequacy—that stand in the way of their being actively self-ruling agents who seek to achieve goals they set for themselves. Since these effects are not only physical but psychological, an ideology of liberation helps people recognize and overcome the damage oppression has done to their psyches by raising their consciousness, that is, by making conscious and articulate what had previously remained unconscious and inarticulate. Finally, liberation ideologies intend not only to inform and educate victims, but their oppressors as well. Oppressors suffer (usually without knowing it) from the stifling and stunting of their moral, intellectual, and civic capacities, just as the master in Hegel's parable (discussed in Chapter 5) oppressed not only his slave, but himself as well.

In all these ways, liberation ideologies try to make people strong enough to bear the burdens and experience the joys of self-rule—of democracy, in other words. Now it might be argued that one of these ideologies—animal liberation—cannot achieve any such end, since it is concerned with the well-being of animals. But this objection, as we have seen, misses the point. The ideology of animal liberation is addressed to human beings with the aim of liberating them as well as other animals. For to the degree that we accept unquestioningly the assumptions of speciesism, animal liberationists say, we remain locked into a false picture of the world and our place in it. This, as we note in the next chapter, is a theme shared with another newly emerging ideology.

NOTES

1. See Marilyn Frye, "Oppression," in Frye, *The Politics of Reality* (Trumansburg, N.Y.: Crossing Press, 1983), pp. 1–16; also in Terence Ball and Richard Dagger, eds., *Ideals and Ideologies: A Reader* (New York: HarperCollins, 1991), selection 46.
2. Quoted in William Barrett, *The Illusion of Technique* (Garden City, N.Y.: Doubleday Anchor, 1978), p. xv.
3. William Grier and Price Cobb, *Black Rage* (New York: Basic Books, 1969).
4. Frantz Fanon, *Black Skin, White Masks* (New York: Grove Press, 1982).
5. Quoted in Taylor Branch, *Parting the Waters: America in the King Years, 1954–1963* (New York: Simon & Schuster, 1988), p. 589.
6. Quoted in Miriam Schneir, ed., *Feminism: The Essential Historical Writings* (New York: Vintage Books, 1972), p. 3.
7. Ibid., Part 4: "Men as Feminists."
8. See Sheila Rowbotham, *Women's Consciousness, Man's World* (Harmondsworth: Pelican Books, 1973).
9. See Emma Goldman, *Anarchism and Other Essays* (1910; repr. New York: Dover Publications, 1969). Two of her essays, "The Traffic in Women" and "Marriage and Love," are included in Schneir, ed., *Feminism*, pp. 308–324.
10. See Shulamith Firestone, *The Dialectic of Sex: The Case for Feminist Revolution* (New York: Morrow, 1970).
11. See Vivien Gornick, *Essays in Feminism* (New York: Harper & Row, 1978).
12. For Greek attitudes toward sexuality and same-sex love (the term *homosexuality* was not coined until the late nineteenth century), see Plato, *The Symposium;* K. J. Dover, *Greek Homosexuality* (Cambridge, Mass.: Harvard University Press, 1978); Michel Foucault, *The History of Sexuality,* vol. 1, trans. Robert Hurley (New York: Pantheon, 1986).

13. Elaine Pagels, *Adam, Eve, and the Serpent* (New York: Random House, 1988), pp. 10–11.
14. See Richard Mohr, *Gays/Justice* (New York: Columbia University Press, 1988); also Ball and Dagger, eds., *Ideals and Ideologies*, selection 47.
15. Phillip Berryman, *Liberation Theology: Essential Facts about the Revolutionary Movement in Latin America—and Beyond* (Philadelphia: Temple University Press, 1987), p. 6.
16. Quoted in ibid., p. 23.
17. Gustavo Gutierrez, *A Theology of Liberation: History, Politics and Salvation*, rev. ed. trans. Sister Caridad Inda and John Eagleson (Maryknoll, N.Y.: Orbis Books, 1988), p. 307; see also Ball and Dagger, eds., *Ideals and Ideologies*, selection 48.
18. Matthew 25:34–40 (revised standard version).
19. Peter Singer and Tom Regan trace some of the sentiments and ideas of animal liberation back as far as Plutarch (ca. 49–119 A.D.) and St. Thomas Aquinas (1224–1274); see Singer and Regan, eds., *Animal Rights and Human Obligations* (Englewood Cliffs, N.J.: Prentice-Hall, 1976), pp. 111–121.
20. Quoted in Peter Singer, *Practical Ethics* (Cambridge: Cambridge University Press, 1979), p. 49.
21. Ibid., p. 50.
22. See the selections from Henry Salt's works in Regan and Singer, *Animal Rights and Human Obligations*, pp. 173–178, 185–189. For a more substantial selection, see George Hendrick and Wilene Hendrick, eds., *The Savour of Salt* (London: Centaur Press, 1989).
23. Peter Singer, *Animal Liberation*, 2nd ed. (New York: Random House, 1990). As a utilitarian, Singer is uncomfortable with the idea of the intrinsic worth of life and the language of rights. He rests his case on the claim that animals, like humans, are capable of experiencing pain and pleasure. An alternative, nonutilitarian case for animal *rights* is made by Tom Regan (see note 24, below).
24. The most systematic philosophical defense of the idea of intrinsic worth and the *rights* of animals is Tom Regan's *Animal Rights* (Berkeley and Los Angeles: University of California Press, 1983). Like Singer, Regan also argues that animal liberation entails the liberation of humans, freeing them from previously unexamined speciesist prejudices and practices.
25. See Malcolm X, *Malcolm X Speaks* (New York: Grove Press, 1966).

FOR FURTHER READING

Black Liberation

Branch, Taylor. *Parting the Waters: America in the King Years, 1954–1963* (New York: Simon & Schuster, 1988).

Carmichael, Stokely, and Charles Hamilton. *Black Power* (New York: Vintage Books, 1967).

Fanon, Frantz. *Black Skin, White Masks* (New York: Grove Press, 1982).

Grier, William H., and Price N. Cobbs. *Black Rage* (New York: Bantam Books, 1969).

King, Martin Luther, Jr. *Why We Can't Wait* (New York: Harper & Row, 1964).

X, Malcolm. *The Autobiography of Malcolm X* (New York: Grove Press, 1965).

———. *Malcolm X Speaks* (New York: Grove Press, 1966).

Women's Liberation

Beauvoir, Simone de. *The Second Sex* (New York: Bantam Books, 1968).

Elshtain, Jean Bethke. *Public Man, Private Woman: Women in Social and Political Thought* (Princeton, N.J.: Princeton University Press, 1981).

Friedan, Betty. *The Feminine Mystique* (New York: Norton, 1963).

Mill, John Stuart. *The Subjection of Women* (1869).

Mitchell, Juliet. *Woman's Estate* (New York: Vintage Books, 1973).

Schneir, Miriam, ed. *Feminism: The Essential Historical Writings* (New York: Vintage Books, 1972).

Wollstonecraft, Mary. *A Vindication of the Rights of Woman* (Harmondsworth: Penguin, 1982).

Gay Liberation

Mohr, Richard. *Gays/Justice* (New York: Columbia University Press, 1988).

Liberation Theology

Berryman, Phillip. *Liberation Theology: Essential Facts about the Revolutionary Movement in Latin America—and Beyond* (Philadelphia: Temple University Press, 1987).

McGovern, Arthur F. "The Evolution of Liberation Theology," *New Oxford Review*, 17 (June 1990), pp. 5–8.

Pottenger, John. *The Political Theory of Liberation Theology* (Albany, N.Y.: State University Press of New York, 1989).

Animal Liberation

Amory, Cleveland. *Man Kind?* (New York: Harper & Row, 1974).

Coats, C. David. *Old MacDonald's Factory Farm* (New York: Continuum Books, 1989).

Frey, R. G. *Interests and Rights: The Case against Animals* (Oxford: Oxford University Press, 1980).

Regan, Tom. *The Case for Animal Rights* (Berkeley and Los Angeles: University of California Press, 1983).

——, and Peter Singer, eds. *Animal Rights and Human Obligations* (Englewood Cliffs, N.J.: Prentice-Hall, 1976).

Singer, Peter. *Animal Liberation*, 2nd ed. (New York: Random House, 1990).

Chapter
9

Green Politics: Ecology as Ideology

Only connect . . .

E.M. Forster, *Howards End*

All ideologies are born of crisis. Starting from a shared sense that some-thing is wrong, that the world is not as it should be, all ideologies attempt to explain or account for puzzling or problematic features of people's lives; then, on the basis of these explanations, they offer diagnoses and prescriptions for the ills of a troubled time. The ideology we examine in the present chapter is certainly no exception to this rule. Although many of its ideas are quite old, this ideology is quite new—so new, in fact, that it has, as yet, no generally agreed-upon name. But because many within this movement call their actions and perspective **Green politics,** and themselves *Greens*, we refer to them and their ideology in this way.[1]

The crisis out of which a broadly based Green movement has emerged is the environmental crisis. Actually, this is not a single crisis, but a series of crises arising in connection with the ecological and environmental damage wrought by overpopulation, pollution of air and water, the destruction of the tropical rain forests, the rapid extinction of entire species of plants and animals, the "greenhouse effect" (the warming of the earth's atmosphere), the destruc-tion of forests and lakes by acid rain, the depletion of the earth's protective ozone layer, and other by now familiar instances of environmental damage and degradation.

These crises are interconnected. All, moreover, are the result of human actions and practices over the last two centuries. Many are by-products of tech-nological innovations, such as the internal combustion engine. But the causes of these environmental crises, according to many environmentalists, are as much ideological as they are technological. They stem, that is, from ideas and ideolo-gies that place human beings above or apart from nature. Against these, the emerging Green movement proposes its own counterideology, which has two main aspects. This counterideology consists, first of all, of a critique of some of the key assumptions underlying the ideologies that have dominated modern politics. And second, it attempts to offer a more positive and hopeful vision of human beings' relation with the natural environment and with one another.

THE GREEN CRITIQUE OF OTHER IDEOLOGIES

To devise and act upon an alternative environmental ideology, say the Greens, is not merely one option among many. It may be the only remaining chance that human beings have to save the planet and its myriad species—including the human species itself. This is because the human species is linked to, and deeply dependent upon, other species of plants and animals. To see this dependence in action, consider the tale of the tree. Trees are not only a source of shade and lumber, but of oxygen, which they exchange for the carbon dioxide (CO_2) that is a by-product of burning and other processes of oxidation, including our own breathing: approximately twenty times per minute we breathe in a mixture of oxygen and nitrogen, exhaling CO_2 with every breath. To clear tropical rain forests, for instance, or to destroy northern forests with acid rain is therefore to reduce the amount of oxygen available for us to breathe. This, in turn, increases the amount of carbon dioxide in the atmosphere, which results in the further warming of the earth's atmosphere known as the **greenhouse effect.** Global warming then brings drought and turns formerly fertile land into deserts and dust bowls, thereby reducing crop production and causing humans and other animals to starve. It will also bring in its wake the gradual melting of the polar ice caps, thereby raising sea levels and permanently flooding many low-lying coastal areas, including most of Florida and much of countries like Bangladesh.

The moral of the tale of the tree is simply this: all things are connected. Or, to put the point another way: what goes around, comes around. In one sense, of course, this is not an entirely new message. All the world's great religions have said much the same thing in one way or another. "Whatsover a man soweth, that shall he also reap" (Galatians 6.7). This is true not only of individuals, but of human beings from one generation to another. "The fathers have eaten sour grapes and their children's teeth are set on edge" (Ezekiel 18.2). In other words, what human beings do in one time and place will affect other human beings, and other species, in other times and places.

But while the world's major religions have taught that all things are interconnected, most of the major modern ideologies have not. The Greens, therefore, tend to be quite critical of other ideologies, **right** and **left** alike. They criticize not only the specific beliefs and doctrines of those other ideologies, but, no less importantly, their *unexamined assumptions* as well.

Consider, for example, the assumptions about nature and human beings' relationship to nature shared by several modern ideologies. Liberals, socialists, and individualist conservatives share a similar attitude toward nature, one that celebrates the ever-increasing human "conquest" or "mastery" of nature. They see nature as either a hostile force to be conquered or a resource base to be harnessed for such human purposes as "growth" and "economic development." Technological, scientific, and economic progress is therefore to be measured in terms of the human species' power over nature. Such an adversarial attitude was expressed early on by seventeenth-century thinkers, including Thomas Hobbes' friend Sir Francis Bacon. Indeed, Bacon speaks of nature much as the Marquis de Sade was later to speak of women. Nature (always "her") is haughty and proud but must be subdued, humbled, and humiliated by "man," whose sense of power increases with his "conquest" of nature. Nature must be "interrogated," "subdued," and made to "yield up her secrets" to man, Bacon declared, so that man can then turn nature's secrets against her, "shaping nature as on an anvil." Through their technology men do not "merely exert a gentle guidance over nature's course; they have the power to conquer and subdue her, to shake her to her foundations." Finally, "by art and the hand of man she is forced out of her natural state, and squeezed and moulded" for human purposes.[2] Similarly, though less "sadistically," John Locke believed that nature in itself was without value. It is only when people put "waste" land and resources to human use that they acquire whatever "value" they have: "land that is left wholly to nature, that hath no improvement of pasturage, tillage, or planting, is called, as indeed it is, waste; and we shall find the benefit of it amount to little more than nothing."[3] And Karl Marx, critical as he was of capitalism and the liberal ideology that justified it, nevertheless waxed enthusiastic about the increased power over nature that capitalism had brought about:

> The bourgeoisie, during its rule of scarce one hundred years, has created more massive and more colossal productive forces than have all preceding generations together. Subjection of nature's forces to man, machinery, application of chemistry to industry and agriculture, steam navigation, railways, electric telegraphs, clearing of whole continents for cultivation, canalization of rivers, whole populations conjured up out of the ground—what earlier century had even a presentiment that such productive forces slumbered in the lap of social labor?[4]

In light of these views, the Greens say that it is scarcely surprising that liberal capitalist and communist societies are alike in sharing an "anthropocentric" or "humanistic" bias.[5] Both tend to prefer economic "growth" and productivity to the protection of the natural environment. Nor is it surprising, they say, that rivers like the Volga and the Mississippi are little more than open sewers, or that the lakes and fish and pine trees of Siberia and New England and Canada are poisoned by acid rain. And although the Soviet Union was the scene of the world's worst nuclear accident to date—at Chernobyl in 1986—the United States came quite close to disaster at Three Mile Island in Pennsylvania in 1979. Past and possible future accidents aside, both the United States and the Soviet Union are producing deadly nuclear and chemical wastes without any means of storing them safely for the hundreds and even thousands of years that they remain highly dangerous to the health of humans and other beings.

From their ecological point of view, the Greens see little difference between communism and capitalism. The ideologies by means of which both systems justify themselves are essentially heedless of the natural environment upon which we and all creatures ultimately rely. Therefore, say the Greens, we need to rethink the assumptions on which these influential ideologies are founded in the first place. More than that, we need to devise an ideology that recognizes and respects nature's delicate system of checks and balances.

TOWARD AN ECOLOGICAL ETHIC

Many Greens prefer not to call their perspective an ideology, but an "ethic." Earlier ecological thinkers, such as Aldo Leopold, spoke of the attitude of reverence and respect for the land as a **land ethic.**[6] Others have spoken, more recently, of an ethic with earth itself at its center,[7] while others, in a similar spirit, speak of an emerging "planetary ethic."[8] Despite differences of accent and emphasis, however, all appear to be alike in several crucial respects.

An environmental or ecological ethic, they say, would at a minimum include the following features. First, such an ethic would emphasize the web of interconnections and mutual dependence within which we and other species live. People are not only connected with one another, but with other species of animals and plants. The latter include not only those that human beings eat—fish, cows, and corn, for example—but the tiny plankton on which whales and ocean fish feed, the insects and minnows eaten by lake and river fish, the worms that loosen and aerate the soil in which the corn grows. The corn feeds the cows that fertilize the fields, and humans eat the fish, the corn, and the cows. All are interdependent participants in the cycle of birth, life, death, decay, and rebirth. And all the participants in this cycle depend upon the air and water, the sunlight and soil, without which life is impossible.

These, the Greens say, are elemental truths that we forget at our peril. Yet forget them we have. In separating ourselves from nature, we have divided our lives and experiences into separate compartments. We think of vegetables and meats as commodities that come from the grocery store wrapped in plastic and styrofoam, for instance, and water as it comes from the faucet or bottle. We rarely pause to reflect upon what makes these things possible and available to us, or of how much we depend on them—and they on us. But this sense of disconnectedness, the Greens charge, is an illusion that, unless dispelled, will doom our species and many others to extinction.

But where do we go to learn about these interconnections? There are many places. There is science, particularly the disciplines of biology, **ecology,** and geology, and also literature, music, and art. Philosophy and various religions also have much to contribute. But one neglected source, the Greens remind us, is to be found in the folk wisdom of native peoples, such as the Indians of North America. According to one account, Chief Sealth (or Seattle) of the Sugamish tribe, replied to an offer from the American government to buy his tribe's land in 1854 by saying that it was not theirs to sell. The land and air and water belongs to everybody and to nobody; nature is not for sale at any price, for it is not a commodity that exists apart from us. On the contrary, Seattle supposedly said,

> We are part of the earth and it is part of us.
> The perfumed flowers are our sisters;
> the deer, the horse, the great eagle,
> these are our brothers.
> The rocky crests,
> the juices of the meadows,
> the body heat of the pony, and man—
> all belong to the same family.

"This we know," he continued. "The earth does not belong to man; man belongs to the earth. All things are connected. . . ."[9] To fail to recognize this interconnectedness, Chief Seattle warned—and Greens today agree—is to doom our own species and all others to increasing misery and eventual extinction.

Several other features of an environmental or Green ethic follow from the recognition of interconnectedness and interdependence. The first of these is a respect for life—not only human life but all life, from the tiniest microorganism to the largest whale. The fate of our species is tied to theirs, and theirs to ours. Since life requires certain conditions to sustain it, a second feature follows: we have an obligation to respect and care for the conditions that nurture and sustain life in its many forms. From the aquifers below to the soil and water and air above, nature nourishes its creatures within a complex web of interconnected conditions. To damage one is to damage the others, and to endanger the existence of all the creatures that dwell within and depend upon the integrity of this delicate, life-sustaining web.

To acknowledge this is not, however, to overlook or deny the enormous power that humans have over nature. On the contrary, it requires that we recognize the extent of our power—and that we take full responsibility for restraining it and using it wisely and well. Greens point out that the fate of the earth and all its creatures now depends, for better or for worse, on human decisions and actions. Not only do we depend on nature, they say, but nature depends on us—on our care and restraint and forbearance. It is within our power to destroy the earth many times over. This we can do very quickly in the case of nuclear war (or rather—since the word "war" implies victors and vanquished, and nuclear war will have no winners—"nuclear omnicide," i.e., the destruction of everything and everyone). Every local conflict, however small at first, could turn into a superpower confrontation, with predictably deadly results. From this emerges a further feature of a green ethic: Greens must work for peace. This is not to say that Greens are to avoid all confrontation or conflict, but that they are to employ the tactics of direct confrontation, of nonviolent protest and resistance, in the manner of Mahatma Gandhi, Martin Luther King, Jr., and others. This many militant Greens have done, not only in antiwar protests, but in attempts to slow or stop the clear-cutting of old-growth forests, the construction of nuclear power plants, and other activities they deem to be destructive of the natural environment.

Such a stance is now necessary, in their view, because the earth and all its inhabitants can be destroyed not only by nuclear omnicide, but by slower, though no less destructive, methods of environmental degradation, including the cumulative effects of small-scale, everyday acts. All actions, however small or seemingly insignificant, produce consequences or effects, sometimes out of all proportion to the actions that bring them about. (Consider, for example, the simple act of drinking coffee from a styrofoam cup. That convenient but nonbiodegradable container will still be around for many hundreds of years after its user's body has been recycled into the soil.) In modern industrial society the old adage, "Mighty oaks from tiny acorns grow," might well be amended to, "Mighty disasters from tiny actions grow." It is from our everyday actions, however insignificant they might appear to be, that large-scale environmental consequences follow. Hence the duty of **stewardship.**

Because each of us is an actor—whether as producer, consumer, or in some other role—each bears full responsibility for his or her actions and, since we live in a democracy, partial responsibility for others' actions as well. Each of us has, or can have, a hand in making the laws and policies under which we live. For this reason Greens give equal emphasis to our collective and individual responsibility for protecting the environment that protects us. Greens are, in short, "small-*d*" democrats whose ethic emphasizes the importance of informed and active democratic citizenship. But as to what that ethic consists of, and as regards the best way of informing oneself and others and of being an active citizen, Greens differ among themselves.

UNRESOLVED DIFFERENCES

As a relative newcomer on the political and ideological scene, the Green movement has raised, but not yet answered to everyone's satisfaction, several questions. Let us look briefly at two of these. The first concerns the character of the emerging environmental ethic. Is it sacred, as some Greens suggest, or is it secular and scientific, as others insist? A second question, or rather series of questions, concerns the strategies and tactics to be employed by the environmental movement. Should Greens act in new and different ways or in the way that the various interest groups have traditionally acted? Should they, for example, form their own political party or should they work within existing parties? Should they hire lobbyists to influence legislation, or should they work outside of conventional interest-group politics? After all, as Greens often note, the earth and its inhabitants are hardly a unique "special interest." Let us consider each of these issues in turn.

An environmental ethic, according to some Greens, is in the final analysis religious or spiritual, resting as it does on the virtues of humility, respect, and reverence. An environmental ethic entails humility in the face of our individual mortality and our collective status not as solitary dwellers on or masters of our planet, but as one species and generation among many. An environmental ethic also requires that we respect life in all its forms and the conditions, both animate and inanimate, that sustain and nurture it. And finally, such an ethic entails an attitude of reverence. It requires that we revere, cherish, and care for other people and other species, not only in our own time, but in the generations and ages to come. We have, to paraphrase Edmund Burke, a sacred obligation to leave to future generations a habitation instead of a ruin.

On this much, at least, most Greens probably agree. But beyond this point agreement ends and differences begin to appear as some Greens take a spiritual or religious turn that makes other Greens wary. Some who conceive of an environmental ethic grounded in spiritual or religious values say that we should look upon the earth as a benevolent and kindly deity—the goddess Gaia (from the Greek word for earth)—to be worshipped in reverence and awe. A number of Greens, including some (but not all) of those who call themselves **deep ecologists**—proponents of a *biocentric* perspective that places human beings on a par with other species—suggest this as a way of liberating ourselves from the confines of a purely materialistic or scientific perspective into another state of mind, one more attuned to "listening" to and learning from nature than to talking to and dictating for it.[10] Others, however, seem to speak of the goddess Gaia in a less metaphorical and more literal fashion.[11]

Some deep ecologists, particularly those affiliated with the Earth First! movement, are inclined to speak neither in humanistic nor in religious terms, but in a more Malthusian idiom. Thomas Malthus was the nineteenth-century English cleric and economist who claimed that human population increases geometrically (i.e., at an ever-increasing rate) while the resources available to sustain that population increase at an arithmetic (i.e., steady) rate. Thus, according to **Malthus' law,** the ever-growing human population increasingly outstrips available resources, with widespread hunger and starvation the inevitable result. From widespread starvation comes a further result: a new equilibrium between population and resources. Unfortunately, this short-lived equilibrium ends as population increases, and the cycle begins all over again. Taking their cue from Malthus, the leading thinkers of Earth First!—including the late novelist Edward Abbey and Dave Foreman, editor of the newsletter *Earth First!*—claim that nature is not without its own resources for countering human hubris and error. Famine, floods, the AIDS epidemic—by these and other means nature chastises the heedless human species and punishes at least some of its members for their species' pride, ignorance, and indifference. Although the language of Earth First! is not religious, its vision of dire punishments sometimes seems to come straight from the vengeful God of the Old Testament.

By contrast, ecologists of a more social and secular stripe are apt to regard any talk of religion and goddesses and deep ecology with deep suspicion, if not downright hostility. These critics include social ecologist Murray Bookchin and "ecofeminist" Ynestra King, among others. They contend that talk about goddesses is mystical mumbo-jumbo to be avoided at all costs. And they view Earth First! as an antihuman and inhumane "ecofascist" organization that seeks to remove human beings from the ecological equation entirely. **Social ecologists,** by contrast, acknowledge humanity's dependency and responsibility for the environment, but hold that human life has special importance.

Other differences within the broadly based Green movement are beginning to emerge. Although all agree about the importance of informing and educating the public, they are divided over how this might best be done. Some say that Greens should take an active part in electoral politics. This is the course favored by many European Greens, particularly in Germany, who have organized Green parties. A number of Greens have been elected to various national parliaments. Greens in the United States, mindful of the difficulties facing minority or third parties, have opted for other strategies. The social ecologists, for example, tend to favor local, grassroots campaigns to involve neighbors and friends in efforts to protect the environment. Some, though not all, social ecologists are anarchists who see the state and its pro–growth policies as the problem, rather than the solution, and seek its eventual replacement by a decentralized system of communes and cooperatives.[12]

Other Greens have chosen to pursue quite different strategies. Some groups, such as Greenpeace, favor dramatic direct action calculated to make headlines and capture public attention. Greenpeace activists, for instance, have interposed their bodies between whalers' power harpoons and their prey. They have also confronted hunters in search of baby seals and tracked down and publicly exposed those who illegally dump toxic wastes. These and other tactics have been publicly condemned by the governments of Japan, Iceland, and France, and in 1985 French agents in neutral New Zealand blew up and sank Greenpeace's ocean-going vessel, *The Rainbow Warrior*, killing a crew member. (After that attack, donations poured in, and a new vessel, *Rainbow Warrior II*, was launched and commissioned to continue the work of its predecessor.) Even more militant groups, such as the Sea Shepherd Society and Earth First!, have advocated **ecotage** (ecological sabotage) and "monkey-wrenching" as morally justifiable means of protesting, if not always preventing, injuries and insults to the natural environment. Sea Shepherds sabotage whaling and tuna-fishing fleets. Some members of Earth First! have "spiked"—that is, driven long metal spikes into—thousand-year-old redwood trees to prevent their being cut down by logging companies seeking short-term profits. The spike does no harm to the tree, but it poses a serious danger to any chainsaw or sawmill operator whose blade might strike it. These and other tactics are described, and even celebrated, in Edward Abbey's novel, *The Monkey-Wrench Gang*.

The tactics of Greenpeace and the more militant measures advocated by Earth First! and the Sea Shepherds have been criticized and disowned by other environmental groups, especially those favoring more subtle, low-key efforts to influence legislation and inform the public on environmental matters. The Sierra Club, for example, actively lobbies Congress and state legislatures in hopes of passing laws to protect the natural environment. It also publishes books and produces films about a wide variety of environmental issues. Similar strategies are followed by other groups, such as the Environmental Defense Fund. Another group, The Nature Conservancy, solicits funds to buy land to turn into nature preserves.

Although quite new, the Green movement is already beset by factional infighting. Anarchists are opposed to the tactics favored by environmental lobbyists, social ecologists are appalled by the political pronouncements of Earth First! and other deep ecologists, and the moderate and conservative members of The Nature Conservancy and Sierra Club are embarrassed by all the adverse publicity. Deep ecologists, in turn, are highly critical of the "shallow ecology" of mainstream conservationists. Yet, as Greens are quick to note, the important point is not that environmentalists disagree about means, but that they agree about fundamental assumptions and ends. They are alike in assuming that all things are connected—ecology is, after all, the study of interconnections—and they agree that the maintenance of complex ecosystems is not only a worthy goal, but a necessary one if the human race and other species are to survive.

CONCLUSION

We have seen how and for what reasons the Greens criticize many modern mainstream ideologies. We have also noted their reluctance to view their perspective as an ideology. Is their ethic an ideology? We believe that it is, at least by the criteria that we have proposed for identifying and explicating ideologies. First, an ecological ethic fulfils the four functions of an ideology. Second, it proposes and defends a particular view of liberty or freedom. And finally, it advances a particular conception of democracy. Let us briefly consider each of these features in turn.

Ecology as Ideology

An environmental or Green ideology fulfills the four functions of an ideology, as outlined in Chapter 1. It is, first of all, *explanatory:* it offers an explanation of how the environmental crisis came about. That crisis grew out of the human *hubris,* or pride, that some Greens call "anthropocentrism" and others "humanism." The mistaken belief that human beings are self-sufficient and sovereign masters of nature and our planet underlies modern man's rampant and irresponsible disregard for the delicate and interconnected web of life. Second, the emerging Green ideology supplies a standard for assessing and *evaluating* actions, practices, and policies. It applauds actions that tend to preserve and protect the natural environment—rain forests, wildlife habitats, wetlands, and other ecosystems—and condemns those that damage and destroy the natural environment. Third, this ideology *orients* its adherents, giving them a sense of identity. Greens think of themselves as members of a species whose health and very existence is deeply dependent upon other species and upon the conditions that nourish and nurture them all. Fourth, their ideology gives Greens a *program* of political and social action. They assume a responsibility for, among other things, promoting practices or policies that protect the natural environment and for educating and enlightening people who are heedless of the health of other species and of the natural environment as a whole. As they see it, only a massive and worldwide change of consciousness can save the planet and its species from heedless human depredation.

Ecology, Freedom, and the Democratic Ideal

As we noted in Chapter 1, every ideology subscribes to its own particular conception of freedom. The Green ideology is no exception. Greens believe that human beings and other species can be truly free to flourish and survive only if they overcome, both in theory and in practice, the **arrogance of humanism**— the humanist outlook that ignores the worth of other species and their environment. The Green view of freedom can therefore be encapsulated in our triadic model (Figure 9.1).

Finally, as we noted in Chapter 1, every modern ideology has its own characteristic interpretation of the democratic ideal. Once again, the Greens are no exception. As we noted earlier, the Greens believe that each of us bears a responsibility for protecting and preserving the environment. This includes not only the natural environment that sustains all creatures, but the social, economic, and political environment in which human beings live and work. People can flourish only within a political system that gives everyone a voice and a vote, thereby maximizing individual participation and personal responsibility. That system, say the Greens, is necessarily democratic. And the best kind of democracy, they add, is a decentralized grassroots system that encourages and permits the widest possible participation.[13] Only in such a setting can each of us take our full, fair, and equal share of responsibility for preserving our planet and all its species.

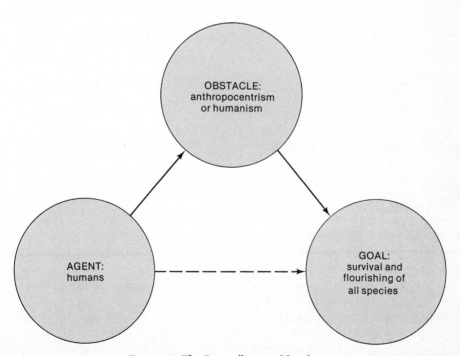

Figure 9.1 The "green" view of freedom.

NOTES

1. Fritjof Capra and Charlene Spritnak, *Green Politics* (New York: Dutton, 1984).
2. Quoted in William Leiss, *The Domination of Nature* (New York: George Braziller, 1972), pp. 58–59.
3. John Locke, *Second Treatise of Government*, para. 42; also in Terence Ball and Richard Dagger, eds., *Ideals and Ideologies: A Reader* (New York: HarperCollins, 1991), selection 12.
4. Karl Marx and Friedrich Engels, *The Manifesto of the Communist Party*, in Lewis S. Feuer, ed., *Marx and Engels: Basic Writings on Politics and Philosophy* (Garden City, N.Y.: Doubleday Anchor, 1959), p. 12; also in Ball and Dagger, eds., *Ideals and Ideologies*, selection 31.
5. David Ehrenfeld, *The Arrogance of Humanism* (New York: Oxford University Press, 1978).
6. Aldo Leopold, *The Sand County Almanac* (New York: Oxford University Press, 1968).
7. See Christopher Stone, *Earth and Other Ethics* (New York: Harper & Row, 1987).
8. Cf. Hans Jonas, *The Imperative of Responsibility* (Chicago: University of Chicago Press, 1984).
9. There is some question about the authenticity of this version of Chief Seattle's Message, which appears in John Seed, Joanna Macy, Pat Fleming, and Arne Naess, *Thinking Like a Mountain* (Philadelphia: New Society Publishers, 1988), pp. 68–71. For a very different version of the speech, see Eva Greenslit Anderson, *Chief Seattle* (Caldwell, Idaho: The Caxton Printers, 1942), pp. 202–211.
10. See John Seed et al., *Thinking Like a Mountain* (Philadelphia: New Society Publishers, 1988).
11. See Judith Plant, ed., *Healing the Wounds: The Promise of Ecofeminism* (Philadelphia: New Society Publishers, 1989).
12. See Murray Bookchin, *The Modern Crisis* (Montreal: Black Rose Books, 1986).
13. See Rudolph Bahro, *Building the Green Movement* (London: G. R. P., 1978); and Jonathon Porritt, *Seeing Green: The Politics of Ecology Explained* (Oxford and New York: Basil Blackwell, 1984).

FOR FURTHER READING

Berry, Wendell. *The Gift of Good Land* (San Francisco: North Point Press, 1981).

Bramwell, Anna. *Ecology in the Twentieth Century: A History* (New Haven, Conn.: Yale University Press, 1989).

Carson, Rachel. *Silent Spring* (Boston: Houghton Mifflin Co., 1962).

Catton, William R. *Overshoot: The Ecological Basis of Revolutionary Change* (Urbana, Ill.: University of Illinois Press, 1980).

Devall, Bill, and George Sessions. *Deep Ecology: Living as if Nature Mattered* (Layton, Utah: Gibbs M. Smith, Inc., 1985).

Ehrenfeld, David. *The Arrogance of Humanism* (New York: Oxford University Press, 1978).

Hardin, Garrett. *Filters against Folly* (New York: Viking Penguin, 1985).

Heilbroner, Robert L. *An Inquiry into the Human Prospect,* 2nd ed. (New York: Norton, 1980).

Leopold, Aldo. *Sand County Almanac* (New York: Oxford University Press, 1968).

Nash, Roderick Frazier. *The Rights of Nature: A History of Environmental Ethics* (Madison, Wis.: University of Wisconsin Press, 1989).

Partridge, Ernest, ed. *Responsibilities to Future Generations: Environmental Ethics* (Buffalo, N.Y.: Prometheus Books, 1981).

Porritt, Jonathon. *Seeing Green: The Politics of Ecology Explained* (Oxford and New York: Basil Blackwell, 1984).

Regan, Tom. *All That Dwell Therein* (Berkeley and Los Angeles: University of California Press, 1982).

————, ed. *Earthbound: New Introductory Essays in Environmental Ethics* (New York: Random House, 1984).

Roszak, Theodore. *Person/Planet* (Garden City, N.Y.: Doubleday Anchor, 1978).

Schumacher, E. F. *Small Is Beautiful: Economics as if People Mattered* (Garden City, N.Y.: Doubleday Anchor, 1973).

Seed, John, Joanna Macy, Pat Fleming, and Arne Naess, *Thinking Like a Mountain* (Philadelphia: New Society Publishers, 1988).

Worster, Donald. *Nature's Economy: A History of Ecological Ideas* (Cambridge and New York: Cambridge University Press, 1977).

Chapter
10

The Future of Ideology

[E]very boy and every gal
  That's born into the world alive
Is either a little Liberal
  Or else a little Conservative!

Gilbert and Sullivan, *Iolanthe*

W hen Gilbert and Sullivan's musical spoof of English politics and society was first performed in 1882, the audience may well have believed that the division between the Liberal and Conservative parties neatly reflected the major ideological divisions of their day. But the range of ideological choices was not so narrow even then. Many socialists were active in North America and Europe—including Karl Marx, who died in England the year following the first performance of *Iolanthe*. Anarchists of different stripes were also active, as were the various nationalists, elitists, and racial theorists who were sowing the seeds of fascism and nazism. Anyone seeking an alternative to liberalism and conservatism did not have far to look.

Even within the ranks of liberals and conservatives, moreover, there was disharmony and disagreement. This was especially true of the liberals, who were arguing among themselves as much as they quarreled with their ideological rivals. Divided into the groups we have called welfare and neoclassical liberals, they agreed on the value of individual liberty, but disagreed strenuously as to whether a strong government was needed to promote liberty—as T. H. Green and the welfare liberals maintained—or, conversely, that the only safe government is a weak government, as Herbert Spencer and the neoclassical liberals insisted.

If the world of political ideologies was more complicated in 1882 than Gilbert and Sullivan made it seem, it is even more so today. To the ideological disputes and divisions of the 1800s, the twentieth century has added new ones. Beginning with fascism and proceeding through the newly emerging ideologies we discussed in Chapters 8 and 9, this century has been a time of ideological ferment. Newer and older ideologies alike have contributed to this ferment as they have responded to changing circumstances by shifting their positions, splitting into factions, criticizing and even borrowing from one another—all of which can easily bewilder someone trying to make sense of any one ideology, let alone the wider world of political ideologies in general. Just as one thinks he or she understands what communism is all about, for example, Gorbachev's *glasnost* and the other remarkable changes of the late 1980s in the communist countries come along to upset all expectations.

This is why we have taken a historical approach to understanding political ideologies in this book. Political ideologies, as we have emphasized, are dynamic; they do not stand still, but change and respond to changing circumstances. Trying to define a particular ideology, then, is, like trying to hit a moving target. But if we look back in history to see how a particular ideology emerged as a political force and how it has responded to changing circumstances and new ideological challenges, we are at least able to use our grasp of what *has happened* to understand what *is happening* now. The past is usually the best guide to the present. Only by knowing what went before can we hope to understand what is likely to happen in the future of political ideologies—a future that, in one way or another, will play a part not only in our own futures, but in those of our children and grandchildren. With that in mind, our purpose in this final chapter is to take stock of the state of political ideologies today and to try to foresee their future.

POLITICAL IDEOLOGIES: CONTINUING FORCES

In Chapter 7 we observed how liberalism and socialism have both followed the lead of the Enlightenment philosophers of the eighteenth century in anticipating continuing and ever-accelerating human progress through the exercise of reason. To some extent, of course, their expectations have been met. Whether measured in terms of religious tolerance, freedom of speech, the right to vote and participate in government, or health and life expectancy, the condition of most people of Europe and North America does indeed seem to be better than it was two centuries ago. In other respects, however, it is clear that things have not turned out as the early liberals and socialists expected. In particular, the forces of nationalism and religion continue to play powerful parts in politics and society.

Liberalism and socialism can both accommodate the kind of local or parochial sentiments that nationalism embodies, but they do so uncomfortably. In different ways, each represents the universalism of the Enlightenment. Liberals do this by stressing individual liberty—not the liberty of Englishmen or Arabs or Chinese or any other group, but of individuals in the abstract. For their part, socialists have sought to promote the interests of the working class, but they have tried to do this by overcoming or eliminating class divisions so that every individual may enjoy a free and fulfilling life. In neither case do national loyalties play a part. Yet nationalism has proved to be a very significant factor in modern politics.

Nationalism and Ideology

The nationalist sentiments and ideologies awakened in the nineteenth century have grown even more vocal and powerful in the twentieth. We noted earlier, in Chapter 7, how nationalism figured in the rise of fascism and nazism in this century, but that is only part of the story. Nationalism has also contributed directly to the attempts to gain independence from foreign powers through **anticolonial movements** in Africa, Asia, and Latin America. In the nineteenth century in Latin America nationalism joined with liberalism as colonists fought to free themselves from Spanish or Portuguese rule. In the twentieth century Marxist movements have more often exhibited a nationalist tendency, drawing especially on Lenin's theory of imperialism and Mao's appeal to the peasants— the "rural proletariat" of countries that are oppressed by the "bourgeois" or "capitalist countries" of Europe and North America. In the years following World War II, in fact, communist uprisings in the so-called Third World usually took the form of anticolonial "wars of national liberation."

By the late twentieth century, however, nationalist impulses seemed as likely to frustrate as to further the spread of Marxist socialism. One sign of this is the continuing conflicts between countries that claim to be communist. The long-standing tension between the Soviet Union and the People's Republic of China is the best example, but not the only one. China has also fought a brief war with its communist neighbor to the south, Vietnam, and Vietnam has invaded another neighbor, Cambodia, in order to overthrow its communist (Khmer Rouge) regime. In all these cases old antagonisms between nations have seemed to be more powerful than allegiance to a common ideology. These antagonisms have also provoked dissension *within* the boundaries of communist countries, particularly in the multinational Soviet Union. About half the population of the Soviet Union is Russian, with the other half consisting of people of various nationalities—Latvian, Ukrainian, Armenian, and many others. Many of these people resent Russian dominance and want greater independence for their own national group. There are also conflicts and bitterness between some of these diverse national groups, with occasional violent outbursts as the result. So by the late twentieth century, nationalism seems to be a divisive force that may be pulling some communist countries apart.

Nor is this a problem only in the communist world. Nationalism continues to be a powerful factor throughout the world, often in the form of **separatist movements.** The Basques in Spain, the Scots and Welsh in Great Britain, the French-speaking Quebecois in Canada—militant members of these and other nationalities occasionally speak up, and in some cases resort to violence, to try to win greater national autonomy or independence for their group. The continuing conflict in Northern Ireland is in part a conflict between nationalities. So, too, are many of the disputes in Africa, the Middle East, and Asia.

All this suggests that nationalism will not simply go away, no matter how much Marxists say that the workers have no fatherland and no matter how much liberals talk about individuals simply as individuals, and not as members of any particular ethnic, racial, or national group. For the near future, at least, nationalism will doubtless continue to complicate matters. Indeed, there is some reason to believe that nationalistic sentiments may become even more significant in the next century. As technological advances in communication and transportation make the world a smaller place, with more people crossing more boundaries in search of political refuge or economic opportunity, nationalistic resentments seem to be coming to the surface. In Europe, resentment directed against so-called guest workers from other countries and of immigrants from former colonies has led to a rekindling of fascist sentiments in Germany and France. Similar concerns about immigration and the growth of Asian-American and Hispanic populations have led in the United States to the passage of "official English" laws and may have sparked renewed activity by the Ku Klux Klan and other white supremacist groups.

For better or worse, then, nationalism promises to be with us for quite some time. Much the same can also be said about religion.

Religion and Ideology

Contrary to most conservatives, who have usually regarded religion as an essential part of the social fabric, many liberals and socialists have wanted or expected religion to fade away. There have been important exceptions, to be sure, but liberals and socialists have tended to look upon religion in one of two ways. The first is to see it as an obstacle to a full and free life—an outmoded superstition, according to some Enlightenment thinkers, or "the opiate of the people" as Marx put it. Once "reason" or "history" or "class struggle" does its work, some said, the obstacle of religion will be removed and left behind. The second way is to declare religion a private matter to be left to the individual's conscience. Even if religion survives, then, it should not be a force in the public arena of politics.

Yet religion has survived, and it continues to play a major role in political controversies around the world. Indeed, many religious people see their religion not as an obstacle, but a pathway to freedom.[1]

Evidence of the continuing strength of religion in politics is abundant. In earlier chapters we discussed the New Right in American conservatism and liberation theology as it has emerged in Latin America. Further evidence can be found in the Middle East, where the conflict between Israel and the surrounding countries has both religious and nationalistic elements, as does the civil strife in Lebanon. But the clearest instance of the political power of religion today is found in the Islamic faith. Because many Westerners find the resurgence of militant Islam confusing and troubling, a brief explanation seems necessary here.

People of the Islamic faith are of many different nationalities and are to be found in almost every part of the globe. Their numbers are concentrated, however, in Northern Africa and the Middle and Near East. Islam has dominated this territory virtually since the religion began around 620 A.D., when the Prophet Mohammed announced in Arabia that he had received a revelation from the Angel Gabriel. The report of this and subsequent revelations make up the Koran, the holy book of Islam that believers (Muslims) take to be the divine word of Allah, or God. Together with Mohammed's own words and deeds (or *Sunna*), which Muslims are supposed to emulate, the Koran forms the basis of the Islamic faith—a monotheistic faith, like Judaism and Christianity, that worships one all-knowing, all-powerful, and merciful God.

Within a century of Mohammed's death in 632 A.D., Islam had spread from Arabia throughout the Middle East, across Northern Africa, and through most of Spain. The Muslim rulers of Spain were generally tolerant of other religions, allowing both Christians and Jews to practice their faiths—a courtesy seldom extended to Jews or Muslims in Christian countries at that time. In this way Spain served as the chief point of contact between Christian Europe and the Islamic world. This was especially significant because it enabled Europeans to enjoy such fruits of Islamic culture as Arabic numerals and algebra. Islamic universities also preserved many of the classical works of western philosophy that were lost to Europe for centuries before being rediscovered through contact with Islamic Spain.

Even before Muslims invaded Spain, however, a split developed in Islam that continues today. This is the split between the Sunni Muslims, by far the larger group, and the Shi'ites. In the beginning the controversy arose over the question of who was to follow in Mohammed's footsteps as *caliph*, or leader of the Islamic community, but it also raised the further question of what the nature of this leadership should be. The Sunnis conceived of the *caliph* as a kind of chief executive, while the Shi'ites insisted that the *caliph* is an infallible *imam*, a divinely gifted leader who must be a member of the house of Ali (Mohammed's son-in-law). More generally, the Shi'ites are the more militant and less accommodating Islamic faction—and easily the dominant faction in Iran.

For Sunnis and Shi'ites alike, religion is not simply a private matter. Islam is a total way of life; it draws no distinction, for instance, between church and state, religion and politics. The law of the land and the precepts of the faith should be one and the same. Thus the Koran prohibits usury, calls for a tax on the wealthy to aid the poor and needy, and prescribes severe punishment for adultery. These and other injunctions are to be enforced by the rulers, who are heads of church and state—or, properly speaking, the church-state. Islam calls for theocracy, in other words, a form of rule in which the law of the land is supposed to follow directly from God's commands.

In the twentieth century the countries of the Islamic world have generally moved away from theocracy as they have begun to distinguish government and politics from matters of faith. In this respect, of course, they have followed the example of Western liberals and socialists. But there has also been a strong reaction against this and other forms of secularism—a reaction most evident in Iran under the regime of the Ayatollah Ruhollah Khomeini (1902–1989). Under his leadership, Iran banned Western music and required women to veil their faces in accordance with Islamic tradition. Khomeini also led Iran through a long and bloody war with Iraq, where the Sunni version of Islam is dominant, and tried to suppress the practice of other religions in Iran. In the last year of his life, Khomeini offered a million dollar reward to anyone who would kill

Salman Rushdie, a British citizen and former Muslim whose novel, *The Satanic Verses*, many Muslims regard as blasphemous.

Although we do not know what direction Iran will take with Khomeini dead, it seems certain that the Islamic faith will be a major factor in determining that direction. Indeed, Islam gives every indication of sharply affecting the pace and direction of social and political change throughout the area where it is the dominant religion—an area that includes sizable parts of the Soviet Union.

As the examples of Islam, liberation theology, and the New Christian Right attest, religion is no more likely than nationalism to lose its political appeal. But this is not because religion is a single, united force. To be sure, there is a sense in which fundamentalists within both Christianity and Islam are reacting against the spread of secularism, or secular humanism. Both believe that there is too much attention to human desires and too little to God's commands. This belief has led Islamic fundamentalists to declare a death sentence on a "blasphemous" writer, while members of the New Christian Right have tried to remove supposedly "immoral" books from public libraries and require the teaching of "creation science" in public schools.

What they have in common as fundamentalists, however, is more than offset by their differences as Muslims and Christians. As liberation theology demonstrates, furthermore, fundamentalism is far from the only active force in religion these days. Liberation theologians and New Right fundamentalists share a commitment to Christianity, but their ideas of what it means to be and act as Christians are very different indeed. Where the New Right calls for a strict or literal reading of the Bible and a return to what they consider to be traditional morality, liberation theology insists that the Bible must be read in the light of the circumstances and knowledge of the day, including knowledge gained from the theories of radicals and atheists such as Karl Marx, and then applied to reshape society in the interests of all, including the poor. Although many other Christians do not go as far as the liberation theologians, they still see their religion as an inspiration to act in unconventional ways. In the 1980s, for instance, the National Conference of Catholic Bishops of the United States condemned as immoral not only nuclear war, but the use of nuclear weapons even as a deterrent or threat. At about the same time, some American Christians organized the Sanctuary movement, which defied the immigration policies of the United States government by helping refugees from Central America enter and live in the United States.

So while religion is alive and well as a political force, it is a force pushing in different directions. Just as a single river may divide into several streams, so religion will continue to affect and influence political ideologies in a variety of ways.

IDEOLOGY AND THE ENVIRONMENT

Despite their disagreements, liberals and socialists and some conservatives, especially the individualists, have shared a faith in material progress. They have believed, that is, that human life can and will become easier—less subject to starvation, disease, and unremitting labor—through the mastery of nature. This is why they have usually encouraged industrial and technological development.

Now, in the last decade of the twentieth century, we can see that material progress is a mixed blessing. Although life is better for many people in many ways, it is clear that much of this improvement has come at the expense of the physical environment. Nature has not proved so easy to "master" or "harness" as the champions of progress had thought. The greenhouse effect, acid rain, toxic wastes of various sorts—these and the other environmental problems we discussed in Chapter 9 leave no doubt that material progress has produced a host of unanticipated and unhealthy consequences. Life may be better for many people in many ways, but the planet is now so crowded that the demands on the earth's resources may soon exceed its capacities.

As the century draws to a close, ecological problems have become political problems as well. All ideologies will have to respond to the challenge of these new circumstances in some fashion. One response, as we saw in Chapter 9, is the emergence of a new Green ideology. Whether this becomes a major ideology in its own right depends in large part on how the "mainstream" ideologies respond to the ecological crisis. If liberalism, socialism, or conservatism manages to address environmental problems in a convincing manner, perhaps by stealing the thunder of the Greens, there will be neither need nor room for a Green ideology as such. If none of them does this, however, we should expect Green Politics to become an increasingly influential presence on the political scene.

Yet another possibility exists. The ecological crisis could conceivably provoke a revival of fascism. According to Robert Heilbroner, it may prove impossible to persuade people to make the sacrifices necessary to meet the ecological crisis.[2] Those of us who have grown used to the benefits of material progress—personal cars and air conditioners, for example—will not want to surrender them, and those who do not now enjoy those benefits will want them as much as we do. Few people will voluntarily give up what they have; indeed, most people will continue to want more and more. But if these demands continue, the ecological crisis will result in outright ecological disaster. The only solution, then, may be coercion. Governments may have to force people to lower their expectations and live more modest lives. In a democracy, Heilbroner says, this will be all but impossible, for the people are unlikely to elect leaders who promise them hardship. Yet they may turn to leaders who promise to protect them and their economic well-being from foreigners who want what they have. Militant nationalism may thus increase, bringing with it a tendency to silence dissenting opinion, to concentrate power in the hands of a few leaders, and to foster hostile relations among the nation-states of the world—a highly unsettling prospect in the age of nuclear weapons.

Heilbroner does not predict that all this will happen, but he does see it as one possible outcome of the environmental difficulties we now face. Even if there is no broad revival of fascism, moreover, many observers believe that ecological pressures pose a serious challenge to those ideologies that embrace democracy.

POLITICAL IDEOLOGIES AND THE DEMOCRATIC IDEAL

And what of the future of democracy? At the end of the twentieth century two things seem clear. The first is that democracy is more popular than ever. There are still fascists and nazis about, but they are relatively few in number. Some conservatives will occasionally question the ability of a democratic regime to preserve peace and stability, and some socialists, like Heilbroner, sometimes wonder whether democracy can survive the challenges of an era of limits—a time, that is, when economic and environmental constraints seem to make it impossible for all people to enjoy all the material comforts they may want. But hardly anyone these days flatly rejects democracy. This is a time, instead, when the ideal of democracy is inspiring challenges to established leaders and regimes around the world. The people who have begun to dismantle the Marxist-Leninist state in Eastern Europe and the Soviet Union, for instance, have acted in the name of democracy, as have those who have revolted against right-wing governments in Latin America and South Africa.

The second thing that seems clear about the future of democracy is that it has no place for one of the three versions of the democratic ideal that have proved dominant this century. This version, **people's democracy,** has fallen victim to the general demise of Marxism-Leninism. As we explained in Chapter 2, a people's democracy is supposed to consist of rule by the Communist party in the interests of the people. In this way, the Communists argued, the party could both speak for the people and use its powers to defeat their counterrevolutionary enemies. As long as the party itself was a democratic institution, with room for debate and disagreement among the friends of the people, the country would be a people's democracy even though no other party was allowed to compete for power. It became increasingly obvious that the party was *not* a democratic institution, however, but a rigid apparatus in which party members clung to power and privilege, exploiting rather than liberating the people. George Orwell developed this theme in the form of a fable, *Animal Farm,* in 1945. The Yugoslavian Marxist Milovan Djilas made this argument in the early 1950s in his book, *The New Class*—and was thrown in prison. The student radicals of the 1960's New Left in the United States and Europe advanced a similar argument. Indirectly, so too did Alexander Dubcek, the Communist leader of Czechoslovakia who took steps to loosen the party's control over his country in 1968, only to be removed from office when the Soviet Union sent tanks and troops into Czechoslovakia to put an end to the reforms of the Prague Spring.

The situation began to change in the 1980s, first with the emergence of the Solidarity trade union in Poland—a noncommunist trade union in a country where the Communist party controlled all unions. Then came Mikhail Gorbachev and *perestroika* in the Soviet Union itself. Gorbachev's "restructuring" of the Soviet Union amounted to an admission that Marxism-Leninism had failed to achieve its promises economically or politically. Some dissidents inside the party dared to say that the people's democracy was no democracy at all. Once it seemed clear that Gorbachev would not use the military might of the Soviet Union to crush any popular uprisings in Eastern Europe, the people's democracies collapsed. Throughout Eastern Europe the walls—legal, political, and physical—came tumbling down. The People's Republic of Hungary even dropped "People's" from its name.

The chief exception to this trend is the People's Republic of China. There, in the country Mao Zedong once called a "people's democratic dictatorship," the protesters who occupied Tiananmen Square in the spring of 1989 called upon Communist party leaders to relinquish some of their power so that China could become a democracy. They demanded not people's democracy, but something like **liberal democracy.** The party responded by sending troops to massacre the demonstrators. Hundreds, perhaps thousands, died in a single night. Other demonstrators have since been arrested, imprisoned, and shot. Party leaders have condemned the protesters' plea for democracy as an attempt at "bourgeois liberalization" and have reaffirmed their commitment to people's democracy. To observers throughout the world—and to many of the one billion people of China, one suspects—the events of Tiananmen Square confirm the view that people's democracy is not democracy at all, but a front behind which an entrenched elite protects its power and privilege.

The decline of people's democracy means that the democratic ideal now survives in two principal forms—*liberal* and **social democracy.** There is some chance that these two forms will converge, since both seem committed to freedom of speech, competition for political office, and other civil and political rights. There is also some sign that socialists are adopting some aspects of a capitalist, or market-oriented economy. But the differences between them are still quite significant. Those who favor liberal democracy continue to stress the importance of privacy, including private property, so that individuals may be free to choose how to live. The proponents of social democracy, however, continue to emphasize equality as necessary to democracy, claiming that people will not be able to rule themselves unless they have something like an equal voice in the decisions that affect their lives. And the people will not have an equal voice, social democrats say, as long as some have far more wealth and property—and therefore more power—than others.

In the near future, then, the ideological contest will probably continue to pit liberalism and socialism against each other, with each proclaiming its devotion to democracy. As more socialists abandon Marxism-Leninism, it is possible that a realignment may take place along lines that reflect the division of liberalism into its welfare and neoclassical wings. Welfare liberals may come to believe that their views of liberty, equality, and democracy are closer to those of the moderate socialists than to the views of the neoclassical liberals. For their part, neoclassical liberals and conservatives may conclude that they should make common cause against those who favor an active government and a more egalitarian society. The first group would then speak for social democracy, the second for liberal democracy.

But what of the liberation ideologies and the Greens? What of religion and nationalism? Almost certainly all will play a part in the politics of the near future. The main question is whether liberalism or socialism or perhaps conservatism will manage to absorb them, or whether these new ideologies will develop sufficient strength and scope to challenge the older or mainstream ideologies. Most liberation ideologies, for instance, share a sense of frustration with liberalism and socialism, but they also owe much of their ideal of liberation to these two ideologies. If either liberalism or socialism can give liberationists— black, women, gay, or animal—reason to believe that they can make that ideal real, then the liberation ideologies could conceivably merge with one of those ideologies. Otherwise, they will probably continue to follow an independent course as challengers to liberalism, socialism, and, of course, conservatism. But if the aforementioned realignment takes place, it is likely that the liberation ideologies would become part of the social democratic alliance of welfare liberals and socialists. Conservatives who favor traditional forms of society and individualists who prefer an individualistic, competitive society would then form the opposition, perhaps in the name of liberal democracy. Or perhaps we shall simply see the world of ideologies splinter into many small fragments, with no ideology popular enough to overwhelm any of the others.

There are, of course, a great many possibilities, and the political world is always capable of surprising us, as the opening of the Berlin Wall and the other unexpected events of 1989 attest. Any predictions, then, should be hedged and qualified, surrounded by "maybe," "if," and "perhaps." But one prediction can be made more boldly: the end of ideology is nowhere in sight.

IDEOLOGIES AND THE END OF IDEOLOGY

Amidst all the talk about the end of communism in the late 1980s, some commentators began to wonder about the end of ideology in general. With the downfall of communism, they declared, not only were the great ideological conflicts of the twentieth century coming to an end, but all significant ideological conflict was evaporating into a widespread consensus on the desirability of liberal democracy. From this time forward, virtually everyone will agree on the general forms and purposes of political life; the only disagreements will be over how best to achieve the goals—especially the goal of individual liberty, including the liberty to own property—that nearly everyone accepts. Since this will leave ideology with no useful function to perform, it will simply disappear.[3]

However interesting and attractive the argument, we cannot accept this conclusion. There are, we believe, three reasons why ideologies cannot and will not end. The first is that the end-of-ideology argument has appeared—and failed—before. In the late 1950s and early 1960s other scholars predicted that a growing consensus on the desirable ends of politics was leading to the end of ideology, at least in the Western world. As Daniel Bell put it in 1960,

Few serious minds believe any longer that one can set down "blueprints" and through "social engineering" bring about a new utopia of social harmony. At the same time, the older "counter-beliefs" have lost their intellectual force as well. Few "classic" liberals insist that the State should play no role in the economy, and few serious conservatives, at least in England and on the Continent, believe that the Welfare State is "the road to serfdom." In the Western world, therefore, there is today a rough consensus among intellectuals on political issues: the acceptance of a Welfare State; the desirability of decentralized power; a system of mixed economy and of political pluralism. In that sense, too, the ideological age has ended.[4]

The consensus was either short-lived or remarkably superficial, however, as the turmoil of the 1960s soon convinced almost everyone that the end of ideology was not yet in sight. It is possible, of course, that the earlier claims were simply premature, so that now, some thirty years later, the end of ideology has truly come.[5] But the fact that the prediction failed once suggests to us that it is likely to fail again.

Besides that, we believe that enough differences remain, even after the demise of Marxism-Leninism, to keep ideological conflict alive for quite some time. This conflict may be less severe and less threatening than it has been in the past, for which we can all be grateful. But socialism, as we suggested in Chapter 6, may well experience a revival of sorts as it sloughs off the burden of Marxism-Leninism. If it does, enough diffferences will remain between socialists, liberals, and conservatives to fuel many an ideological dispute. In addition to disputes *between* ideologies, there will continue to be differences *within* ideologies. The split between welfare and neoclassical liberals, for one, seems deep enough to prevent any widespread consensus on the forms and scope of government activity from emerging. And a great many unresolved issues and tensions continue to press for resolution. What should be the role of religion in public life? Is nationalism something to be encouraged or discouraged? What about the status of those who see themselves as victims—blacks, gays, women, the poor—who have been pushed to the margins of society, prevented from grasping the power they need to liberate themselves? And, as animal rights advocates remind us, what of creatures who cannot speak for themselves? Do they have rights in need of protection? These are among the many questions that must be answered before anything like an ideological consensus can be reached. Yet they seem more likely to provoke conflict than agreement.

Finally, our third reason for believing that ideologies are going to be with us for quite some time is that new challenges and difficulties continue to arise. The clearest evidence of this is the environmental crisis, or crises, that we discussed in Chapter 9. Barring some miraculous discoveries—such as a cheap, safe, and nonpolluting source of energy—this crisis will require a political response. And this response will almost certainly take on an ideological form. In other words, any adequate response must fulfill the four functions of an ideology. First, people will need to have some explanation of the nature of the crisis, along with, second, an evaluation of the situation they face. Third, they will also need orientation—that is, some sense of where they stand with regard to the crisis. Fourth and finally, they will need a program for action telling them what they can, and should, do. And they will need all these things to be set out in fairly simple terms. They will need, in short, the guidance of an ideology.

If more than one ideology offers this guidance, as seems likely, then ideological conflict will certainly persist.

For these reasons, we do not expect to see the end of ideology. Ideologies are too useful, and too important, to wither away. People appear to need ideologies to join thought to action, to provide some vision of human possibilities that will move them to act. As long as humans must act in a complicated and confusing world, full of challenges and conflicts, people will turn to ideologies to explain why social conditions are as they are, to evaluate those conditions, to provide a sense of orientation, and to set out a program of action—an attempt to take the world as it is and to remake it as it should be. People will also rely upon ideologies to give meaning to the democratic ideal and substance to the concept of freedom. With this work to be done, it is difficult to see how human beings can do without them. We must conclude, then, that as long as ideologies have these ends to serve, there will be no end of ideology.

NOTES

1. For example, Martin Luther King, Jr., and many others who were active in the Civil Rights Movement in the United States. For an excellent account of the role of religion in the struggle for civil rights, see Taylor Branch, *Parting the Waters: America in the King Years, 1954–1963* (New York: Simon & Schuster, 1988). For a broader account of the role of religious inspiration in political struggles, see Michael Walzer, *Exodus and Revolution* (New York: Basic Books, 1985).
2. Robert Heilbroner, *An Inquiry into the Human Prospect,* 2nd ed. (New York: Norton, 1980).
3. For a forceful statement of this view, see Francis Fukuyama, "The End of History," *The National Interest* (Summer 1989):3–18; also in Terence Ball and Richard Dagger, eds., *Ideals and Ideologies: A Reader* (New York: HarperCollins, 1991), selection 55.
4. Daniel Bell, *The End of Ideology: On the Exhaustion of Political Ideas in the Fifties,* rev. ed. (New York: Collier Books, 1961), p. 397.
5. Bell revives and defends his end of ideology thesis in "The End of Ideology Revisited (Parts I and II)," *Government and Opposition,* 23 (Spring and Summer, 1988):131–150 and 321–328. A portion of Part II appears in Ball and Dagger, eds., *Ideals and Ideologies,* selection 54.

Glossary

achieved status The condition of earning one's place in society through effort and ability. (Contrast with *ascribed status*.)

affirmative action The attempt to promote equality of opportunity by providing assistance to members of groups, such as women and racial minorities, that have been the victims of discrimination.

alienation Marx adapted this term from Hegel's philosophy to describe the separation or estrangement of persons or classes of people from their human potential. In capitalism, Marx claims, the worker's ability to control his or her labor is alienated, thus frustrating the desire to be a creative, self-directed person.

anarchism From the Greek *an archos*, meaning "no rule" or "no government," anarchism is an ideology that aims to abolish the state, replacing political relations with cooperative or voluntary ones.

anarcho-communism The version of anarchism that aspires to a cooperative society in which property is owned or controlled by the whole community.

anticolonial movements Attempts by people in Third World countries to gain their independence from the rule of (usually European) colonial powers.

apartheid The South African policy of apartness or separate development, which advocates segregating the races, with whites holding political power.

aristocratic privilege Rooted in the belief that one class of people is superior to others, this is the policy of reserving certain rights and opportunities—such as access to governing power—for the exclusive enjoyment of the nobility.

arrogance of humanism The Green charge that a *humanist*, or anthropocentric, outlook ignores or devalues the worth of other species of animals and plants and the environment that sustains them.

Aryans Name given to a group of people from whom all Indo-European languages supposedly derive. Nazis believe that this people and their purest descendants are a "master race" whose destiny is to conquer and rule—or exterminate—"inferior" races.

ascribed status In contrast to *achieved status*, a society is based on *ascribed status* when a person is born into a particular social status—such as noble or serf—with little opportunity either to raise or lower his or her social standing.

atomistic conception of society The view that society consists of individuals who are essentially unconnected to or independent of one other, like marbles on a tray. (Contrast with *organic conception of society*.)

base (also **material-productive base**) Marx's metaphor for the social relations that constitute the real basis or foundation of material production—e.g., the relationship of landowner to farm worker is part of the *base* of an agricultural society. (See *superstructure* and *materialist conception of history*.)

bourgeoisie Originally referred to those who lived in a market town (*bourg*, in French), but later to the middle class—merchants and professional people—in general. In Marx's terms, the *bourgeoisie* is the ruling class in capitalist society because it controls the *forces* (or *means*) of production.

capitalism An economic system in which the major means of production are privately owned and operated for the profit of the owners or investors.

center The moderate or middle-of-the-road position in political terms, as opposed to the more extreme positions of the *left* and *right*.

centralized control Socialists who favor *centralized control* want to concentrate the control of all resources and all decisions concerning production and distribution of goods in the central government.

class A key concept in socialist, and particularly Marxian, analysis, *class* refers to one's socially determined location in the structure of social-economic relations. If you are part owner of the *forces* (or *means*) of production, you are a member of the *bourgeoisie* or *capitalist* class; if you are yourself a means of production, then you are a member of the working class, or *proletariat*.

classical (or **traditional**) **conservative** Someone, like Edmund Burke, who believes that the first aim of political action must be to preserve the social fabric by pursuing a cautious policy of gradual *reform*.

command economy Favored by the proponents of *centralized control*, this is the attempt to plan and direct economic production and distribution instead of relying on market forces.

communism Originally used to describe any scheme of common or social control of resources, this term is now associated with Marxian socialism. For Marx and the Marxists, the communal ownership and control of the *forces* (or *means*) of production represents the fulfillment of human history. The culmination of a long-term revolutionary sequence, communist society subscribes to the principle, "From each according to ability, to each according to need."

corporativism A policy Benito Mussolini instituted in Italy in an attempt to bring owners, workers, and government together to promote economic production and harmony.

Counter-Enlightenment This term refers to a diverse group of thinkers in the early and mid-nineteenth century who rejected some of the leading ideas of the *Enlightenment* philosophers.

cultural conservatism Closely connected to *classical conservatism*, this brand of conservatism is particularly suspicious of commerce, industry, and "progress," which threaten, it says, our relationship with nature and our respect for cultural pursuits.

cunning of reason Hegel's phrase for the process by which intentional actions produce unintended, but nonetheless "rational," consequences that promote the development of Spirit through history.

decentralized control In contrast to *centralized control*, some socialists want to disperse power by placing control of resources and production in the hands of people at the lowest possible level, such as the town or workplace.

deep ecologists This term refers to the proponents, within the Green movement, of a "biocentric" or life-centered philosophical, ethical, and political perspective, placing the welfare of human beings on a par with other species and the conditions that nurture and sustain them.

democratic centralism Lenin's attempt to combine democracy with central control of the revolutionary *vanguard party*. The party should encourage debate and discussion within its ranks before decisions are made, Lenin said. Once the leadership reaches a decision, however, debate must stop and all members must obey.

dialectic Different versions of this method of reasoning are found in Socrates, Plato, Hegel, and Marx, among others. Generally speaking, *dialectic* is the process whereby opposite views or forces come into conflict, which eventually leads to the overcoming or reconciliation of the opposition in a new and presumably higher form.

dialectical materialism (or **DiaMat**) The Soviet Marxist-Leninist view that traces all social, economic, and political phenomena to physical matter and its motions. The phrase, never used by Marx, became standard during Stalin's era.

ecology As a scientific discipline, *ecology* is the study of the connections, interdependencies, and energy flows within and between species and ecosystems. In its more recent political sense, however, *ecology* refers to a perspective that values the protection and preservation of the natural environment.

ecotage Short for ecological sabotage, this is a form of direct action practiced by Earth First! and other militant environmentalist groups. Such sabotage ranges from "monkey wrenching" ("decommissioning" bulldozers, cutting power lines, etc.) to "spiking" old-growth trees to save them from loggers.

elitism Elitists believe that in any society a small number of people (an "elite") either should or necessarily will lead or rule the rest.

empirical A statement or proposition is *empirical* if it describes or explains how things are (e.g., "It is hotter in Arizona than in Minnesota."). Usually contrasted with *normative* or evaluative.

Enlightenment The influential philosophical movement of the eighteenth century, especially in France, that proclaimed the triumph of reason and science over custom and superstition.

essentially contested concept A concept (e.g., art, religion, democracy) that generates controversy because it lacks a complete set of clear standards for determining when something falls under the concept. Indeed, this openness or indeterminacy seems to be the nature or essence of these concepts.

Fabian socialism The British brand of socialism emphasizing the peaceful, piecemeal, and gradual transition from a capitalist to a socialist society.

false consciousness A Marxian phrase referring to the false or distorted beliefs of members of a subordinate class who fail to understand their true position in society. These false beliefs work to the advantage of the ruling class because they prevent the subordinate class from seeing the real cause of its oppression.

feudalism Specifically, the social and economic system of medieval Europe that centered on the relationship of the lord, who promised protection and the use of land in exchange for service, and the vassal. More generally, *feudalism* refers to any similar agricultural society in which a relatively small number of people control the land while most others work it as tenants or serfs.

gay The tendency to favor exclusive sexual relations with persons of the same sex.

glasnost The Russian word for openness used by Mikhail Gorbachev to signal a policy of greater tolerance and freedom in the USSR.

green politics The use of various strategies to put environmental concerns at or near the top of the political agenda.

greenhouse effect The gradual warming of the earth's atmosphere due to the build-up of carbon dioxide (CO_2) that results from the burning of fossil fuels (oil, gas, coal, etc.) and the destruction of forests.

harm principle The principle, defended by John Stuart Mill and others, that we should be allowed to do whatever we want unless our actions harm or threaten harm to others.

homophobia The fear of homosexuals and their influence.

ideological superstructure (also **superstructure**) Marx's metaphor for the set of beliefs, ideas, and ideals that justifies or legitimizes the social arrangements that constitute the foundation or *base* of society. (See *materialist conception of history*.)

immiseration of the proletariat The Marxian prediction that the condition of the working class or *proletariat* would become progressively worse under *capitalism*.

imperialism According to Lenin, the policy whereby capitalist countries conquer, colonize, and exploit Third World countries. It represents, in Lenin's view, the highest and last stage of capitalist domination of the world economy. Also a central concept for Mao Zedong and other Marxist-Leninists.

individualist conservative Someone who believes that government should promote individual liberty by protecting against foreign threats, but otherwise leave people alone to do as they see fit. Such a person may be closer to *neoclassical liberalism* than to other forms of conservatism.

innovation According to Edmund Burke, *innovation* is change for the sake of change or novelty. The desire to innovate, Burke says, leads people to neglect or reject their time-tested customs. (Contrast with *reform*.)

irrationalism The belief, associated with thinkers like Freud and Le Bon, that human beings are moved more by instincts, urges, or subconscious forces than by reason.

land ethic A phrase coined by ecologist Aldo Leopold to refer to an attitude of reverence and respect for the land and the myriad life forms it sustains.

left (or **left-wing**) In political terms a leftist is one who believes a significant, perhaps even radical, change in a new direction will lead to great improvement in social and economic arrangements. In general, socialists are on the *left*, not the *right* or *center*.

levelling The effort, criticized by many conservatives, to diminish or eliminate the gap between the wealthiest and poorest members of a society. Critics maintain that these efforts promote mediocrity and reduce everyone to the same miserable level.

liberal democracy In contrast to *people's* and *social democracy*, *liberal democracy* emphasizes the importance of individual rights and liberty, including the right to own private property.

libertarianism Generally, the desire to expand the realm of individual liberty. More specifically, another name for *neoclassical liberals*, who argue that the only legitimate power of government is to protect the persons and property of its citizens. Some libertarian *anarchists* believe that all governments are illegitimate and immoral.

Malthus' Law The claim that human population tends to grow faster than the resources required to sustain it.

market socialism The attempt to combine some features of a competitive market economy with public control of resources.

mass society According to some critics, the abolition of traditional social hierarchies has produced a dangerously unstable society in which the common people, and the politicians and advertisers who appeal to their tastes, bring everything and everyone down to their own level.

master-slave dialectic Hegel's account of the confrontation between an all-powerful master and his presumably powerless slave. The conflict between the two reveals that the master is dependent upon his slave, and the slave, by winning his struggle for freedom and recognition, liberates both himself and the master. Marx and later liberation ideologists also employ this parable of emancipation.

material forces of production (also **forces of production, means of production,** or simply **productive forces**) Marx's phrase for the material means or resources that labor transforms into useful goods or commodities. Examples include trees that are transformed into lumber, ores that are transformed into metal, and the labor necessary to accomplish the transformation.

materialism The philosophical doctrine that all reality—social, political, and intellectual—is ultimately reducible to combinations of physical matter. Different versions can be found in Hobbes, in Engels, and in twentieth-century *dialectical materialists*.

materialist conception (or **interpretation**) **of history** The Marxian framework for interpreting or explaining social change. The central idea is that changes in the material-productive *base* bring about changes in the *social relations of production* and the *ideological superstructure*.

mercantilism The economic policy of promoting a country's wealth at the expense of others' by establishing *monopolies* and regulating foreign trade to favor domestic industry.

mixed constitution (or **government**) The *republican* policy of combining or balancing rule by one, by the few, and by the many in a single government, with the aim of preventing the concentration of power in any person or social group.

monopoly Exclusive control of a commodity or market.

nationalism The belief that people fall into distinct groups, or nations, on the basis of a common heritage or birth. Each nation is then supposed to form the natural basis for a separate political unit, or nation-state.

nation-state A political unit that unites the members of a single nation, or people.

natural right A right that everyone has simply by virtue of being a person. Such a right can neither be granted nor legitimately denied by any person or political authority.

negative freedom In contrast to *positive freedom*, this is the absence of restraint. You are free, in this view, if no one else is preventing you from doing what you want to do.

neoclassical liberalism The belief that government is a necessary evil that should do nothing but protect the persons and property of its citizens. (See *libertarianism*.)

neoconservatism Beginning among disenchanted *welfare liberals* in the 1960s, *neoconservatism* advocates less reliance on government, an anticommunist foreign policy, and an emphasis on the value of work, thrift, family, and self-restraint.

New Christian Right The movement by evangelical fundamentalists, such as the Moral Majority, to restore what they take to be traditional family values.

normative A statement or proposition is *normative* if it prescribes how things should be or judges what is good or bad; e.g., lying is wrong. Usually contrasted with *empirical*.

opiate of the masses (or **people**) Marx's phrase for religion, which he believed dulled the critical capacity of oppressed people by directing their attention and hopes away from this life.

organic conception of society In contrast to the *atomistic conception*, this view holds that the members of a society are connected and interdependent, like the parts of the body, and society itself is more than merely the sum of its parts.

original sin The belief in Christian theology that the first sin—Adam and Eve's defiance of God in the Garden of Eden—has somehow infected all humanity.

orthopraxis Literally, correct practice or action. Liberation theologians urge the Catholic church, and Christians in general, to do what is right by working for justice for the poor and an end to oppression.

people's democracy Favored by Marxist-Leninists, this is the view that democracy is government by the Communist party in the interests of the working class.

perestroika The Russian word for restructuring, used by Mikhail Gorbachev to refer in particular to the restructuring of the Soviet Union's economy.

Physiocrats French economic theorists of the eighteenth century who believed that land is the basis of wealth and that unrestricted competition promotes prosperity.

political absolutism Any form of government in which the ruler (or rulers) has nearly complete power, unrestrained by law or other governing bodies.

polity In Aristotle's theory, this is generally the best form of government: rule by the many, who are neither wealthy nor poor, in the interests of the whole community.

positive freedom In contrast to *negative freedom*, this is the belief that freedom is not simply the absence of restraint, but also the power or ability to act and to develop one's capacities.

prejudice In Burke's theory, this is the "latent wisdom" that societies accumulate through long experience and that usually provides a useful guide to conduct and policy.

proletariat Originally the lowest class in ancient Rome, this is Marx's word for wage-laborers, the industrial working class.

racism The belief that one race (usually one's own) is innately superior to other races or ethnic groups.

reactionary Someone who wants to return to an earlier form of society or government. More generally, an extreme conservative.

reform A gradual and cautious change that corrects or repairs defects in society or government and, according to Edmund Burke, is safer and wiser than *innovation*.

religious conformity The policy of requiring everyone in a society to follow or acknowledge the same religious beliefs.

republic A form of government by the people that includes the rule of law, a *mixed constitution*, and the cultivation of an active and public-spirited citizenry.

revisionists The name given to later Marxists who attempted to amend or revise Marxian theory in light of developments after Marx's death.

revolution Originally used to describe an attempt to restore or revolve back to a previous condition, since the French Revolution this word has meant a sweeping or fundamental transformation of a society.

revolutionary dictatorship of the proletariat (also **dictatorship of the proletariat**) The form of government that Marx expected to provide the transition from the revolutionary overthrow of the *bourgeoisie* to the eventual coming of communist society. This interim or transitional state will presumably *wither away*.

right (or right-wing) In opposition to the *left* and *center*, the people who occupy the *right* end of the political spectrum typically oppose change and prefer an established social order with firmly rooted authority. Both conservatives and fascists are usually considered *right-wing* despite their differences.

separatist movements The attempt by a group of people who see themselves as a distinct nation to break away from another country in order to form their own *nation-state*.

sexism The belief that one sex is innately superior to the other.

social contract How do some people acquire authority over others? Some theorists, such as Thomas Hobbes and John Locke, have answered that individuals in a *state of nature* have in some way entered into an agreement, or social contract, to form political societies and establish governments, thus creating political authority.

Social Darwinists A group of *neoclassical liberals* of the late nineteenth and early twentieth centuries who adapted Darwin's theory of evolution to social and political life, concluding that the struggle for survival is a natural feature of human life and government should not intervene.

social democracy In this view, democracy requires a rough equality of power or influence for every citizen, which may require in turn the redistribution of wealth and the social control of resources and property. (Contrast with *liberal* and *people's democracies*.)

social ecologists In contrast to *deep ecologists*, their view attaches special importance to human life, but also holds that humanity is dependent upon, and responsible for, the environment that sustains it and other species of life.

social relations of production (or **relations of production**) Marx's phrase describing the social division of labor (e.g., investors, managers, supervisors, laborers) required to transform the *material forces of production* into useful goods.

speciesism The belief that the human species is innately superior to other animal species.

state of nature In the theories of Thomas Hobbes, John Locke, and Robert Nozick, among others, this is the condition in which people live before they create society and government. Everyone is free and equal in this state, and no one has authority over anyone else.

stewardship An orientation emphasizing human beings' responsibility for protecting, preserving, and sustaining the natural and social environment for the sake of future generations.

Tory democracy This policy, initiated by the British Conservative leader Benjamin Disraeli, supported voting rights and other benefits for the working class in order to forge an electoral alliance between the upper and the working class against the Liberal party.

totalitarianism The attempt to control every aspect of a country's life (e.g., military, press, schools, religion, economy) by a single all-powerful party that systematically smothers all opposition.

traditional (or **classical**) **conservative** Someone, like Edmund Burke, who believes that the first aim of political action must be to preserve the social fabric by pursuing a cautious policy of *reform*.

utilitarianism The view that individuals and governments should always act to promote *utility* or, in Bentham's terms, the greatest happiness of the greatest number.

utility Anything that has value for anyone has utility.

utopia A term coined by Thomas More from Greek words meaning either *good place* or *no place*. It now refers to a perfect society from which greed, crime, and other social ills have been banished.

utopian socialism A phrase Marx and Engels used to denote the moralistic and unrealistic schemes of earlier socialists, such as Charles Fourier and Robert Owen.

vanguard party Lenin's term for the communist party, which is to take a tutelary or leading role in the overthrow of capitalism and the transition to communism.

welfare (or **welfare-state**) **liberalism** In contrast to *neoclassical liberalism,* this form of liberalism regards government as a tool to be used to promote individual freedom, welfare, and equality of opportunity.

withering away of the state Marx's description of the process whereby the interim *revolutionary dictatorship of the proletariat* loses its reason for being and gradually ceases to exist.

Name Index

Abbey, Edward, 232–233
Adams, Abigail, 207
Adams, John, 36, 104, 207
Alexander the Great, 26
Ali, house of, 242
Amory, Cleveland, 225
Anderson, Eva Greenslit, 236n
Anthony, Susan, B., 207
Aquinas, Saint Thomas, 224n
Arendt, Hannah, 21, 198
Aristotle, 25–27, 30, 31, 106, 131, 211
Ashcraft, Richard, 89
Avineri, Shlomo, 142

Bacon, Sir Francis, 228
Bahro, Rudolph, 236n
Bailyn, Bernard, 45n
Bakunin, Mikhail, 143, 164–165
Baldwin, James, 204
Ball, Terence, 89n, 142, 173n
Barrett, William, 223n
Beauvior, Simone de, 225
Bebel, August, 145
Becker, Carl, 88n
Bell, Daniel, 20n, 112, 247–249
Bellamy, Edward, 166–167
Bentham, Jeremy, 71–72, 87, 218
Berlin, Isaiah, 21, 89, 142, 173n, 197n
Bernstein, Eduard, 148–150, 152, 155
Berry, Wendell, 236
Berryman, Phillip, 224n, 225

Biko, Steve, 207
Bismarck, Otto von, 78, 103, 149, 180
Blake, William, 122, 202
Boff, Leonardo, 215
Bonaparte, Napoleon, 5–6, 18, 67, 70, 100, 180
Bookchin, Murray, 21, 232
Bonald, Louis Gabriel de, 179
Bramwell, Anna, 236
Branch, Taylor, 223n, 224, 249n
Brandt, Conrad, 174n
Bullock, Alan, 198
Burke, Edmund, 93–100, 104, 107, 110–111, 231
Burns, Mary, 144
Bush, George, 8
Butler, Melissa, 89n

Caesar, Julius, 28
Calvin, Jean, 55–56
Capra, Fritjof, 236n
Carmichael, Stokely, 224
Carr, E. H., 174
Carson, Rachel, 236
Carter, April, 21
Carver, Terrell, 142, 174
Catton, William R., 236
Chiang Kai-shek, 160, 162
Charlemagne, 30
Charles I, 33, 57
Charles II, 33, 59

259

Subject and Title Index